T0305384

Econometrics as a Con Art

Exposing the Limitations and Abuses of Econometrics

Imad A. Moosa

Professor of Finance, Royal Melbourne Institute of Technology (RMIT), Australia

Edward Elgar
PUBLISHING

Cheltenham, UK • Northampton, MA, USA

Published by
Edward Elgar Publishing Limited
The Lypiatts
15 Lansdown Road
Cheltenham
Glos GL50 2JA
UK

Edward Elgar Publishing, Inc.
William Pratt House
9 Dewey Court
Northampton
Massachusetts 01060
USA

A catalogue record for this book
is available from the British Library

Library of Congress Control Number: 2017931767

This book is available electronically in the **Elgar**online
Economics subject collection
DOI 10.4337/9781785369957

ISBN 978 1 78536 994 0 (cased)
ISBN 978 1 78536 995 7 (eBook)

Typeset by Servis Filmsetting Ltd, Stockport, Cheshire

Contents

Preface

When in the early 1970s I decided to study econometrics as an elective in my undergraduate economics degree, I was asked if I could invert a matrix. When I proved that I could do that, I was allowed to be one of the few (those who could, amongst other things, invert a matrix) to study econometrics as an elective. How things have changed since that time, as econometrics has become a necessity for those studying economics, surpassing in terms of importance economic statistics, history of economic thought, economic history and applied economics. Econometrics has since changed from a means to become an end by itself, to the extent that I know of at least one major university that has a Department of Econometrics. We have reached a stage where we are expected to have more faith in the results of econometric estimation and testing than theory, intuition and common sense. This cannot be a positive development for the study of the "dismal science".

When I started my econometrics classes, I was told that econometrics consisted of three elements: economic theory, mathematics and statistics – economic theory came first. Since then, economic theory has paled into insignificance as emphasis shifted to the development of econometric methods and pure mathematical abstraction. Econometric methods are described as statistical methods developed to deal with economic data, which may sound plausible but the problem is that statistical methods are designed to analyse experimental data. Econometricians, however, believe that they are capable of devising econometric methods that can deal with the problems associated with historical economic and financial data, including errors of measurement and unobservable variables. This is an illusion or wishful thinking.

When I was in investment banking for ten years I used my knowledge of econometrics twice. On the first occasion, I ran a simple OLS regression to explain variations in the dollar's effective exchange rate in terms of the interest rate and growth, hoping to find an explanation for the extraordinary strength of the US currency in the first half of the 1980s. On the second occasion, I ran a series of OLS regressions to reveal the exchange rate regime followed by a particular country, with the objective of taking advantage of arbitrage opportunities. In both cases the results turned out to be useful, and in both cases the exercise involved no more than running simple regressions and reporting the results (in English, not econometrics) to senior management. However, I recall conducting a study whose results were subsequently used to design a profitable trading strategy. That study was based on correlation analysis, which is simple statistics, not econometrics.

When I took the heroic decision to join academia in the early 1990s, I had to take econometrics seriously, both in my teaching and research. With the passage of time, I became increasingly sceptical of the usefulness of econometrics until I realized that reality was far away from what econometricians had led us to believe. I realized that progress in the development of econometric methods was disproportional to our understanding of the working of the economy and financial markets. More seriously, I became increasingly convinced that econometrics provided the means of producing results that support prior beliefs. Eventually, I reached a stage when I started to believe that the rise of econometrics to prominence has been detrimental to the progress of economics. As a result, I have decided to write this book to expose the limitations and abuses of econometrics and to demonstrate that it is a con art that can be used to prove almost anything.

Writing this book would not have been possible without the help and encouragement I received from family, friends and colleagues. My utmost gratitude must go to my wife, children and grandson (Afaf, Nisreen, Danny and Ryan) who are my source of joy. As usual, Afaf was instrumental in helping me finish the manuscript by providing technical support in various shapes and forms, particularly graphics. I would also like to thank my colleagues and friends, including John Vaz, Kelly Burns, Vikash Ramiah, Mike Dempsey, Larry Li, Liam Lenten and Brien McDonald. I am grateful to Somaiya Al-Alami for providing some of the data used for empirical illustrations.

In preparing the manuscript, I benefited from an exchange of ideas with members of the Table 14 Discussion Group, and for this reason I would like to thank Bob Parsons, Greg O'Brien, Greg Bailey, Bill Breen, Paul Rule, Peter Murphy, Bob Brownlee and Tony Paligano. Parts of this book were written while I was on a study leave at the Gulf University for Science and Technology (Kuwait) where I received help from several people. Hence I would like to thank Salah Al-Sharhan, Fida Karam, Tony Simintiras, Sulaiman Al-Abduljader, Hana Derbas and Hiba Shehab.

My thanks also go to friends and former colleagues who live far away but provide help via means of telecommunication, including Kevin Dowd (whom I owe intellectual debt), Razzaque Bhatti, Ron Ripple, Bob Sedgwick, Sean Holly, Dan Hemmings and Ian Baxter. Last, but not least,

I would like to thank Alex Pettifer, editorial director of Edward Elgar, who encouraged me to write this book.

Naturally, I am the only one responsible for any errors and omissions that may be found in this book. It is dedicated to my daughter, Nisreen, my son, Danny, and my grandson, Ryan.

Imad A. Moosa
2017

To Nisreen, Danny and Ryan

1. The nature and evolution of econometrics

1.1 ECONOMETRICS OR ECONOMIC-TRICKS?

In the 1940s the term "econometrics" was a *neologism* (a new word), consisting of two Greek words: *oikonomia* (meaning administration or economics) and *metron*, which means measure (for example, Chait, 1949). In English, the literal meaning of "econometrics" is "economic measurement", although measurement may not appear explicitly as a function of econometrics. Today, econometrics is about more than measurement, and for the sceptics it is effectively "economy-tricks" (or "economic-tricks"), a collection of "tricks" used by economists to prove what they want to prove. Even econometrics enthusiasts refer to tricks in econometrics (for example, Varian, 2014). McAleer et al. (1985) start their paper by telling a story about a new typist for Carl Christ (a famous econometrician) who actually typed "econometrics" as "economic tricks" – for the sceptics the typist must have been observant and foresighted. For the time being, this cynical view of econometrics is put aside by considering what the discipline is all about from a historical perspective.

Although econometric techniques are widely used by both practitioners and academics, no generally accepted definition of econometrics exists – this is why Tintner (1953) referred to "the difficult problem of defining econometrics". To do that, he proceeded by giving a "preliminary definition", but the proper definition proposed by Tintner came only after presenting a definition of economics, identifying the forerunners of econometrics, defining quantitative economics (which presumably encompasses econometrics), and tracing the origin of the word "econometrics". Tintner suggested reasons as to why he preferred the definition of econometrics as a combination of economics, mathematics and statistics, which are the three pillars or components of econometrics as recognized universally. He argued that while the definition of econometrics was of some importance, it was to a certain extent arbitrary, but then he described econometrics as being related to economics in the same manner as psychometrics is related to psychology, sociometrics to sociology, and biometrics to biology. Typically, when it comes to defining econometrics, the tendency

1

is to identify the sub-divisions (or branches) of the discipline, its pillars (or components), and the tasks (functions) that can be executed by using econometric techniques.

Econometrics has become a household term that can be found as an entry in the *Collins Dictionary*, where it is emphasized that the term is singular (www.collinsdictionary.com). The definition found in the *Collins Dictionary* is that econometrics is "the application of mathematical and statistical techniques to economic problems and theories". This brief definition overlaps with the definitions of related disciplines using quantitative techniques such as mathematical economics and operational research. However, it is typical that a description of what econometrics is all about gives rise to the problem of distinguishing econometrics from similar and close disciplines such as mathematical economics, statistics, economic statistics, mathematical statistics, statistical economics, quantitative economics, analytical economics, empirical economics, empirical econometrics, and perhaps operational research. The emphasis by the *Collins Dictionary* that the term "econometrics" is singular is due to the fact that many authors take the word to be the plural of "econometric". For example, Baltagi (2002) starts section 1.4 of his book by saying that "econometrics have experienced phenomenal growth in the past 50 years". I suppose that the word "econometric" is an adjective and adjectives have no plurals.

A large number of definitions can be found in the academic and professional literature – these definitions have common elements and they shed some light on the nature of econometrics. For example, the popular website *Investopedia* (www.investopedia.com) adopts the following definition of econometrics:

> Econometrics is the application of statistical and mathematical theories to economics for the purpose of testing hypotheses and forecasting future trends. Econometrics takes economic models and tests them through statistical trials. The results are then compared and contrasted against real-life examples. Econometrics can be subdivided into two major categories: theoretical and applied.

Two characteristics of econometrics are embodied in this definition. The first is that econometrics consists of econometric methods (theoretical econometrics) and applied econometrics. Theoretical econometrics is about the development of estimation, testing and model evaluation procedures, whereas applied econometrics is about the application of econometric methods to economic issues. We will see later that econometric methods and applications evolved contemporaneously. The second characteristic is that econometric methods are designed to deal with either hypothesis testing or forecasting, although the two functions are related. This definition therefore identifies the branches of econometrics (methods and applications or theoretical and applied) and the functions that can be executed by using econometric techniques (hypothesis testing and forecasting). It is, however, not clear what is meant by "comparing and contrasting with real-life examples" – perhaps it means that when a model is used to generate forecasts, the predictive power of the model is assessed by comparing the forecasts with the corresponding actual (observed) data.

Another definition of econometrics, which can be found on lexicon. ft.com, is the following:

> Econometrics is the art and science of using data to test various economic theories. More specifically, econometrics can be viewed as the use of mathematics and sophisticated statistical modelling to test economic or financial theories as well as forecast the effects of changes in economic or financial factors under various scenarios. . . . Econometrics is an inter-disciplinary effort to understand economic and financial behaviour through the use of data, economic theory, mathematics, statistical methods, and other quantitative techniques.

This definition describes econometrics as art and science, but it does not tell us whether it is more like art or science. This is an important issue that will be examined later on when it is argued that neither econometrics nor economics is a science – at least not in the same sense as physics is a science. The definition also points to the main functions of hypothesis testing and forecasting and identifies the components of econometrics as economic theory, mathematics and statistics. However, the term "other quantitative techniques" may extend econometrics out of its natural boundaries. For example, some of the quantitative operational research techniques used to solve management problems include scheduling, transportation and network analysis. These techniques typically fall out of the realm of econometrics, which means that not all of quantitative techniques are used by econometricians. This is another issue that will be dealt with later.

1.2 MORE DEFINITIONS

Hansen (2011) contends that the best way to define econometrics is to go back to its roots, to the words of the "founding father", Ragnar Frisch (1895–1973), who was one of the three principal founders of the Econometric Society, the first editor of *Econometrica*, and a co-winner of the first Nobel Prize in economics in 1969. In an editorial of the first issue of *Econometrica*, Frisch (1933a) wrote the following:

A word of explanation regarding the term econometrics may be in order. Its definition is implied in the statement of the scope of the [Econometric] Society, in Section I of the constitution, which reads: "The Econometric Society is an international society for the advancement of economic theory in its relation to statistics and mathematics. . . . Its main object shall be to promote studies that aim at a unification of the theoretical-quantitative and the empirical-quantitative approach to economic problems.

This definition identifies the components of econometrics as economic theory, mathematics and statistics. However, Frisch argued that each of the three components was a necessary, but not by itself a sufficient condition for a real understanding of quantitative relations in modern economic life. Hence, he concluded that it was the unification of the three components that constituted econometrics. For Hansen (2011), "this definition remains valid today, although some terms have evolved somewhat in their usage". He goes on to define econometrics as "the unified study of economic models, mathematical statistics, and economic data", suggesting that the sub-divisions and specializations encompassed by econometrics are (1) econometric theory, which is about the development of tools and methods; and (2) applied econometrics, which is about the development of quantitative economic models and the application of econometric methods to these models using economic data. In his definition, Hansen adds data as a component of econometrics and lumps statistics and mathematics into one term, "mathematical statistics".

Several definitions come from recognized econometricians. For example, Haavelmo (1944) defined econometrics as a "conjunction of economic theory and actual measurements, using the theory and technique of statistical inference as a bridge pier". Samuelson, Koopmans and Stone (1954) stated that "econometrics may be defined as the quantitative analysis of actual economic phenomena based on the concurrent development of theory and observation, related by appropriate methods of inference". Spanos (1986) defined it as the systematic study of economic phenomena using observed data.

In a comprehensive survey of the discipline, Geweke et al. (2006) define econometrics more broadly by identifying its aims "to give empirical content to economic relations for testing economic theories, forecasting, decision making, and for ex post decision/policy evaluation". They also suggest that "econometrics calls for a unification of measurement and theory in economics", which is appealing because neither "theory" nor "measurement" on their own is sufficient to boost our understanding of how the economy works.

A detailed description of econometrics can be found in the *International Encyclopaedia of the Social Sciences* (www.encyclopedia.com), which describes econometrics in detail as follows:

Succinctly defined, econometrics is the study of economic theory in its relations to statistics and mathematics. The essential premise is that economic theory lends itself to mathematical formulation, usually as a system of relationships which may include random variables. Economic observations are generally regarded as a sample drawn from a universe described by the theory. Using these observations and the methods of statistical inference, the econometrician tries to estimate the relationships that constitute the theory. Next, these estimates may be assessed in terms of their statistical properties and their capacity to predict further observations. The quality of the estimates and the nature of the prediction errors may in turn feed back into a revision of the very theory by which the observations were organized and on the basis of which the numerical characteristics of the universe postulated were inferred. Thus, there is a reciprocating relationship between the formulation of theory and empirical estimation and testing. The salient feature is the explicit use of mathematics and statistical inference. Nonmathematical theorizing and purely descriptive statistics are not part of econometrics.

This extended definition identifies the components of econometrics as economic theory, statistics and mathematics and recognizes the nature of observations (data) used for the purpose of estimating and testing economic functional relations. The definition (description) also identifies the "essential premise" that economic theory lends itself to mathematical formulation, which is not universally acceptable. Non-mathematical theory is excluded from econometrics, implying that mathematical economic theory (mathematical economics) is part of it. Also excluded are "purely descriptive statistics", presumably a reference to economic statistics. In this encyclopaedia entry, it is stated explicitly that "much of what is commonly known as econometrics is mathematical economic theory that stops short of empirical work" and that "some of what is known as econometrics is the statistical estimation of *ad hoc* relationships that have only a frail basis in economic theory". The implication of this definition is that the presentation of an economic theory by using diagrams and confronting it with observed data do not constitute econometric analysis. It is not clear if the implication of this description is that descriptive economic theory and economic statistics are not sophisticated enough, which makes it useless. A large number of econometricians and mathematical economists seem to think along these lines.

Perhaps the best way to understand what econometrics is all about is to describe it in terms of its branches (econometric methods and applied econometrics), functions (hypothesis testing and forecasting) and components (economic theory, mathematics and statistics). But even this description has significant overlapping with related disciplines as we are going to see later. The evolution of econometrics has led to a shift of emphasis in favour of econometric methods, as the development of new methods has become the end rather than the means to an end, and away from economic theory to pure mathematics and statistics. An Australian university is probably the only university in the world that has a separate department of econometrics, a department where the academics often brag about not using real data. If this is the case, where is measurement in econometrics?

1.3   THE EARLY YEARS OF ECONOMETRICS

Appendix Table 1A.1 displays a time line for the evolution of econometrics, going back to the works of Yule (1895) and Hooker (1901). While the term "econometrics" was used for the first time by Pawel Ciompa in 1910, it was Ragnar Frisch who established the discipline as we know it today (Bjerkholt, 1995). The precursor to econometrics was quantitative research in economics, the origins of which can be traced at least as far back as the work of the 16th-century political arithmeticians who analysed data in their studies of taxation, money and international trade. Geweke et al. (2006) suggest that two political arithmeticians (William Petty and Gregory King) presented the earliest unified quantitative/theoretical approach to economics. In the latter part of the 17th century William Petty published work on *political arithmetic*, which was econometric in its methodological framework even from the modern point of view.

Schumpeter (1954) argued that the "works of the political arithmeticians illustrate to perfection what Econometrics is and what Econometricians are trying to do". According to Charles Davenant (1698), Gregory King was the first to fit a linear function of changes in corn prices on deficiencies in the corn harvest, effectively estimating an excess demand function (for corn). Geweke et al. (2006) contend that the early empirical work of King and others "seems to have been the discovery of 'laws' in economics, very much like those in physics and other natural sciences". It will be argued later that there are no laws in economics and that the desire to make economics look like physics is probably due to inferiority complex on the part of economists going down that slippery slope. The proposition that there are laws in economics is ludicrous, to say the least (more about this in Chapters 3 and 4).

The use of mathematics in economics preceded the use of statistics – for example, in 1711 Giovanni Ceva, an Italian engineer, advocated the use of mathematics in economic theory. However, it was Leon Walras, the French economist credited for the formulation of the marginal theory of value and general equilibrium theory, who erected the foundations of modern mathematical economics. Although his work was removed from any immediate statistical application, he developed a comprehensive system of relations between economic variables (including money) in order to explain the mutual determination of prices and quantities of commodities and the capital goods produced and exchanged.

The birth of modern statistics in the late 19th century was pivotal for the emergence of econometrics, as econometric methods are essentially statistical methods modified to deal with economic relations. The earliest applications of simple correlation analysis in economics was carried out by Yule (1895) who examined the relation between pauperism (widespread and extreme poverty) and the method of providing relief, and by Hooker (1901) who investigated the relation between the marriage rate and the general level of prosperity. Henry Moore (1914, 1917) was the first to place the statistical estimation of economic relations at the centre of quantitative analysis in economics. Moore carried out econometric work on business cycles, the determination of wages, and the demand for certain commodities (see, for example, Stigler, 1962).

Moore's work was taken further by Schultz (1938), Allen and Bowley (1935), Wright (1915, 1928), Working (1927), Tinbergen (1930) and Frisch (1933b) who worked on the measurement of demand, family expenditure, and the problem of identification. Early empirical work in finance was carried out by Louis Bachelier (1900) who recognized the random walk character of stock prices, leading eventually to the emergence of the efficient market hypothesis as developed by Eugene Fama in the late 1960s and early 1970s. In macroeconomics, Clement Juglar (1819–1905) discovered the Juglar cycle, an investment cycle of about 7–11 years' duration, leading eventually to the work of Mitchell (1928) and Burns and Mitchell (1947) on the business cycle.

1.4   SUBSEQUENT DEVELOPMENTS

Econometrics as we know it today began to emerge in the 1930s and 1940s with the foundation of the Econometric Society and Cowles Commission. The Econometric Society was established to confront theoretical economics with reality and the advancement of economic theory in its relation to statistics and mathematics (Fisher, 1933). The Cowles Commission for Research in Economics was founded in Colorado Springs in 1932 by Alfred Cowles, a businessman and economist. In 1939 the Commission moved to the University of Chicago. In 1943 Jacob Marschak, who had left Oxford University to move to the US in 1939, became the director of the Cowles Commission, a post that he held until 1948 when he was succeeded by Tjalling Koopmans. Under Marschak's directorship, the Commission began an intensive study of the problems of estimation and identification associated with simultaneous equation systems. In 1948 Koopmans became the director of the Commission, playing an instrumental role in the development of work on the estimation of simultaneous equations. That work was published in three monographs: *Statistical Inference in Dynamic Economic Models* (edited by Koopmans, 1950), *Economic Fluctuations in the United States, 1921–1941* (Klein, 1950), and *Studies in Econometric Method* (edited by Hood and Koopmans, 1953).

Rising opposition to the Cowles Commission by the Department of Economics at the University of Chicago during the 1950s encouraged the Cowles group to move to Yale University in 1955, where the Commission was reincarnated as the Cowles Foundation. The idea of the joint or simultaneous determination of certain economic variables was met with a degree of resistance from several parties, most notably from Wold (1949), who argued that multi-equation econometric models should be structured in a recursive manner, such that the inputs to each equation would be predetermined by preceding equations. In other words, the solution for the *n*th endogenous variable in a recursive system involves only the first *n* equations. Wold rejected simultaneity, the notion that everything occurs at the same time on the grounds that the true description of economic events must be along a temporal sequence.

Initially, emphasis was placed on the development of econometric methods. It was the probabilistic rationalizations of regression analysis, advanced by Koopmans (1937) and Haavelmo (1944), that formed the basis of modern econometrics. Haavelmo (1944) defended the probability approach by arguing that the use of statistical measures (such as the mean, standard error and correlation coefficient) for inferential purposes is justified only if the process generating the data can be cast in terms of a probability model and that the probability approach is not suitable for the analysis of the dependent and non-homogeneous observations often encountered in economic research. Tinbergen (1937) saw the role of the econometrician as a passive one of estimating the parameters of an economic relation already specified on a priori grounds by an economist (although these days it is not clear who is an economist, who is an econometrician and who is both). Although he discussed the problems of the determination of time lags, trends, structural stability and the choice of functional forms, he did not propose any systematic methodology for dealing with them.

Keynes (1939) was critical of econometrics, mainly with respect to the technical difficulties associated with the application of statistical methods to economic data, emphasizing the problems of misspecification, multi-collinearity, functional form, dynamic specification, structural stability, and the difficulties associated with the measurement of theoretical variables. In response to the criticism directed by Keynes at Tinbergen's work,

Haavelmo (1943) recognized the need for a general statistical framework to deal with these criticisms, suggesting that the technical problems raised by Keynes could be dealt with by means of formal probabilistic models. Keynes was demonized by some econometricians for daring to criticize econometrics.

Geweke et al. (2006) recognize Haavelmo's contribution as marking "the beginning of a new era in econometrics", paving the way for the rapid development of the discipline. Specific developments cover the areas of (1) identification of structural parameters, (2) estimation and inference in simultaneous equation models, and (3) developments in time series econometrics. In the field of identification of structural parameters, important contributions were made by Koopmans, Rubin and Leipnik (1950), Wegge (1965) and Manski (1995). These contributions were about devising the rank and order conditions for the identification of a single equation in a system of simultaneous linear equations and structural parameters in the context of semiparametric models. Developments in applications or applied econometrics occurred simultaneously.

1.5 MACROECONOMETRICS, MICROECONOMETRICS AND FINANCIAL ECONOMETRICS

Significant changes took place in the global economic environment in the 1970s, arising largely from the breakdown of the Bretton Woods system and the quadrupling of oil prices – these developments had implications for the direction of research in econometric methods and applications. Mainstream macroeconometric models had been built and tested in the 1950s and 1960s, when economic stability prevailed under conditions of stable energy prices and fixed exchange rates. The prestige of large-scale macroeconometric models was damaged severely in the 1970s when it was revealed that their forecasting performance was often far inferior to that of the simple unconditional time series models of the autoregressive moving average (ARMA) variety, which were popularized in the 1970s by Box and Jenkins (1970). Pollock (2014) explains this observation by suggesting that, unlike ARMA models, the equations of the macroeconometric models did not address even the simple laws of linear dynamic systems.

In the 1970s and early 1980s, the Cowles Commission approach to the identification and estimation of simultaneous macroeconometric models was questioned by Lucas (1976), Lucas and Sargent (1981) and Sims (1980). The response to the Lucas critique has been to treat the structural change emphasized by Lucas as a potential econometric problem.

There was also a move away from macroeconometric models towards microeconometric research. The emphasis gradually shifted from estimation and inference based on a given tightly parameterized specification to diagnostic testing, specification searches, model uncertainty, model validation, parameter variations, structural breaks, and to semiparametric and nonparametric estimation. These developments had an adverse effect on the role of economic theory as emphasis shifted to the invention of new econometric methods using advanced mathematical statistics.

The Lucas critique of mainstream macroeconometric modelling led some econometricians, notably Sims (1980, 1982), to be sceptical about the validity of the Cowles Commission style of achieving identification in econometric models. As an alternative, he suggested the use of a vector autoregressive (VAR) specification. In the "structural VAR" (SVAR) approach, it is assumed that structural shocks are orthogonal, but a mixture of short-run and long-run restrictions are used to identify the structural model. The focus of the SVAR literature has been on impulse response analysis and forecast error variance decomposition, with the aim of estimating the time profile of the effects of monetary policy, oil price or technology shocks on output and inflation.

Partly as a response to the dissatisfaction with macroeconometric time series research and partly in view of the increasing availability of micro data and computing facilities, interest shifted to the analysis of micro data. Important micro data sets have become available on households and firms in such areas as housing, transportation, labour markets and energy. These data sets include various longitudinal surveys (for example, the University of Michigan Panel Study of Income Dynamics and the Ohio State National Longitudinal Study Surveys), cross-sectional surveys of family expenditure, and population and labour force surveys. While opening up new possibilities for analysis, the increasing availability of micro data has also raised a number of new econometric issues primarily originating from the nature of the data. The models and issues considered in the microeconometric literature are wide ranging and include fixed and random effect panel data models (for example, Mundlak, 1961, 1978), logit and probit models and their multinominal extensions, discrete choice or quantal response models (Manski and McFadden, 1981), continuous time duration models (Heckman and Singer, 1984), and microeconometric models of count data (Hausman et al., 1984; Cameron and Trivedi, 1986).

Studies of the efficient market hypothesis (EMH) provided the impetus for the application of time series econometric methods in finance (hence the rise of the so-called financial econometrics). The EMH was built on the work of Bachelier (1900) and evolved in the 1960s from the random walk theory of asset prices advanced by Samuelson (1965). By the early 1970s a consensus had emerged among financial economists suggesting that stock prices could be well approximated by a random walk model and that changes in stock prices were basically unpredictable. Further developments in financial econometrics include equilibrium asset pricing models, modelling of asset return volatility (Engle, 1982, Bollerslev, 1986), analysis of high frequency intraday data, and market microstructure. Unfortunately, these developments have nothing to do with our ability to anticipate financial crises or devise a profitable trading strategy. As a matter of fact, work on the EMH in particular led to erroneous policies and the advent of the global financial crisis. We do not need financial econometrics to realize that greed-triggered fraud leads to financial mishaps. We do not need financial econometrics to find out that deregulation can bring about financial disasters. And we do not need financial econometrics to recognize the fact that bailing out (or bailing in) failed financial institutions under the pretext of too big to fail creates a moral hazard that perpetuates the occurrence of financial crises.

1.6   RECENT DEVELOPMENTS

Recent work in econometrics has been predominantly about the development of new estimation and testing methods without corresponding advances in empirical work on the working of the economy and financial system. In 1982 Robert Engle suggested the autoregressive conditional heteroscedasticity (ARCH) model to represent volatility clustering, which opened the floodgates for a non-stop emergence of ARCH-like models. Bollerslev (2008) argues that what he calls "Rob Engle's seminal Nobel Prize winning 1982 Econometrica article" spurred a virtual "arms race" into the development of "new and better" procedures for modelling and forecasting time-varying financial market volatility. He contends that the output of this "industry" is a "perplexing alphabet-soup of acronyms and abbreviations used to describe the plethora of models and procedures that have been developed over the years". There have been more sequels to ARCH than to *Jaws*, *Rocky*, *Rambo* and *Die Hard* put together. As for "better" models, it is not obvious to me in what way the extensions and alternative are better – it has been an extravaganza that served no purpose whatsoever, apart from providing the means whereby students get their PhDs and academics get their promotions. What Bollerslev (2008) calls an "arms race" has been a total waste of brain power as we moved from ARCH to other versions of volatility models obtained by simple tweaks. The development of these models has dominated econometrics in the last 30 years or so, taking us from ARCH to its disciples as shown in Figure 1.1

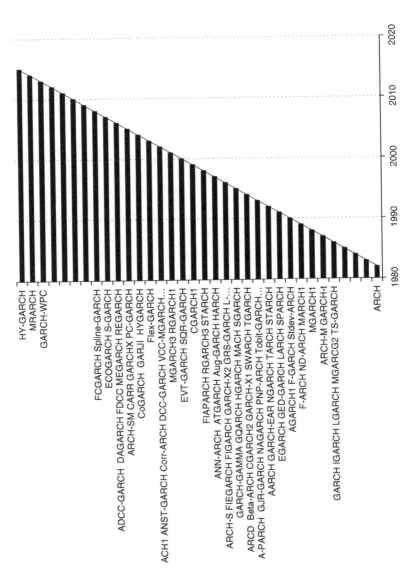

Figure 1.1   The growth of the ARCH industry

(which, by the way, does not represent an exhaustive list of ARCH models). It looks absolutely ridiculous, to say the least.

Extravaganza in estimation and testing methods continues – we used to have the instrumental variables method, now we have "jackknife instrumental variable estimation". Other new estimation methods include estimation with overidentifying inequality moment conditions, Bayesian estimation of dynamic discrete models, superparametric estimation of bivariate Tobit models, quantile regression for dynamic panel data with fixed effects, nonparametric instrumental regression, local GMM estimation, and many more. As for testing, recent developments include testing models of low-frequency variability, unit root quantile regression testing, specification tests of parametric dynamic conditional quantiles, and testing for common conditionally heteroscedastic factors. Even cointegration, which has proved to be a notion of dubious usefulness, has gone through some recent developments. In fact the *Journal of Econometrics* ran a special issue on cointegration in September 2010, dealing with topics such as likelihood testing for no fractional cointegration, which followed work on quantile cointegration regression and structural nonparametric cointegrating regression. All of these developments represent no more than extravaganza that has contributed nothing to our understanding of economics and finance.

1.7   THE ALLEGED SUCCESS OF ECONOMETRICS

Econometricians typically hail the evolution of econometrics as a "big success". For example, Geweke et al. (2006) argue that "econometrics has come a long way over a relatively short period". As indicators of the success of econometrics, they list the following: (1) applications of econometric methods can be found in almost every field of economics; (2) econometric models have been used extensively by government agencies, international organizations and commercial enterprises; (3) macroeconometric models of differing complexity and size have been constructed for almost every country in the world; and (4) both in theory and practice econometrics has already gone well beyond what its founders envisaged. Other measures of the success of econometrics include the observation that there is now scarcely a field of applied economics into which mathematical and statistical theory has not penetrated, including economic history. Pagan (1987) declares econometrics as an "outstanding success" because the work of econometric theorists has become "part of the process of economic investigation and the training of economists". Yet another indicator of the success of econometrics is the observation of excess demand for well-trained econometricians.

These claims represent no more than self-glorifying rhetoric, which at the limit considers the discovery or invention of ARCH to be as worthwhile of the Nobel Prize as the discovery or invention of Penicillin. The widespread use of econometrics is not indicative of success, just like the widespread use of drugs does not represent social success. Applications of econometric methods in almost every field of economics is not the same as saying that econometrics has enhanced our understanding of the underlying issues in every field of economics. It only shows that econometrics is no longer a means to an end but rather the end itself. The use of econometric models by government agencies has not led to improvement in policy making, as we move from one crisis to another. Constructing models for almost every country in the world has not helped alleviate poverty or solve recurring economic problems.

The observations that econometric theory has become part of the training of economists and that of excess demand for well-trained econometricians are far away from being measures of success. Including more and more statistical and mathematical material in curriculums amounts to squeezing out theoretical and applied courses (recall the concept of opportunity cost). While core microeconomics and macroeconomics courses remain, students do not have many electives left over to study things like labour economics, welfare economics, public economics, energy economics, case studies in economic policy, and so on. As a result of the alleged success of econometrics, courses in economic history and the history of economic thought have all but disappeared from the curriculum. The alleged success of econometrics has led to the production of economics graduates who may be good at number crunching but do not know much about various economic problems faced by humanity. How many universities in the world have a course in applied economics these days?

Doing sophisticated econometric work has nothing to do with the quest for the truth, but rather more with getting a paper accepted, which often involves confirmation bias. The use of econometrics and quantitative methods in general has become a minimum requirement to have a paper accepted in a highly-rated academic journal. According to Blommestein (2009), "this premium on quantification has had serious adverse consequences, including a misallocation of research efforts in economics". These days, a typical paper in economics follows a highly stylized structure involving the formulation of a theory in mathematical form followed by the construction of an empirical model, then comes the discussion of the empirical results. Whether or not these results contribute to our understanding of economic theory is a different matter – actually, it is totally irrelevant.

The alleged success of econometrics has led to adverse consequences, starting with the brain drain inflicted on society by the movement of physicists, mathematicians and engineers to economics and finance, particularly looking for lucrative jobs in the financial sector. Instead of doing work to improve the fuel efficiency of the internal combustion engine, some innovative people originally working in science and technology have chosen to use their skills to indulge in the parasitic activity of developing new financial products and selling them as high-return, low-risk securities. At the same time, some good economists have left the field or retired early because they could not cope with the success of econometrics. On the other hand, good economists who do not do econometrics are looked down upon by the establishment. For example, Richard Posner, who is a non-believer in the efficient market hypothesis, made some sarcastic comments about the hypothesis in an interview with Cassidy (2010). When Cassidy interviewed Fama, the efficient market guru, he reacted rather furiously to Posner's comments, claiming that Posner is "not an economist" but rather "he's an expert on law and economics". This means that if your analysis does not involve "sophisticated quantitative work", you are not an economist, but if you hide behind equations you are a good economist. As a matter of fact, it is the brand of economics that Fama believes in (the physics-like economics) that has led to the mess we are in now. And it is the brand of economics that Posner believes in that will hopefully get us out of the mess.

Perhaps the success of econometrics can be measured by the increasing number of Nobel Prize winners awarded to econometricians for inventing ARCH, cointegration, causality, GMM, and various econometric methods. However, a Nobel Prize in economics (and peace for that matter) means nothing. Thompson et al. (2006) argue that the Nobel Prize has been awarded for nonsense, referring in particular to the Nobel Prize winning work in finance. Bergmann (1999) suggests that "we economists ought to open our eyes and see that having a Nobel Prize for economics is making the economics profession look ridiculous". She further refers to the embarrassment arising from the need to explain to the public the alleged achievement of the newest laureate. As examples, she mentions the prize won by economists telling us that "politicians and bureaucrats act in their own interest", that "people do the best they can in doping out what to do" and that "people save and spend their savings at different times in their lives". The Nobel Prize was even awarded to an economist who came up with the unethical conclusion that slavery was a good business, at least for those with the whip.

We must not forget that another Nobel Prize was awarded for the invention of that weapon of mass destruction, the efficient market hypothesis and other theories that are used to justify deregulation. Although the title of her article is "Abolish the Nobel for Economics", Bergmann suggests, as an alternative to abolishing the economics Nobel Prize, that the prize should not be awarded every year but rather only when work that advances economics as an empirical science appears. As long as neoclassical economics represents the mainstream, this is unlikely to happen because the research output will be about distilling complicated phenomena into simplistic representations of cheeringly optimal processes by using the available tools of econometric testing (Bergmann, 1999). Econometrics has not been a success because of the Nobel Prizes awarded to econometricians.

1.8   THE MOVE TOWARDS ABSTRACTION

Econometrics is no longer about measurement in economics as it has become too abstract. The meaning of the word "econometrics" is typically stretched to cover mathematical economics and the word "econometrician" refers to an economist, or otherwise, who is skilled and interested in the application of mathematics, be it mathematical statistics, game theory, topology or measure theory. Baltagi (2002) argues that research in economics and econometrics has been growing more and more abstract and highly mathematical without an application in sight or a motivation for practical use. In most cases, however, mathematization is unnecessary and a simple idea that can be represented by diagrams is made much more complex and beyond the comprehension of the average economist, let alone policy makers.

Heckman (2001) argues that econometrics is useful only if it helps economists conduct and interpret empirical research on economic data. Like Baltagi, Heckman warns that the gap between econometric theory and empirical practice has grown over the past two decades. Although he finds nothing wrong, and much potential value, in using methods and ideas from other fields to improve empirical work in economics, he does warn of the risks involved in uncritically adopting the methods and mindset of the statisticians. Econometric methods adapted from statistics are not useful in many research activities pursued by economists. A theorem-proof format is poorly suited for analysing economic data, which requires skills of synthesis, interpretation and empirical investigation. Command of statistical methods is only a part, and sometimes a very small part, of what is required to do useful empirical research.

The trend towards more abstract work can be seen in the contents of *Econometrica*. Table 1.1 lists the titles of selected articles from *Econometrica* in 1936, 1945, 1946, 2012, 2013 and 2016. In the 1930s and 1940s, *Econometrica* published papers on economics, dealing with microeconomic issues like the

Table 1.1   The changing contents of Econometrica

Year	Title
1936	Demand for Boots and Shoes as Affected by Price Levels and National Income
	Pareto's Sociology
	Vertical and Horizontal Shifts in Demand Curves
1945	Multiplier Effects of a Balanced Budget
	Measuring Marginal Utility by Reactions to Risk
	Liquidity Preference of Large Manufacturing Corporations (1921–1939)
1946	Theory of the Firm and Investment
	Capital Expansion, Rate of Growth and Employment
2012	Noisy Stochastic Games
	Reputational Bargaining with Minimal Knowledge of Rationality
	Mechanism Design with Renegotiation and Costly Message Timing and Self-Control
	Inference of Signs of Interaction Effects in Simultaneous Games with Incomplete Information
	Stability and Preference Alignment in Matching and Coalition Formation
	Definable and Contractible Contracts
2013	Efficiency in Games with Markovian Private Information
	Calibrated Incentive Contracts
	Discounted Stochastic games with No Stationary Nash Equilibrium
2016	Reputational Bargaining and Deadlines
	Robust Contracts in Continuous Time
	Stochastic Learning Dynamics and Speed of Convergence in Population Games

demand for boots and macroeconomic issues like the multiplier effect of a balanced budget. In recent volumes most of the papers are too abstract, use no data and do not provide new econometric methods that can be used in empirical work. Notice in particular the frequency of papers on game theory, which is supposed to be a branch of mathematics. Recent issues of *Econometrica* are dominated by what a frustrated academic economist once called "data-free mathematical masturbation", suggesting that it was not his "source of enlightenment" (Mason et al., 1992). This is why a joke goes as follows: during the rule of Nicolai Ceausescu in Romania, the government banned all "western" economics journals – the exception was *Econometrica* because it had nothing to do with economics.

Another adverse consequence of the alleged success of econometrics is that we have become slaves, believing in its power and following blindly the implications of empirical results. When the results do not make sense, we do not reject them because common sense says so, we try to find an explanation for the results. For example, Moosa (2016a) has demonstrated that if we believe the results of empirical testing at the expense of common sense, we will believe that spending on science and technology leads to a higher rate of suicide and that the consumption of margarine is conducive to divorce. This has happened because of the dwindling role of economic theory in empirical work.

1.9   ECONOMETRICS AS A TOOL TO PROVE ANYTHING

Econometrics has been a success only in the limited sense that it can be used to prove almost anything. I have always challenged seminar present-ers, saying that if they let me have their data I could turn their results upside down and come up with a different conclusion. Econometrics is very useful for those wanting to prove a pre-conceived belief or find results that support an ideologically driven hypothesis. Take, for example, Brexit, which had proponents and opponents. The empirical results produced by the opponents on the effect of Brexit on the British economy of leaving the EU are all over the place but ideological bias is conspicuous. For example, the Confederation of British Industry (2013), which is against Brexit, estimated the net benefit to Britain of EU membership to be in the region of 4 per cent to 5 per cent of GDP – that is, between £62 billion and £78 billion per year. Conversely, Congdon (2014) puts the cost of Britain's membership of the EU at 10 per cent, attributing this cost to regulation and resource misallocation. Congdon's estimates were prepared for the United Kingdom Independence Party (UKIP), which has a strong anti-Europe stance.

Last, but not least, econometrics has been used to make outrageous claims and justify draconian economic policy. Econometrics has been used to justify inequality and defend the top 1 per cent. Econometrics has been used to justify tax cuts for the rich and support the trickle-down effect, which is no less than the rich pissing on the poor. Econometrics has been used to support the so-called "great moderation" and justify wholesale financial deregulation, the very policies that have led to growing poverty. When Ronald Reagan wanted to cut taxes for the rich, he hired the services of an economic outfit that produced results showing that cutting taxes for the rich would benefit the poor, which is a travesty in every sense of the word. George Bush Junior did the same, despite opposition from some high-calibre economists who argued that things did not work as envisaged by Bush and his advisers.

Econometrics has succeeded in one sense – it has succeeded as a con art, enabling anyone to prove anything. To be fair, econometrics has been a blessing, providing the means to get PhDs and academic promotions. This is what Richard Posner said in his comments on the efficient market hypothesis when he was interviewed by Cassidy (2010):

> Well, one possibility is that they have learned nothing. . . because market correctives work very slowly in dealing with academic markets. Professors have tenure. They have lots of graduate students in the pipeline who need to get their Ph.D.s. They have techniques that they know and are comfortable with. It takes a great deal to drive them out of their accustomed way of doing business.

There is no wonder then that the likes of Richard Posner are not considered economists because they do not use econometrics. By the logic of this argument, neither Adam Smith nor John Maynard Keynes were economists because they did not use econometrics.

1.10 CONCLUDING REMARKS

We have been so obsessed with the success of econometrics that we even test the untestable. For example, numerous studies have been conducted to test covered interest parity, producing the usual mixed bag of results. When the results do not support CIP, those doing the research seek an explanation, thus producing a menu of why we observe deviations from CIP such as transaction costs, taxation, market imperfection, political risk, and so on. But the fact of the matter is that CIP is not a testable hypothesis. It is a definitional equation, an identity that represents the mechanism whereby bankers quote forward rates for their clients. Instead of testing CIP, an econometrician can ask a banker about the process whereby the forward rate is determined. The banker will tell him that it is calculated by adjusting the spot rate by a factor that reflects the interest rate differential, and that will be the end of the matter. But no, we have to "test, test and test", because econometrics is all about testing.

All it takes is to formulate a hypothesis, get data, test the hypothesis and generate forecasts. The more sophisticated it sounds the better it is. But in terms of advancing our knowledge of the working of the economy and financial markets, the contribution of econometrics has been zero at best and negative at worst. What have we learned about the working of financial markets by the progress made by moving from ARCH to GARCH and onwards to IGARCH, MGARCH, TS-GARCH, F-ARCH, AGARCH, LARCH, SPARCH, AARCH, QTARCH, STARCH, NAGARCH, PNP-ARCH, and so and so forth? Yes, econometrics has been quite a success, but only as a con art.

APPENDIX

Table 1A.1   Time line for the evolution of econometrics

Year	Development	Author(s)
1895	Application of correlation analysis in economics	Yule (1895)
1900	The random walk character of stock prices	Bachelier (1900)
1901	Application of correlation analysis in economics	Hooker (1901)
1907	Using multiple regression in economics	Benini (1907)
1913	The problem of identification	Lenoir (1913)
1914	The foundations of statistical economics	Moore (1914,1917)
1915	The problem of identification	Wright (1915, 1928)
1927	The problem of identification	Working (1927)
1928	Analysis of the business cycle	Mitchell (1928)
1929	The problem of identification	Tinbergen (1930)
1930	Distributed lag models	Fisher (1930)
1933	The problem of identification	Frisch (1933b)
1935	Analysis of family expenditure	Allen and Bowley (1935)
1937	Probabilistic rationalizations of regression analysis	Koopmans (1937)
1937	The arithmetic lag distribution	Fisher (1937)
1938	The theory and measurement of demand	Schultz (1938)
1941	Developing the instrumental variable (IV) method	Reiersol (1941, 1945)
1944	Probabilistic rationalizations of regression analysis	Haavelmo (1944)
1944	Necessary and sufficient conditions for identification	Haavelmo (1944)
1945	Bunch map analysis	Stone (1945)
1947	Analysis of the business cycle	Burns and Mitchell (1947)
1947	The construction of macroeconometric models	Klein (1947, 1950)
1948	The autocorrelation pattern of economic time series	Orcutt (1948)
1949	Limited Information Maximum Likelihood (LIML)	Anderson and Rubin (1949)
1949	The instrumental variable (IV) method	Geary (1949)

Table 1A.1 (continued)

Year	Development	Author(s)
1949	Autocorrelation of the error term	Cochrane and Orcutt (1949)
1949	Recursive systems of simultaneous equations	Wold (1949)
1950	The rank and order conditions for the identification	Koopmans (1949)
1950	Full Information Maximum Likelihood (FIML)	Koopmans et al. (1950)
1950	Testing for residual autocorrelation	Durbin and Watson (1950, 1951)
1952	The hypothesis of habit persistence	Brown (1952)
1954	Two-Stage Least Squares (2SLS)	Theil (1954, 1958)
1954	The geometric distributed lag model	Koyck (1954)
1956	The demand for money under hyperinflation	Cagan (1956)
1957	Two-Stage Least Squares (2SLS)	Basmann (1957)
1957	Econometric analysis of consumption behaviour	Friedman (1957)
1958	Generalized IV estimator	Sargan (1958)
1958	k-class estimators	Theil (1958)
1958	Modelling the cobweb phenomenon	Nerlove (1958a)
1958	The partial adjustment model	Nerlove (1958b)
1958	The censored regression model	Tobin (1958)
1960	Generalization of the geometric distributed lag model	Solow (1960)
1960	Spurious regression	Champernowne (1960)
1960	Modelling structural breaks	Chow (1960)
1961	Non-nested model selection tests	Cox (1961, 1962)
1961	Panel data models	Mundlak (1961, 1978)
1962	Three-Stage Least Squares method	Zellner and Theil (1962)
1962	Seemingly unrelated regressions	Zellner (1962)
1963	The partial adjustment model	Eisner and Strotz (1963)
1964	Error correction modelling	Sargan (1964)
1965	Other solutions to the identification problem	Wege (1965)
1965	Generalization of the arithmetic lag distribution	Almon (1965)

22

Year	Topic	Reference
1966	Other solutions to the identification problem	Fisher (1966)
1966	Generalization of the geometric distributed lag model	Jorgenson (1966)
1969	Causality	Granger (1969)
1969	General specification tests	Ramsey (1969)
1970	Iterated instrumental variables	Lyttkens (1970)
1970	ARIMA models	Box and Jenkins (1970)
1970	Random coefficient models	Swamy (1970)
1971	Iterated instrumental variables	Brundy and Jorgenson (1971)
1971	Iterated instrumental variables	Dhrymes (1971)
1971	System k-class estimators	Srivastava (1971)
1971	The multivariate flexible accelerator model	Treadway (1971)
1972	Causality	Sims (1972)
1972	Causality	Engle et al. (1983)
1973	The proportional hazards model	Cox (1972)
1973	System k-class estimators	Savin (1973)
1973	General specification tests	Wu (1973)
1974	Spurious regression	Granger and Newbold (1974)
1975	Semiparametric estimation	Manski (1975, 1985)
1976	The Lucas critique	Lucas (1976)
1978	Economic theory and econometric models	Leamer (1978)
1978	General specification tests	Hausman (1978)
1979	Unit root testing	Dickey and Fuller (1979, 1981)
1979	Censored regression models	Buckley and James (1979)
1979	The bootstrap	Efron (1979)
1980	VAR models	Sims (1980, 1982)
1980	Diagnostic tests	Breusch and Pagan (1980)
1981	Discrete choice or quantal response models	Manski and McFadden (1981)
1982	The generalized method of moments (GMM)	Hansen (1982)
1982	Disequilibrium models	Quandt (1982)
1982	Model evaluation criteria	Hendry and Richard (1982)
1982	Diagnostic tests	Godfrey and Wickens (1982)
1982	ARCH models	Engle (1982)

Table 1A.1 (continued)

Year	Development	Author(s)
1983	Estimation of simultaneous nonlinear equations	Amemiya (1983)
1983	Exposing con practices in econometrics	Leamer (1983)
1983	Exogeneity	Engle et al. (1983)
1983	Disequilibrium models	Maddala (1983, 1986)
1983	Small sample theory	Phillips (1983)
1983	Semiparametric estimation	Cosslett (1983)
1984	Small sample theory	Rothenberg (1984)
1984	Bayesian VAR models	Doan et al. (1984)
1984	Continuous time duration models	Heckman and Singer (1984)
1984	Micro-econometric models of count data	Hausman et al. (1984)
1984	Least absolute deviations estimator	Powell (1984, 1986)
1985	Bayesian VAR models	Litterman (1985)
1985	Model evaluation criteria	McAleer et al. (1985)
1985	Econometric analysis of pseudo panels	Deaton (1985)
1985	Dymimic models	Engle et al. (1985)
1985	Adaptive Conditional Heteroskedasticity	McCulloch (1985)
1986	Spurious regression	Phillips (1986)
1986	Count regression models	Cameron and Trivedi (1986)
1986	Cointegration	Granger (1986)
1986	GARCH models	Bollerslev (1986)
1986	IGARCH (Integrated GARCH)	Engle and Bollerslev (1986)
1986	Log-GARCH (Logarithmic GARCH)	Geweke (1986)
1986	MGARCH2 (Multiplicative GARCH)	Geweke (1986)
1986	TS-GARCH (Taylor–Schwert GARCH)	Taylor (1986)
1987	Cointegration	Engle and Granger (1987)
1987	ARCH-M (ARCH-in-Mean)	Engle et al. (1987)
1987	The GARCH-t model	Bollerslev (1987)

Year	Model / Topic	Reference
1988	Econometric models of auction pricing	Hendricks and Porter (1988)
1988	Cointegration	Johansen (1988, 1991)
1988	MGARCH1 (Multivariate GARCH)	Bollerslev et al. (1988)
1989	Modelling structural breaks	Nyblom (1989)
1989	TS-GARCH (Taylor–Schwert GARCH)	Schwert (1989)
1989	Structural VAR models	Blanchard and Quah (1989)
1989	Structural time series models	Harvey (1989)
1989	F-ARCH (Factor ARCH)	Diebold and Nerlove (1989)
1989	N-dimensional factor ARCH	Diebold and Nerlove (1989)
1989	MARCH1 (Modified ARCH)	Friedman et al. (1989)
1989	The method of simulated moments (MSM)	McFadden (1989)
1989	The method of simulated moments (MSM)	Pakes and Pollard (1989)
1990	Fully modified ordinary least squares	Phillips and Hansen (1990)
1990	AGARCH1 (Asymmetric GARCH)	Engle (1990)
1990	F-GARCH (Factor-GARCH)	Engle et al. (1990)
1990	Stdev-ARCH (Standard deviation ARCH)	Schwert (1990)
1991	Cointegration	Phillips (1991)
1991	EGARCH (Exponential GARCH)	Nelson (1991)
1991	Generalized Error Distribution GARCH	Nelson (1991)
1991	LARCH (Linear ARCH)	Robinson (1991)
1991	SPARCH (Semi-parametric ARCH)	Engle and Gonzalez-Rivera (1991)
1992	AARCH (Augmented ARCH)	Bera, Higgins and Lee (1992)
1992	GARCH-EAR (GARCH Exponential AutoRegression)	LeBaron (1992)
1992	NGARCH (Nonlinear GARCH)	Higgins and Bera (1992)
1992	QTARCH (Qualitative Threshold ARCH)	Gourieroux and Monfort (1992)
1992	STARCH (Structural ARCH)	Harvey et al. (1992)
1993	Modelling structural breaks	Andrews (1993)
1993	A-PARCH models	Ding et al. (1993)
1993	GJR-GARCH	Glosten et al. (1993)
1993	NAGARCH (Nonlinear Asymmetric GARCH)	Engle and Ng (1993)
1993	PNP-ARCH (Partially Non-Parametric ARCH)	Engle and Ng (1993)

Table 1A.1 (continued)

Year	Development	Author(s)
1993	Tobit-GARCH	Kodres (1993)
1993	VGARCH1	Engle and Ng (1993)
1993	Weak GARCH	Drost and Nijman (1993)
1994	ARCD (Autoregressive Conditional Density)	Hansen (1994)
1994	β-ARCH (Beta ARCH)	Guégan and Diebolt (1994)
1994	CGARCH2 (Composite GARCH)	Den Hertog (1994)
1994	GARCH-X1	Lee (1994)
1994	SWARCH (regime Switching ARCH)	Cai (1994)
1994	TGARCH (Threshold GARCH)	Zakoïan (1994)
1995	Econometric models of auction pricing	Laffont et al. (1995)
1995	DSGE models	Kim and Pagan (1995)
1995	GARCH-Γ (GARCH Gamma)	Engle and Rosenberg (1995)
1995	GQARCH (Generalized Quadratic ARCH)	Sentana (1995)
1995	HGARCH (Hentschel GARCH)	Hentschel (1995)
1995	MACH (Moving Average Conditional Heteroskedastic)	Yang and Bewley (1995)
1995	SGARCH (Stable GARCH)	Liu and Brorsen (1995)
1996	Structural break in macroeconomic time series	Stock and Watson (1996)
1996	ARCH-Smoothers	Nelson (1996)
1996	FIEGARCH (Fractionally Integrated EGARCH)	Bollerslev and Mikkelsen (1996)
1996	FIGARCH (Fractionally Integrated GARCH)	Baillie et al. (1996)
1996	GARCH-X2	Brenner et al. (1996)
1996	GRS-GARCH (Generalized Regime-Switching GARCH)	Gray (1996)
1996	Level-GARCH	Brenner et al. (1996)
1996	PGARCH1 (Periodic GARCH)	Bollerslev and Ghysels (1996)
1996	VSGARCH (Volatility Switching GARCH)	Fornari and Mele (1996)
1997	ANN-ARCH (Artificial Neural Network ARCH)	Donaldson and Kamstra (1997)
1997	ATGARCH (Asymmetric Threshold GARCH)	Crouhy and Rockinger (1997)
1997	Aug-GARCH (Augmented GARCH)	Duan (1997)
1997	HARCH (Heterogeneous ARCH)	Müller et al. (1997)

Year		Reference
1998	Structural breaks and forecast failure	Clements and Hendry (1998, 1999)
1998	Modelling structural breaks	Bai and Perron (1998)
1998	ACD (Autoregressive Conditional Duration) models	Engle and Russell (1998)
1998	FIAPARCH (Fractionally Integrated Power ARCH)	Tse (1998)
1998	RGARCH3 (Root GARCH)	Gallant and Tauchen (1998)
1998	STGARCH (Smooth Transition GARCH)	Gonzalez-Rivera (1998)
1999	CGARCH1 (Component GARCH)	Engle and Lee (1999)
2000	EVT-GARCH (Extreme Value Theory GARCH)	McNeil and Frey (2000)
2000	SQR-GARCH (Square-Root GARCH)	Heston and Nandi (2000)
2001	Non-nested model selection tests	Pesaran and Weeks (2001)
2001	MGARCH3 (Mixture GARCH)	Wong and Li (2001)
2001	RGARCH1 (Randomized GARCH)	Nowicka-Zagrajek and Weron (2001)
2002	Weak instrument problem	Stock et al. (2002)
2002	ACH1 (Autoregessive Conditional Hazard)	Hamilton and Jordà (2002)
2002	ANST-GARCH (Asymmetric Nonlinear Smooth Transition GARCH)	Nam et al. (2002)
2002	CorrARCH (Correlated ARCH)	Christodoulakis and Satchell (2002)
2002	DCC-GARCH (Dynamic Conditional Correlations)	Engle (2002a)
2002	VCC-MGARCH (Varying Conditional Correlation)	Tse and Tsui (2002)
2002	DTARCH (Double Threshold ARCH)	Li and Li (1996)
2002	GO-GARCH (Generalized Orthogonal GARCH)	van der Weide (2002)
2002	MEM (Multiplicative Error Model)	Engle (2002b)
2002	RGARCH2 (Robust GARCH)	Park (2002)
2002	Structural GARCH	Rigobon (2002)
2002	Panel unit root tests	Levin et al. (2002)
2003	Model uncertainty in cointegrating VARs	Garratt et al. (2003, 2006)
2003	DSGE models	Smets and Wouters (2003)
2003	Flex-GARCH (Flexible GARCH)	Ledoit et al. (2003)
2003	Panel unit root tests	Im et al. (2003)
2004	CAViaR (Conditional Autoregressive Value at Risk)	Engle and Manganelli (2004)
2004	COGARCH (Continuous GARCH)	Klüppelberg et al. (2004)
2004	COGARCH	Klüppelberg et al. (2004)
2004	GARJI	Maheu and McCurdy (2004)
2004	HYGARCH (Hyperbolic GARCH)	Davidson (2004)

Table 1A.1 (continued)

Year	Development	Author(s)
2005	Modelling structural breaks	Pesaran and Timmermann (2005, 2007)
2005	DSGE models	Christiano et al. (2005)
2005	ARCH-SM (ARCH Stochastic Mean)	Lee and Taniguchi (2005)
2005	CARR (Conditional Autoregressive Range)	Chou (2005)
2005	GARCHX	Hwang and Satchell (2005)
2005	PC-GARCH (Principal Component GARCH)	Burns (2005)
2006	Random coefficient models	Hsiao and Pesaran (2006)
2006	Model uncertainty in cointegrating VARs	Strachan and van Dijk (2006)
2006	ADCC-GARCH (Asymmetric Dynamic Conditional Correlations)	Cappiello et al. (2006)
2006	DAGARCH (Dynamic Asymmetric GARCH)	Caporin and McAleer (2006)
2006	FDCC (Flexible Dynamic Conditional Correlations)	Billio et al. (2006)
2006	GDCC (Generalized Dynamic Conditional Correlations)	Cappiello et al. (2006)
2006	Matrix EGARCH	Kawakatsu (2006)
2006	REGARCH (Range EGARCH)	Brandt and Jones (2006)
2007	ECOGARCH (Exponential Continuous GARCH)	Haug and Czado (2007)
2007	S-GARCH (Simplified GARCH)	Harris et al. (2007)
2007	Testing for regime switching	Cho and White (2007)
2007	Least squares model averaging	Hansen (2007)
2008	Spline-GARCH	Engle and Rangel (2008)
2008	Dynamic quantile models	Gourieroux and Jasiak (2008)
2008	Testing models of low-frequency variability	Müller and Watson (2008)
2009	FCGARCH (Flexible Coefficient GARCH)	Medeiros and Veiga (2009)
2009	Estimation with overidentifying inequality moment conditions	Moon and Schorfheide (2009)
2009	Unit root quantile autoregression testing using covariates	Galvao (2009)
2009	Functional-coefficient cointegration models	Xiao (2009a)
2009	Quantile cointegrating regression	Xiao (2009b)
2009	Structural nonparametric cointegrating regression	Wang and Phillips (2009)
2009	Bayesian estimation of dynamic discrete choice models	Imai et al. (2009)
2009	Testing models with multiple equilibria by quantile methods	Echenique and Komunjer (2009)

Year	Description	Reference
2010	Specification tests of parametric dynamic conditional quantiles	Escanciano and Velasco (2010)
2010	Regression models with mixed sampling frequencies	Andreou et al. (2010)
2010	Likelihood based testing for fractional cointegration	Lasak (2010)
2010	Instrumental variable models for discrete outcomes	Chesher (2010)
2011	Bayesian inference in a time varying cointegration model	Koop et al. (2011)
2011	Semiparametric estimation of bivariate Tobit models	Chen and Zhou (2011)
2011	Instrumental variable estimation in the presence of moment conditions	Okui (2011)
2011	Quantile regression for dynamic panel data with fixed effects	Galvao (2011)
2011	Nonparametric Instrumental Regression	Darolles et al. (2011)
2012	Local GMM estimation models with conditional moment restrictions	Gospodinov and Otsu (2012)
2012	Kernel-weighted GMM estimators	Kuersteiner (2012)
2012	Model selection with multiple breaks	Castle et al. (2012)
2012	Dynamic misspecification in nonparametric cointegrating regression	Kasparis and Phillips (2012)
2012	Sequential estimation of structural models with a fixed point constraint	Kasahara and Shimotsu (2012)
2012	Functional differencing	Bonhomme (2012)
2013	Complete subset regressions	Elliott et al. (2013)
2013	GARCH models without positivity constraint	Francq et al. (2013)
2013	Bayesian semiparametric multivariate GARCH models	Jensen and Maheu (2013)
2013	Panel unit root tests in the presence of a multifactor error structure	Pesaran and Smith (2013)
2013	Testing for common conditionally heteroskedastic factors	Dovonon and Renault (2013)
2013	Nonparametric Estimation in Random Coefficients Binary Choice Models	Gautier and Kitamura (2013)
2014	Multivariate rotated ARCH models	Noureldin et al. (2014)
2014	Integrated modified OLS for cointegrating regressions	Vogelsang and Wagner (2014)
2014	Time-varying sparsity in dynamic regression models	Kalli and Griffin (2014)
2014	Conditional moment models under semi-strong identification	Antoine and Lavergne (2014)

Table 1A.1   (continued)

Year	Development	Author(s)
2015	Panel non-parametric regression with fixed effects	Lee and Robinson (2015)
2015	Hyperbolic GARCH model	Li et al. (2015)
2015	Quantile cointegration in the ARDL model	Cho et al. (2015)
2015	Instrumental variable estimation in functional linear models	Florens and van Bellegem (2015)
2015	Jackknife instrumental variable estimation	Bekker and Crudu (2015)
2015	Bootstrap testing of hypotheses on cointegration relations in VAR models	Cavaliere et al. (2015)
2015	Estimation of nonparametric models with simultaneity	Matzkin (2015)
2016	Covariance breakdowns in multivariate GARCH models	Jin and Maheu (2016)
2016	Continuous time models with mixed frequency data	Chambers (2016)
2016	Multivariate and multiple permutation tests	Chung and Romano (2016)
2016	Smoothed quantile regressions for panel data	Galvao and Kato (2016)
2016	Heterogeneous panels with structural breaks	Baltagi et al. (2016)

2. Components, functions and related disciplines

2.1 COMPONENTS AND FUNCTIONS OF ECONOMETRICS

While most of the definitions and descriptions of econometrics identify the components of the discipline as economic theory, statistics and mathematics, other variations can be observed. In some cases the components are identified as theory (presumably economic theory), statistics and data (for example, Brown, 2010). In other places mathematics is replaced with mathematical economics.

The functions of econometrics are typically taken to be hypothesis testing and forecasting. Brown (2010) adds estimation as the first function although estimation is a step that should precede hypothesis testing and forecasting. Sometimes the functions are stated as (1) formulation and specification of econometric models, (2) estimation and testing of models, and (3) use of models. Schneider (1952) identified the three parts of econometric investigation as (1) quantitative formulation of the relations between variables (construction of models); (2) formulation of the equations and the numerical determination of the coefficients; and (3) hypothesis testing. Although forecasting may not appear explicitly, one can assume that the "use of the model" covers forecasting. However, there is no explicit or implicit mentioning of forecasting in Schneider's identifications of the functions of econometrics. Individual econometricians place emphasis on different functions – for example, Brown (2010) argues that forecasting is "perhaps the main reason for econometrics", whereas Hendry (1980) emphasizes testing by suggesting that "the three golden rules of econometrics are test, test and test".

Sometimes, forecasting appears under "measurement". For example, Baltagi (2002) contends that econometrics provides quantitative estimates of price and income elasticities of demand, estimates of returns to scale in production, technical efficiency, and the velocity of money, implying that measurement follows from model estimation and testing. He adds that econometrics "provides predictions about future interest rates, unemployment, or GNP growth". This is the forecasting function, which again follows from estimation and hypothesis testing. However, a model that performs well in hypothesis testing (where what matters are the significance of the estimated coefficients and the diagnostics tests) does not necessarily perform well in forecasting, in the sense of producing small forecasting errors and the ability to predict the direction of change. For example, Moosa and Vaz (2016a) find that cointegration (which is a hypothesis testing issue) does not matter for forecasting accuracy by examining the relation between the stationarity and size of the forecasting error. In another paper, Moosa and Vaz (2016b) show that poor predictive power cannot be attributed to failure to account for cointegration when it is present (that is, by generating forecasts from a straight first difference model rather than an error correction model).

As a component of econometrics, Chait (1949) uses the term "political economy" rather than "economic theory" to refer to the economics component of econometrics. Political economy is an old name for economics, dealing with the conditions of production organization, as in the works of Adam Smith, David Ricardo and Karl Marx. Distinction can be made between political economy and economic theory as follows. Political economy involves the analysis of linkages between politics and economics, encompassing the principles of economics and law as well as political and social sciences. While economic theory traditionally focuses on market decisions, political economy deals with situations where the market does not produce the desired outcome. In a way, this is a distinction between positive economics (what is) and normative economics (what ought to be).

2.2 DATA AS A COMPONENT OF ECONOMETRICS

Whether or not data is considered as an explicit component of econometrics, it is an input in econometric analysis that causes most of the problems and it is perhaps the prime reason why econometrics is not a scientific discipline. The data used by econometricians or economists conducting empirical work may be time series data, cross-sectional data or pooled data. Time series data represent repeated observations of a variable in subsequent time periods. Cross-sectional data represent a set of observations of some variable at one specific point in time over several agents (countries, companies, markets, consumers and so on). A pooled data set comprises both time series and cross-sectional data.

A special case of pooled data is panel data, which consist of observations of the same set of agents over time. A set of pooled data is a time series of cross sections but the observations in each cross section do not necessarily refer to the same unit. A set of panel data, on the other hand, consists of samples of the same cross-sectional units observed at multiple points in time. A panel data observation may be denoted x_{it} where i and t refer to the unit in the cross section and time, respectively, such that $i = 1,\ldots N$ and $t = 1,\ldots T$ A balanced panel has every observation from 1 to N recorded in every period 1 to T. An unbalanced panel, on the other hand, has missing observations.

Experimental Data

In the natural sciences investigators make their own measurements through experiments (as in testing Boyle's law) and other scientific procedures – for example, by measuring the distance from earth to a certain galaxy or the height of a mountain. In economics, however, the economy itself generates data in vast quantities. In essence, economists use accounting data representing recorded transactions and activities. The problem with accounting data is that they are not collected specifically for the purposes of the econometrician, which causes all sort of problems, as the econometrician does not have any control over non-experimental data. Econometrics is used to deal with or solve problems such as measurement errors, but whether or not the treatment is adequate is a different matter. For example, an item called "errors and omissions" is used to balance the balance of payments, but it is typically the case in the balance of payments statistics that this item is huge. It is not clear how econometrics can deal with errors and omissions when a regression is run involving capital flows, which are not measured accurately because of errors and omissions. If anything, the best way to deal with this problem is to improve the quality of the data and reduce the size of errors and omissions. This is a function of economic statistics, not econometrics, which means that the rise of econometrics and the demise of economic statistics (as academic disciplines) represent an adverse development.

Statistical methods are designed for experimental data, in which case it may be inappropriate to claim that econometric methods are statistical methods adapted to deal with the specific nature of economic functional relations. Econometricians also claim that since the data used in econometric work is non-experimental, economic theory is used to adjust for the lack of proper data (Brown, 2010). However, theory is often ignored and most econometricians are not well-trained in economic theory although they are well-trained in mathematical statistics. Furthermore, cross-sectional studies in particular are not based on any theoretical model, which is the essence of the Leamer critique and his call to take the con out of econometrics (Leamer, 1983). There is also the claim that although the data used by econometricians are non-experimental, the collection of data for applied econometric research resembles what astronomers do when they gather data without conducting experiments. This claim is far-fetched because astronomers use instruments at the cutting edge of technology to measure distances from earth to planets and galaxies whereas econometricians have to be content with balance of payments data that have a very large component of errors and omissions.

The "Badness" of Economic Data

Baltagi (2002) argues that the data collected for applied econometric research are not ideal for the economic question at hand because they were posed to answer legal requirements or comply to regulatory agencies. Griliches (1986) describes the situation as follows:

> Econometricians have an ambivalent attitude towards economic data. At one level, the 'data' are the world that we want to explain, the basic facts that economists purport to elucidate. At the other level, they are the source of all our trouble. Their imperfections make our job difficult and often impossible. . . . We tend to forget that these imperfections are what gives us our legitimacy in the first place. . . . Given that it is the 'badness' of the data that provides us with our living, perhaps it is not all that surprising that we have shown little interest in improving it, in getting involved in the grubby task of designing and collecting original data sets of our own. Most of our work is on 'found' data, data that have been collected by somebody else, often for quite different purposes.

Griliches' depiction of the data issue sounds like means justifying ends – that is, we choose to deal with contaminated and inaccurate data (the means) for survival (the end). This perhaps explains why econometrics has killed economic statistics. The implication of Griliches' depiction of the situation is that econometricians resist improvement in the data while claiming that the data problem can be tackled by developing "novel" econometric methods. At best this is doing the wrong thing for the right reason. The word "legitimacy" has no place here.

Baltagi (2002) observes that economists are increasingly getting involved in collecting their data and measuring variables more accurately, but this is counterfactual as indicated by the rapid growth of theoretical econometrics and the demise of economic statistics, which is the field that looks at the collection and presentation of data. Econometrics is a paramount component in economics degrees curriculums these days, but economic statistics as a subject has all but disappeared. Even worse, good econometricians are not supposed to deal with data and concentrate on the development of methods that eventually end up on *Eviews* for the use of "working-class" people, the humble economists doing empirical work.

To do what scientists do, Griliches (1986) goes on to say the following:

> The encounters between econometricians and data are frustrating and ulti-mately unsatisfactory both because econometricians want too much from the data and hence tend to be disappointed by the answers, and because the data are incomplete and imperfect. In part it is our fault, the appetite grows with eating. As we get larger samples, we keep adding variables and expanding our models, until on the margin, we come back to the same insignificance levels.

There is always this contrast between economic theory and econometrics because of data imperfection. In economic theory a model may be rep-resented by the linear equation $y_t = a + bx_t$, but when this model is con-fronted with the data the relation appears as, $y_t = a + bx_t + \varepsilon_t$, where the error term ε accounts for the observed deviation of the data points from the straight line representing the hypothesized relation between y and x. Econometrics is all about the behaviour of the error term, and the quality of an estimated model is judged in terms of the properties of the error term.

Unobservable and Unmeasurable Variables

One must not forget that some of the variables appearing in economet-ric models are unobservable and unmeasurable. For example, a model relating y to x may be specified as $y_t = a + bx_{t+1} + \varepsilon_t$, where x_{t+1} is the expected value of x, which is not observed at t. This means that it has to be estimated somehow, typically in an arbitrary manner, which gives rise to all possibilities when the model is estimated. Consequently, the slope coefficient b (which is used to measure elasticity, or the response of y to a change in x) may turn out to be significantly positive, significantly negative or statistically insignificant. The explanatory variable x may be unmeas-urable, such as consumer sentiment, in which case it has to be proxied somehow, again giving rise to a divergent set of results. On the other hand, the variable x may be measurable but defined in various ways, again allow-ing the econometrician to pick the set of results that he likes. A special case is that of the news model of financial prices where x is modelled sepa-rately, for example as an autoregressive process, then y is specified to be a function of the unanticipated component of x proxied by the residual of the autoregressive process, which represents "news". In reality, the unan-ticipated components can only be measured as the difference between the realized and previously anticipated values obtained from opinion surveys.

A Dismal Situation

Econometricians have to live with the serious problem arising from measurement errors but it is typically swept under the carpet. Unlike a scientist who has the instruments that allow her to measure the height of Mount Everest with a high degree of precision, econometricians do not have this "luxury". Furthermore, economic data cannot be replicated and may not have enough variation to discriminate between two competing theories. But then who cares if faulty data proves that more guns lead to fewer murders (which makes the gun-lobby happy) and that cutting taxes for the top 1 per cent benefits the society as a whole?

2.3 RELATED AND OVERLAPPING DISCIPLINES

It is not obvious from the definitions of econometrics what the discipline includes and what it excludes. For example, are the models used in operational research econometric models? Are econometric models necessarily empirical? What distinguishes econometrics from other quantitative disciplines?

Tintner (1953) argued that it is not easy to delaminate econometrics from quantitative economics, statistical economics and mathematical economics, but he did not consider econometrics as being identical to quantitative economics. Mills (1940) identified several views of the meaning of quantification: (1) the employment of techniques of observations that involve enumeration or measurement; (2) the utilization in observation of objectively functioning instruments permitting verification of one observer's result by another; (3) the building-up of a body of substantive knowledge composed of entities and relations defined in quantitative terms; (4) the expression of conclusion in quantitative terms; and (5) the testing of conclusion through numerical comparisons. Chait (1949) expressed a view of "yes but", when he said:

> Strictly, econometrics is quantitative economics. But in the same way as with other words, this expression indicates only imperfectly the meaning. This meaning is richer and more precise. We can understand it in its full sense if we remember that econometrics is a synthesis of four disciplines: political economy, mathematical economics, statistical analysis, mathematical analysis. Each one of these disciplines is used for the solution of specific difficulties which arise in concrete problems.

It is not clear from this description what the difference is between mathematical economics and mathematical analysis – after all econometrics pertains to the estimation and testing of economic theory, which makes the item "mathematical analysis" redundant.

The Views of Frisch, Baltagi and Tintner

Frisch (1933a) held the view that there were several aspects of the quantitative approach to economics, and no single one of these aspects, taken by itself, should be confounded with econometrics. Econometrics in Frisch's view can be summarized as follows: (1) econometrics is by no means the same as economic statistics; (2) it is not identical with general economic theory, although a considerable portion of this theory has definitely quantitative character; and (3) econometrics should not be taken as synonymous with the application of mathematics to economics (mathematical economics). On the basis of these qualifications, Baltagi (2002) describes an econometrician to be a "competent mathematician and statistician who is an economist by training". But this characterization is not valid – most econometricians are not economists by training. As a matter of fact, the word "econometrician" these days is taken to imply that the person has a good knowledge of econometric methods but does not know much economics (and some econometricians are proud of it). Typically, research collaboration in empirical work involves an economist who suggests a testable hypothesis and interprets the results produced by an econometrician who carries out the number crunching. It is typical these days to attend a presentation by someone who makes the following statement: "questions about the econometrics used in this paper should be directed at my co-author who is not present".

Tintner (1953) believed that econometrics is neither economic statistics nor quantitative or mathematical economics and advocated the definition of econometrics as pertaining to investigations that utilize mathematics, economics and statistics, which are different from investigations in quantitative economics where no mathematics is used. Mathematical economics, he believed, is quantitative, but not empirical and uses no statistics – hence it is not econometrics. Econometrics is different from theoretical work in statistics, which involves mathematics (hence mathematical statistics) but in general it is unrelated to economic theory. Tintner (1953) also referred to "synthetic economics", which he called the "more immediate forerunner of econometrics". According to him, synthetic economics implies: (1) the use of simultaneous equations to express the consensus of exchange, production, capitalization and distribution; (2) extension of the use of mathematical synthesis into economic dynamics where all of the variables in the constituent problems are treated as functions of time; and (3) further extension of the synthesis to the point of giving the equations concrete statistical forms.

The Disciplines

Appendix Table 2A.1 presents the definitions of econometrics and related disciplines, including economic theory, statistics, mathematics, economic statistics, mathematical statistics, applied mathematics, financial econometrics, mathematical economics, quantitative economics, experimental economics, empirical economics, operational research, financial modelling and management science.

Economic statistics is about the collection and presentation rather than the analysis of data. As argued before, the demise of economic statistics is a step backwards, because no sophisticated econometric technique will tell us anything informative if the data are faulty, despite the claim that econometric methods can deal with measurement errors. Applied mathematics is relevant here because the implication of the ever increasing mathematization of economic theory is propelled by the belief that economics, like mechanics and physics in general, is a branch of applied mathematics, not a social science.

Financial econometrics arose only because some econometricians wanted to move to finance – if financial econometrics makes sense then we should have labour econometrics, international econometrics, welfare econometrics, and so on and so forth. Finance, or financial economics, is a branch of economics, which means that finance should not have its own brand of econometrics. The distinction between quantitative economics and econometrics seems to be blurred – at present the Econometric Society has two journals that publish more or less similar articles: *Econometrica* and *Quantitative Economics*. Empirical economics is the same as applied econometrics while operational research and management science can be distinguished from econometrics.

One would tend to think that econometrics and mathematical economics differ in that econometrics is about measurement, which means that econometric methods are developed to analyse economic data. Mathematical economics, on the other hand is data-free, abstract treatment of economic theory. These days it is hard to distinguish what is published in *Econometrica*, the journal of the Econometric Society, and the *Journal of Mathematical Economics* or the *Journal of Economic Theory*. This can be verified by browsing through recent issues of these journals (Table 2.1). Maddala (1999) argues that "in recent years the issues of Econometrica have had only a couple of papers in econometrics (statistical methods in economics) and the rest are all on game theory and mathematical economics". He adds that "if you look at the list of fellows of the Econometric Society, you find one or two econometricians and the rest are game theorists and mathematical

Table 2.1 *Sample contents of journals*

Econometrica	Journal of Economic Theory	Journal of Mathematical Economics
Robust Contracts in Continuous Time	Graphical Potential Games	Repeated Two-person Zero-sum Games with Unequal Discounting and Private Monitoring
Berk–Nash Equilibrium: A Framework for Modelling Agents With Misspecified Models	Informed Seller with Taste Heterogeneity	Relational Contracts and the First-order Approach
Reputational Bargaining and Deadlines	Continuous Markov Equilibria with Quasi-Geometric Discounting	Decentralized Pricing and the Equivalence between Nash and Walrasian Equilibrium
Utilitarian Preferences With Multiple Priors	Common Belief Foundations of Global Games	Duality and Anti-duality in TU Games Applied to Solutions, Axioms, and Axiomatizations
Menu-Dependent Stochastic Feasibility	Ordinal Bayesian Incentive Compatibility in Restricted Domains	An Envelope Approach to Tournament Design
A Rational Theory of Mutual Funds' Attention Allocation	Endogenous Information Acquisition in Bayesian Games	Lattice-based Monotone Comparative Statics on Saving with Selden/ Kreps–Porteus Preferences
Stochastic Learning Dynamics and Speed of Convergence in Population Games	A Non-cooperative Bargaining Theory with Incomplete Information: Verifiable Types	Bargaining with Incomplete Information: Evolutionary Stability in Finite Populations
Asset Markets with Heterogeneous Information	Bounded Depths of Rationality and Implementation with Complete Information	Games with Incomplete Information when Players are Partially aware of Others' Signals
Information in Tender Offers with a Large Shareholder	Bayesian Persuasion with Heterogeneous Priors	Additive Representation for Preferences over Menus in Finite Choice Settings
Relational Incentive Contracts with Persistent Private Information	Self-control and Bargaining	Bounded Response of Aggregated Preferences
Search with Adverse Selection	How Fast do Equilibrium Payoff sets Converge in Repeated Games?	Bayesian Nash Equilibrium and Variational Inequalities

economists". It remains to say that game theorists are notorious for criticizing "human players" when their actions fail to correspond to the strategies employed in a particular game's equilibrium state (Murphy, 2002).

2.4   THE HAZARD OF USING ECONOMIC DATA

The main proposition presented in this book is that econometrics can be used to support any hypothesis by abusing the data. In this section we present a taste of things to come, starting with a demonstration of how economic data can be used to present and support an ideologically-driven belief.

Some time ago I attended a presentation by a right-wing economist who challenged the view that fiscal stimulus was necessary in the aftermath of the global financial crisis. After telling the audience that Keynes did not know anything about anything because someone he knew had proved that, he proceeded to present a graph taken from a study conducted by an economist who believes that fiscal stimulus works. The graph was a scatter diagram of some measure of fiscal stimulus on GDP growth rate based on cross-sectional data for about 20 countries, showing positive correlation between the two variables. The presenter said that that picture was biased because it did not contain every country in the world. So he enlarged the sample to cover every country in the world and, as expected, he showed that correlation was almost zero. He further explained that fiscal stimulus would not work because the recipients of government funds would spend their money on tattoos.

My reaction to the presentation was that it was a con job. To start with, no one should expect a scatter diagram of two macroeconomic variables to show anything because economies differ drastically, which means that a relation that may work for a somewhat homogeneous set of countries does most likely not work for all countries. The scatter diagram of the first author was more valid because it covered OECD countries only. The fact of the matter is that fiscal stimulus works if government funds are spent on things like infrastructure, depending mostly on local materials and labour – no empirical evidence is needed to support this proposition. Naturally an increase in government expenditure on imported tanks and guns will not stimulate the domestic economy but it will stimulate the economy of the country from which the tanks and guns are imported (and boost the commissions received by arms dealers). Even if some money is spent on tattoos, that still works because the tattooer will spend his money (or some of it) on the purchase of goods and services, boosting the incomes of others, and so on. This line of reasoning makes sense and does not require supportive empirical evidence, which is easy to obtain.

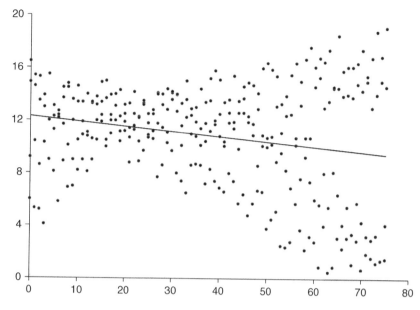

Figure 2.1 A scatter diagram for the overall sample

An Illustration

Using economic data in a selective manner provides the means to support or debunk any proposition. Consider Figure 2.1, which represents a scatter diagram of two variables. Obviously, by looking at the diagram we reach the conclusions that the two variables are uncorrelated. However, we can select various sets of observations from the overall sample and reach any conclusion that we want to reach. In Figure 2.2, we observe scatter diagrams plotted by using four different sub-samples from the overall sample shown in Figure 2.1. It can be claimed, according to which sub-sample is selected, that the two variables are related positively, negatively or by a nonlinear relation, which can be represented by a U-shaped or an inversed U-shaped curve. It can always be claimed that the selected data set is the only thing that is available.

Alternatively we may pick a relation that holds universally (on average), yet we may select sub-samples showing that it does not work as envisaged. Take, for example, the relation between the growth rate of the money supply and CPI inflation rate as portrayed by the quantity theory of money. This relation does not work on a month-to-month or year-to-year basis for every country. Yet it tends to work on average over a number of years. In Figure 2.3 we observe this relation for 147 countries at different

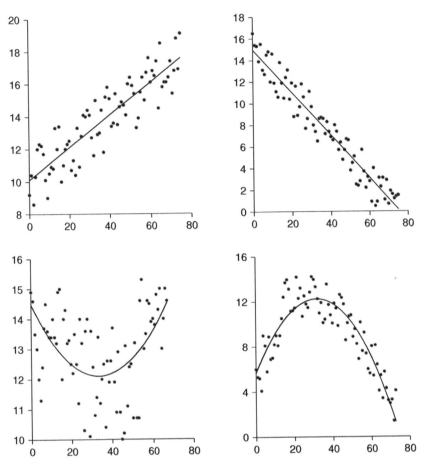

Figure 2.2   Scatter diagrams for sub-samples

stages of development from every continent. The numbers are averages of annual data covering the period 1990–2003. While a positive association between inflation and monetary growth is quite conspicuous, it is possible, by a careful selection of data points, to show that this relation does not hold or that it is negative.

The moral of the story is that economic data can be used to convey any message that the researcher wants to convey. The econometrics enthusiasts would respond to this argument by suggesting that it is not possible to derive inference from a two-variable relation and that we should "control" for other determining variables, which would take us to the realm of multiple linear regression. But we will find out that multiple regression

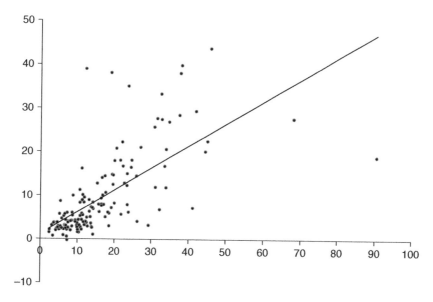

Figure 2.3   A scatter diagram of inflation on monetary growth

enhances our ability to abuse the data and arrive at the desired results. We will see, for example, that multiple regression is used to prove that guns and murders are negatively related and that any one of two competing theories can be proved to be valid for the same data set. Welcome to the world of the con art of econometrics.

APPENDIX

Table 2A.1   Description of econometrics and related disciplines

Discipline	Description
Econometrics	The use of mathematics to represent a model suggested by economic theory, then statistical methods are used to estimate, test and use the model for forecasting.
Economic Theory	Economic theory relies upon quantitative economic models that encompass the assumption of *ceteris paribus*, which means holding constant explanatory variables other than the one under consideration.
Statistics	The collection, classification, analysis and interpretation of numerical data. The theories of probability are used to impose order and regularity on aggregates of more or less disparate elements.
Mathematics	The study of the measurement, relations, and properties of quantities and sets, using numbers and symbols. Arithmetic, algebra, geometry, and calculus are branches of mathematics.
Economic Statistics	The collection, analysis, interpretation, presentation and organization of economic and financial data. Economic data or economic statistics may refer to data (quantitative measures) describing an actual economy, which may also be collected from surveys.
Mathematical Statistics	The application of mathematics to statistics, including mathematical analysis, linear algebra, stochastic analysis, differential equations, and measure-theoretic probability theory.
Applied Mathematics	A branch of mathematics that deals with mathematical methods that find use in science, engineering, business, computer science and industry. It is a combination of mathematical science and specialized knowledge.
Financial Econometrics	The application of econometric methods to financial data. Financial econometrics differs from general econometrics because the emphasis is usually on analysing the prices of financial assets traded at competitive, liquid markets. Financial econometrics is used in risk management to determine how often bad investment outcomes are expected to occur in the future.
Mathematical Economics	The application of mathematical methods to represent theories and analyse problems in economics. By convention, applied methods refer to those beyond simple geometry, such as differential and integral calculus, difference and differential equations, matrix algebra, mathematical programming, and other computational methods.

Quantitative Economics	Mathematical and statistical analysis of economic phenomena and problems, including economic statistics, optimization theory, economic modelling, and economic forecasting and evaluation.
Experimental Economics	The application of experimental methods to study economic issues where data are collected from experiments with the objective of testing the validity of economic theories.
Empirical Economics	The use of econometric and statistical methods to fill the gap between economic theory and observed data. It involves statistical and econometric analysis, policy simulations, strategic modelling, experimental research and qualitative analysis.
Operational Research	A discipline that deals with the application of advanced analytical methods to help make better decisions. It encompasses a wide range of problem solving techniques and methods such as simulation, mathematical optimization, queuing theory and other stochastic-process models, Markov decision processes, econometric methods, data envelopment analysis, neural networks, expert systems, decision analysis, and the analytic hierarchy process. These techniques involve the construction of mathematical models to describe the system.
Financial Modelling	The building of models designed to represent (a simplified version of) the performance of a financial asset, a portfolio of assets, a project, or any other investment.
Management Science	The broad interdisciplinary study of problem solving and decision making in organizations, with strong links to economics, business, engineering and other sciences. It involves the use of analytical methods including mathematical modelling, statistics and numerical algorithms to improve an organization's ability to enact rational and meaningful management decisions by arriving at optimal or near optimal solutions to complex decision problems.

3. Econometrics as a science

3.1 ECONOMETRICS LOOKS LIKE SCIENCE

The claim that econometrics is a science may be based on the observation that a paper dealing with an econometric issue (particularly in econometric theory) looks as "sciency" as a paper appearing in a physics journal. Consider the following two equations:

$$\overline{Z}_{jk}(y) := \sqrt{s_j} \int Z_j(y,x) dF_{Xk}(x) + \sqrt{s_k} G_k(F_{\gamma j} |X_j(y)|.))$$ (3.1)

and

$$Q(\lambda,\gamma) = \int_{-\infty}^{\infty} \frac{dx}{2\pi} \exp\left[ix\{V_\gamma(\Gamma)\} - \frac{x^2}{2}\sigma^2 u_\gamma(\Gamma) \right]$$ (3.2)

One of these equations is taken from *Econometrica* and the other from the *Journal of Experimental and Theoretical Physics*. Can you tell which is which? Well, equation (3.1) is taken from a paper in *Econometrica*, whereas equation (3.2) is taken from the physics journal (Chernozhukov et al., 2013 and Avetisov et al., 2009, respectively). They look pretty similar, although econometrics is supposed to be about measurement in economics where outcomes are determined by human behaviour while physics deals with the laws of nature.

This observation is not limited to these two equations because if you browse through any recent issue of *Econometrica* (where recent means the last 25 years or so), you will find that a typical page of this journal is indistinguishable from a typical page of a journal of physics or even pure mathematics. It may be argued therefore that since econometrics provides as quantitatively rigorous treatment of economic issues as physics provides in dealing with natural phenomena, econometrics must be a science that is no different from physics. Since econometrics, as the name implies, is about measurement, it must be necessarily a science.

After all, Lord Kelvin (1824–1907) emphasized measurement as a criterion of being scientific when he said the following:

> I often say that when you can measure what you are speaking about, and express it in numbers, you know something about it; but when you cannot measure it, when you cannot express it in numbers, your knowledge is of a meagre and unsatisfactory kind. (https://en.wikiquote.org/wiki/William_Thomson)

Lord Kelvin was right about the measurement of the speed of light, the speed of sound, acceleration under gravity and the thrust of a jet engine – this is the kind of measurement that we find in science. Econometricians, on the other hand, measure (imprecisely, to say the least) the response of unemployment to changes in economic growth and some bizarre items such as the rise in productivity as a result of the closure of a regulatory agency, or the drop in the number of murders as a result of gun ownership (which is counterfactual, anyway).

Elements of Science and Art

The true believers claim that econometrics is a science because it looks "sciency", but is it? We start by going back to the data issue discussed in Chapter 2, which is relevant to the question whether econometrics is an art or a science. A discussion of the data problem readily reveals that econometrics lacks the precision associated with science. Even some econometricians do not hold strong views about the scientific nature of econometrics. For example, Baltagi (2002) contends that while econometrics is based on scientific principles (the use of mathematics), it still retains a certain element of art. According to Malinvaud (1966), the art in econometrics is trying to find the right set of assumptions which are sufficiently specific, yet realistic to enable us to take the best possible advantage of the available data (which is typically of poor quality and riddled with measurement errors). While a physicist does not have to worry about the quality of a set of experimental data, which can be replicated easily, an econometrician has to devise methods to deal with errors of measurement. Davis (1941) assumed that the phenomena of economics, as they apply to sufficiently large collections of individuals, are amenable to measurement but he admitted that the measurement of these phenomena is not as exact as that found in the physical sciences. Rather, he refers to "determinate values which may be ascertained within definite limits of error". In any case, Ehrbar (2000) contends that "one cannot expect econometrics to automatically become a science just because it deals with data" and that "such an expectation commits the ontic fallacy, i.e., it assumes that the ontological makeup of the world necessarily generates correct scientific methods".

A number of distinguished economists are sceptical about power of econometrics to yield sharp predictions. In his presidential address to the American Economic Association, Wassily Leontief (1971) characterized econometric work as follows:

> An attempt to compensate for the glaring weakness of the data base available to us by the widest possible use of more and more sophisticated techniques.

Alongside the mounting pile of elaborate theoretical models we see a fast growing stock of equally intricate statistical tools. These are intended to stretch to the limit the meagre supply of facts.

Expressing ideas in exact mathematical form is a strict requirement of science. Tinbergen (1951) described econometrics as a "name for a field of science in which mathematical-economic and mathematical-statistical research are applied in combination". He went on to say the following:

> Econometrics forms a borderland between two branches of science, with the advantages and disadvantages thereof; advantages, because new combinations are introduced which often open up new perspectives; disadvantages, because the work in this field requires skill in two domains, which either takes up too much time or leads to insufficient training of its students in one of the two respects.

However, Mitchell (1937) suggested that "there is slight prospect that quantitative analysis will ever be able to solve the problems that qualitative analysis has framed, in their present form". Econometrics, it seems, was created by the desire to make economics as scientific as physics, which is neither necessary nor realistic. The problem is that while there are laws in physics, there are no laws in economics – at best econometrics provides empirical regularities or stylized facts. This is a point that we will come back to later in Chapter 4.

The Scientific Procedure

The claim that econometric work constitutes science is that economic theories are written in mathematical form and are then estimated and tested by using statistical methods, which sounds like the representation and testing of Boyle's law. A theory is rejected if a model estimated from observed data is found to be incompatible with its predictions, and vice versa. This is indeed a scientific procedure, but its application in econometrics is not straightforward.

It is typically the case that insufficient or poor-quality data are available, which means that the theory cannot be tested in the first place or that testing gives flawed results, which have little or no value. Even worse, if policy action is based on such flawed results, the consequences can be serious. Testing may not be possible because of the problem of multicollinearity, which is dealt with by using principal component analysis. This procedure, however, amounts to testing by using artificially generated data, which not even some econometricians agree with (for example, Pagan, 1984). Then there are a large number of problems including specification errors and measurement errors as well as the problems of identification and aggregation. More importantly, however, testing an economic theory can produce any set of results – hence the expression "mixed bag", which cannot be found in science.

Even representation is different in econometrics from what it is in science, as we are going to see. For example, while Boyle's law is written as an exact relation between the volume of gas and the pressure exerted on it, Okun's law is written as a stochastic equation with an error term. Econometrics is primarily concerned with the properties and behaviour of the error term, and this is why econometricians are generous in providing a menu of estimation methods. In science the error term is not encountered and simple curve fitting by ordinary least squares (OLS) is adequate. The problem of multicollinearity is not encountered in science as a two-variable relation (for example, the volume of gas and the pressure exerted on it) can be isolated from the effects of other variables (for example, temperature). This is a better solution for multicollinearity than what is provided by econometricians.

3.2 THE DEBATE

In view of the remarks made so far, Falk (1995) concludes that "econometrics has not contributed to the scientific status of economics". While scientists do not claim to be able to test all their theories empirically, they are generally able to acquire more consistent and accurate results than those acquired from the work of econometricians. Economics is a social science where the behaviour of agents is not governed purely by economic considerations but also by social and psychological factors, which are not amenable to econometric testing. This is why no economic theory holds everywhere all the time. And this is why the results of empirical testing of economic theories can be a mixed bag. And this is why econometricians use time-varying parametric estimation to account for changes in the values of estimated parameters over time. And this is why there are so many estimation methods that can be used to produce the desired results. In physics, on the other hand, a body falling under the force of gravity travels with an acceleration of 32 feet per second per second – this is true anywhere any time. In physics also, we can predict with accuracy the boiling point of water under any level of atmospheric pressure.

Unlike physicists, econometricians are in a position to obtain the desired results, armed with the arsenal of tools produced by econometric theory. When an econometrician fails to obtain the desired results, he or she may try different functional forms, lag structures and estimation methods, and indulge in data mining until the desired results are obtained. If the empirical work is conducted for the purpose of writing an academic paper, the researcher will seek results that are "interesting" enough to warrant publication or results that confirm the view of the orthodoxy or the findings of a potential referee. And it is typically the case that the results cannot be replicated. Physicists do not have this luxury – it is unthinkable and easily verifiable that a physicist manipulates data (by using principal components or various transformations) to obtain readings that refute Boyle's law. Economists study the behaviour of consumers, firms and governments where expectations and uncertainties play key roles in the translation of economic theory into real world economics. These uncertainties mean that econometric modelling cannot produce accurate representation of the working of the economy.

The Response

An econometrics enthusiast, Kearns (1995), goes on the defensive and disagrees with the propositions put forward by Falk (1995). He starts by defining science as "any mode of investigation by which impartial and systematic knowledge is acquired". This definition is adequate for rejecting the proposition that empirical work in economics is a scientific endeavour because the knowledge acquired from empirical results is neither impartial nor systematic. For one thing, econometrics has become a tool that serves ideology. For example, a government wishing to cut taxes on the rich would argue that a policy action like this is likely to stimulate growth because rich people use the extra income they obtain as a result of the tax cuts to start projects that employ poor people and get growth going. Hence cutting taxes on the rich will not lead to a widening of the budget deficit, but rather to an improvement resulting from higher tax revenue that accompanies growth. A proposition like this does not need empirical testing because we know that this is not how things work. Higher after-tax income for the rich will find its way to stock markets, or to Panama and other tax havens. However, an econometrician can always find evidence supporting the hypothesis that lower taxes boost growth and the fiscal balance. This econometrician will undoubtedly find evidence against the hypothesis but that evidence will not be reported. In physics, on the other hand, no one can produce results that do not support Boyle's law. In science the motivation is a quest for the truth but in econometrics the motivation is to prove a pre-conceived belief, which means that any evidence that does not support the pre-conceived belief will be hidden away.

Two of the characteristics of a scientific discipline are identified by von Mises (1978) and Schumpeter (1978). For von Mises, a scientific method requires the verification of a proposition by numerous sets of data pertaining to sufficiently comparable situations. For Schumpeter (1978) correct prediction is the best or only test of whether a science has achieved its purposes, which means that correct prediction, within the bounds of what one can reasonably expect of an uncertain future, is a requisite for scientific status. Kearns (1995) argues that the two characteristics of a scientific discipline noted by von Mises and Schumpeter are found in econometrics. Hendry (1980) contends that it is possible to verify results consistently by using "rigorously tested models, which adequately described the available data, encompassed previous findings and were derived from well based theories would greatly enhance any claim to be scientific". This makes sense but the reality of econometric testing is far away from Hendry's description. While it is possible that a proposition can be verified, the same proposition can be rejected by using a different set of data, econometric technique or model specification. I am yet to see a hypothesis in economics or finance that has been supported or rejected universally. Take any literature review on any topic in economics and you will quickly reach the conclusion that the results are a mixed bag (try purchasing power parity or the J-curve effect).

The Quantity Theory versus Boyle's Law

Even the quantity theory of money, which is written in such a way as to look like a law of physics using the precise equation $MV = PY$, does not command overwhelming support when it is subject to empirical testing. In fact, when the quantity theory is tested it is written as a stochastic equation with an error term and implicit assumptions. For example, it is assumed that the velocity of circulation (V) is constant and that output (Y) is at the natural long-run level, which means that the ratio (V/Y) is constant. Hence the quantity theory is reduced to a direct proportional relation between the price level (P) and the money supply (M). When this relation is written in a stochastic form and tested empirically, the results are highly supportive only under the extreme conditions of hyperinflation, and even then the relation does not necessarily turn out to be proportional. In contrast, Boyle's law holds when the underlying experiment is conducted in Europe or Asia, in winter or summer, and whether it is conducted in a country experiencing hyperinflation or otherwise.

Furthermore, the quantity theory, unlike Boyle's law, cannot be tested in its full form using data on the four variables M, V, P and Y. This is because the velocity of circulation, V, is not observable, typically calculated as a residual item from the other three variables. By contrast, both the volume of gas and the pressure exerted on it, the two variables in Boyle's law, are observable and easily measurable. No matter where the relation is tested, the same results are obtained – that is, the law holds perfectly. No politician can hire a physicist to demonstrate, for some reason, that the relation between volume and pressure can be represented by a straight line with a positive slope.

Science or Witchcraft?

As for forecasting, a look at the literature on exchange rate economics gives us an idea of how bad econometric forecasting is. We can predict precisely when a falling object will hit the ground and where a projectile will land, but we cannot predict with a reasonable level of confidence whether a currency will appreciate or depreciate on the announcement of unemployment data – that is, we cannot even predict the direction of change, let alone the magnitude of change. I must admit, however, that economists (or applied econometricians) are good at finding explanations for currency appreciation or depreciation in response to the announcement of unemployment data – only after the fact, of course. It all depends on what the researcher wants to prove and if that turns out not to be the case, an explanation is found for why it did not turn out to be the case, sometimes blaming the unwanted results on econometrics itself (such as the low power of the test). This is not science – it is witchcraft.

3.3   ECONOMETRIC WORK AS A SCIENTIFIC ENDEAVOUR

An argument that can be put forward in favour of the proposition that econometric work represents a scientific endeavour is based on the desirable properties of econometric models as identified by Koutsoyiannis (1977). The desirable properties are (1) theoretical plausibility, in the sense that the model must describe adequately the underlying economic phenomena; (2) explanatory ability, in the sense that the model should be able to explain the observations of the real world; (3) accuracy of the estimates of the model parameters, which should converge as far as possible on the true parameters of the model (that is, they should be efficient, consistent and unbiased); (4) forecasting ability, as the model should provide satisfactory predictions of future values of the dependent variable; and (5) simplicity, as the model should represent the economic relations with maximum simplicity.

Anyone who has found an econometric model that meets these criteria should be given the next Nobel Prize in economics (although this does not say much, given that the Prize has been awarded for nonsense). However, I doubt very much if anyone is capable of coming up with such an econometric model, at a time when all of these desirable properties are met by the models describing the laws of physics. An example is the model describing the movement of a projectile that is launched at an angle to the horizon and rises upwards to a peak while moving horizontally. This model predicts with a high level of accuracy the time of flight, the horizontal range, and the peak height of the projectile. The same can be said about a model describing a projectile that is launched with an initial horizontal velocity from an elevated position and follows a parabolic path to the ground. Can any econometric model predict with a fraction of the accuracy of these models by how much unemployment would fall if growth went up by one percentage point? Economists cannot agree on whether inflation and unemployment move in the same direction or in different directions – it all depends!

Kearns (1995) argues that econometric models provide the ability to make predictions, the accuracy of which is constrained only by the practicing econometrician and the economic theory upon which the model is based. This is a caveat-laden issue of "if, but", and it is typically a big if. Only if the econometrician is good enough and the theory is valid, will the model produce accurate predictions. Hendry (1980) argues that "the ease with which spurious results could be created suggested alchemy, but the scientific status of econometrics was illustrated by showing such deceptions are testable". Econometricians keep telling us that cointegration can distinguish between spurious and genuine relations, but this is not so (see, for example, Moosa 2016a). In any case, most of the econometric models of today are not theory-based. Furthermore, econometricians do not seek to use better theory to boost predictive power – rather, they do that by resorting to an old trick, that of inserting (without theoretical justification) a lagged dependent variable.

Unlike the models of science, econometric models typically fail to explain what happens in the real world, let alone predict what may or can happen. Blommestein (2009) refers to the "common situation where the empirical results of different studies of a similar topic have often a very wide range of outcomes and values for structural parameters" (and without a convincing or clear explanation why this is the case), arguing that "such a situation would be unthinkable and unacceptable in the physical sciences". If a physicist obtains different outcomes when addressing a similar problem, this would be a key reason for an urgent scientific debate until the discrepancy in results has been resolved. Unlike scientists, Blommestein argues, "economists are prone to an attitude where they stick to their favourite theories and models come hell or high water and where no mountain of evidence can move them".

Econometrics is Not a Science

Econometrics is not a science because economics is not a science, at least not in the same sense as physics is a science. The desire to elevate econometrics and economic theory to the status of science may be motivated by some sort of inferiority complex. Ritholtz (2009) emphasizes this point by arguing that "economics has had a justifiable inferiority complex versus real sciences the past century". The science-like quantification of economics has created barriers to entry into the economics profession, impeded endeavours to integrate economics with other social sciences and learn from them, led some good non-quantitative economists to leave the profession, led to a brain drain by attracting people from science and engineering, and led "scientific economists" to follow empirical results blindly, sometimes with serious adverse consequences (it was all fine before the global financial crisis!). All of this was for nothing, as the excessive quantification of economics has not contributed anything to our knowledge of the economy and financial markets. After all, those few economists who warned of an impending crisis and the few traders who predicted the crisis and made money out of it are not science-like people. Nouriel Roubini, for example, warned of the possibility of a housing market crash and a looming crisis, but he was not taken seriously because he does not use equations in his analysis.

3.4   THE MATHEMATIZATION OF ECONOMICS

If mathematics is the language of science and if economics is amenable to mathematization, it follows that mathematics is the language of economics, which makes economics and hence econometrics a science. Mathematical economics, which predates econometrics, has its roots in the works of classical economists such as W.S. Jevons, Carl Menger and Leon Walras. Irving Fisher (1892) described Jevons' book, *A General Mathematical Theory of Political Economy*, as the start of the mathematical method in economics. In his book, Jevons made the case that economics as a science concerned with quantities, is necessarily mathematical – in doing so, he expounded upon the marginal utility theory of value. Carl Menger contributed to the development of the theory of marginal utility, which rejected the cost-of-production theories of value as put forward by the classical economists such as Adam Smith and David Ricardo. Independently of Jevons and Menger, Leon Walras formulated the marginal theory of value and pioneered the development of general equilibrium theory.

The Evolution of Mathematical Economics

Debreu (1991) measures the development of mathematical economics in the more recent past in terms of the total number of pages published each year by the "leading periodicals in the field", originally *Econometrica* and the *Review of Economic Studies*. From 1933 (the year when they both started publication) to 1959, these two journals published more than 700 pages in 1935 to the lowest point, below 400 pages in 1943–1944. Debreu marks 1944 as a sharp turning point in the history of mathematical economics and the beginning of a period of explosive growth. *Econometrica* and the *Review of Economic Studies* were joined in 1960 by the *International Economic Review*, in 1969 by the *Journal of Economic Theory*, and in 1974 by the *Journal of Mathematical Economics*. In 1977 these five journals together published over 5,000 pages. During the period 1944–1977, the number of pages (which he calls the "index") more than doubled every nine years. The year 1944 was significant for the development of mathematical economics also because it was the year when John von Neumann and Oskar Morgenstern published a landmark study in mathematical economics, *The Theory of Games and Economic Behavior*, in which they extended functional analytic methods related to convex sets and topological fixed-point theory to economic analysis.

The rapid growth in mathematical economics is not only reflected in the number of pages in the five journals, as even mainstream journals started to publish abstract mathematical papers or at least papers that use equations and mathematical jargon. Take, for example, the *American Economic Review*: in 1940 less than 3 per cent of the pages of volume 30 included rudimentary mathematical expressions, but 50 years later nearly 40 per cent of the pages of volume 80 displayed mathematics of a more elaborate type. Sutter and Pjesky (2007) examine papers published in 2003 and 2004 to measure the extent of mathematics-free research in top economics journals. Of more than 1200 papers published in ten top journals, 6 per cent met a weak criterion of mathematics-free, 3 per cent met an intermediate criterion, and only 1.5 per cent met a strong criterion. They reached an interesting conclusion: if Adam Smith were alive today, he would need to learn mathematics to survive despite his mastery of literature, history and ethics. This has become the status quo: if you do not know advanced mathematics you are not an economist. And if you criticize this trend, it is because you cannot understand the "new economics".

The Contribution of Samuelson

In the post-war period, it was Paul Samuelson who took the lead in making economics a mathematical discipline. In his first major work, *Foundations of Economic Analysis*, Samuelson (1947) insisted that mathematics was essential to understanding what economics was all about. Earlier, J.M. Keynes had written the following in *The General Theory* (1936):

> It is a great fault of symbolic pseudo-mathematical methods of formalising a system of economic analysis . . . that they expressly assume strict independence between the factors involved and lose their cogency and authority if this hypothesis is disallowed; whereas, in ordinary discourse, where we are not blindly manipulating and know all the time what we are doing and what the words mean, we can keep "at the back of our heads" the necessary reserves and qualifications and the adjustments which we shall have to make later on, in a way in which we cannot keep complicated partial differentials "at the back" of several pages of algebra which assume they all vanish. Too large a proportion of recent "mathematical" economics are merely concoctions, as imprecise as the initial assumptions they rest on, which allow the author to lose sight of the complexities and interdependencies of the real world in a maze of pretentious and unhelpful symbols.

In response to the criticisms directed at the mathematization of economic theory, Samuelson (1952) argued that the language of mathematics is sometimes necessary for representing substantive problems and that mathematical economics has led to conceptual advances in economics. With reference to microeconomics, Samuelson asserted that "few people are ingenious enough to grasp [its] more complex parts. . . without resorting to the language of mathematics, while most ordinary individuals can do so fairly easily with the aid of mathematics" (see also Bushaw and Clower, 1957). Like Samuelson, Robert Solow (1988) concluded that mathematical economics was the core "infrastructure" of contemporary economics. He wrote:

> Economics is no longer a fit conversation piece for ladies and gentlemen. It has become a technical subject. Like any technical subject it attracts some people who are more interested in the technique than the subject. That is too bad, but it may be inevitable. In any case, do not kid yourself: the technical core of economics is indispensable infrastructure for the political economy. That is why, if you consult [a reference in contemporary economics] looking for enlightenment about the world today, you will be led to technical economics, or history, or nothing at all.

Down-to-earth economists would definitely disagree with Solow. The mathematization of economics is neither inevitable nor indispensible.

The View of Contemporary Economists

The excessive mathematization of economics is resented by most contemporary economists, including those who know how to solve partial differential equations. Blommestein (2009) suggests that the mathematization of economics has led to a new form of "mental gymnastics" of a "peculiarly depraved" type. David Hendry, who knows his mathematics rather well, declared in an interview with *Econometric Theory* in 2004 that "many American economists now rely heavily on abstract economic reasoning, often ignoring institutional aspects and inter-agent heterogeneity, as well as inherent conflicts of interest between agents" (Hendry, 2004). In his piece, *The Unreasonable Ineffectiveness of Mathematics in Economics*, Velupillai (2005) argues that "the headlong rush with which economists have equipped themselves with a half-baked knowledge of mathematical traditions has led to an un-natural mathematical economics and a non-numerical economic theory". He further says the following:

> Mathematical economics is unreasonably ineffective. Unreasonable, because the mathematical assumptions are economically unwarranted; ineffective because the mathematical formalisations imply non-constructive and uncomputable structures. A reasonable and effective mathematisation of economics entails Diophantine formalisms. These come with natural undecidabilities and uncomputabilities. In the face of this, [the] conjecture [is] that an economics for the future will be freer to explore experimental methodologies underpinned by alternative mathematical structures.

In response, Focardi and Fabozzi (2010) admit that "economic science is generally considered less viable than the physical sciences", and that "sophisticated mathematical models of the economy have been developed but their accuracy is questionable to the point that the [2007–2008] economic crisis is often blamed on an unwarranted faith in faulty mathematical models". Nevertheless they claim that

> The mathematical handling of economics has actually been reasonably successful and that models are not the cause behind the present crisis. The science of economics does not study immutable laws of nature but the complex human artefacts that are our economies and our financial markets, artefacts that are designed to be largely uncertain... and therefore models can only be moderately accurate. Still, our mathematical models offer a valuable design tool to engineer our economic systems. But the mathematics of economics and finance cannot be that of physics. The mathematics of economics and finance is the mathematics of learning and complexity, similar to the mathematics used in studying biological or ecological systems.

The response to the claims made by Focardi and Fabozzi (2010) is easy. To start with, there is no such thing as "economic science" or "science of economics". They do not tell us in what sense "the mathematical handling of economics has actually been reasonably successful" and how "mathematical models offer a valuable design tool to engineer our economic systems". Are these claims valid, given that we have been moving from one crisis to another? No one suggests that mathematical models are "the" cause of the present crisis, but these models led to complacency and faulty policy prescriptions that contributed significantly to the advent of the crisis (they represent a contributory factor to, not the cause of, the crisis).

The proposition that "models can only be moderately accurate" cannot be substantiated with evidence, when the models used by LTCM and AIG, among others, led to spectacular collapses. The claim that "the mathematics of economics and finance cannot be that of physics" is counterfactual for a number of reasons: (1) the mathematization of economics was driven by the desire to make economics as "sciency" as physics; (2) mathematical economists use every mathematical technique under the sun; (3) they import concepts from physics (such as signal extraction and the laws of thermodynamics); and (4) a typical mathematical economist is most likely trained in physics, mathematics or engineering. Partial differential equations, which are normally associated with physics (particularly fluid mechanics and dynamics), are used heavily in mathematical economics. It does not stop there, however – rather it goes further to topology and measure theory. In his brilliant book, *Two Centuries of Parasitic Economics*, Basil Al-Nakeeb (2016) has the following to say about this issue:

> Another grim problem facing macroeconomics is an unwarranted mathematical complexity that ignores Leonardo da Vinci's wise advice: simplicity is the ultimate sophistication. Complexity has been the fashion for some time; its practitioners are typically the first to get lost in the intricate math they weave, arriving at wrong conclusions and misguided policy recommendations. They fail to observe two universal tests for any fruitful endeavour: relevance and common sense. As John Maynard Keynes observed, "good or even competent economists are the rarest of birds". The economic muddle in the West today is testimony to the accuracy of this assessment. The risk to the majority of people and the economy is the dearth of good economists and mathematicians.

The Influx of Mathematics into Economics

Three arguments that can be made to justify the influx of mathematics into economics: (1) mathematics is useful; (2) mathematics is useful for studying economics; and (3) mathematics is more useful than any other discipline for the use of economists. No one can dispute the first point that mathematics is useful – after all it is the language of science. If it was not for mathematics, we would still be riding camels and horses, let alone being able to travel from Sydney to London in less than 24 hours. Technology has progressed by applying the heavily mathematical principles of physics. But economics is not physics, it is not science, and it is not technology.

As for point (2), mathematics is useful for studying economics, but this is true only to a limited extent and so far as using it as a tool. For example, simple differential calculus makes it easier to understand why the profit maximization condition is the equality of marginal cost and marginal revenue. It is not that economics is a science, and requires abstraction to make sense of so many variables. But what we have witnessed is that the use of mathematics in economics has become the end rather than the means to an end. Mathematics, Romer (2015) argues, can help economists to clarify their thinking and reasoning. However, the ubiquity of mathematical theory in economics also has serious downsides: it creates a high barrier to entry for those who want to participate in the professional dialogue, and makes checking someone's work excessively laborious, if at all possible.

Interestingly, Klein and Romero (2007) reach the conclusion that what is published in the *Journal of Economic Theory* has nothing to do with economic theory. Drawing on the work of people with strong mainstream reputations, they distinguish between "model" and "theory", arguing that a model may qualify as theory only if it purports to answer three questions: (1) theory of what?, (2) why should we care?, and (3) what merit in your explanation? They examine the 66 regular articles appearing in the 2004 issues of *Journal of Economic Theory* and apply the three requirements to find that 27 articles fail the first test (theory of what?) and 58 articles fail at least one of the three requirements. Thus, 88 per cent of the articles do not qualify as theory (the "pass" rates would be even lower if one were to exclude the special issue and include short notes). They contend that the journal's claim to scientific status is doubtful, as well as the very title of the journal. A more appropriate title would be *Journal of Economic Model Building*. More generally, they challenge calling model building "theory".

The third point that mathematics is more useful than any other discipline for the study of economics is only accepted by mathematical economists who only know mathematics and resist learning anything else. If this proposition were valid, then any mediocre mathematical economist of these days must be a better economist than Adam Smith, Karl Marx and Joan Robinson. The problem is that belief in point (3) has been reflected in the design of curriculums in graduate programmes in North America in particular. For a PhD programme that requires a year of calculus, it necessarily neglects history, sociology, logic, philosophy, and so on.

The argument that a good economist should have a greater knowledge of mathematics than any other discipline is not that convincing. It is rather perplexing that this belief is still widespread in the aftermath of the global financial crisis. Lawson (2015) suggests that many economists use mathematical methods just because this is what is required of them, not because of any deep belief in their relevance or utility and that those with power allow almost no leeway for the undertaking of alternative approaches to formalistic modelling and act as very restrictive gate keepers. From an academic perspective, the opportunity cost of the mathematization of economics is the neglect of other relevant disciplines. In an interview with Levinovitz (2016), Paul Romer said the following: "Somebody came and said: Look, I have this Earth-changing insight about economics, but the only way I can express it is by making use of the quirks of the Latin language". In response, Romer believes, "we'd say go to hell, unless they could convince us it was really essential".

3.5   RAMIFICATIONS OF THE MATHEMATIZATION OF ECONOMICS

Mathematization has had some ramifications, some of which are detrimental to the progress of economics, both as an academic discipline and as the framework of analysis used to formulate public policy. The following are some of these consequences, which are discussed in turn.

The Use of Unrealistic Assumptions

Mathematical analysis is supposed to be a tool that helps understand economics and economies. However, what has happened as a result of the mathematization of economics is that theory is twisted to fit a mathematical framework, including the use of unrealistic assumptions. For example, the assumption of profit maximization is used in microeconomics because it makes the underlying issue more suitable for differential calculus. Mathematical economists confine themselves to their offices and theorize about how firms make their production and pricing decisions rather than simply asking firms what they actually do. Many down-to-earth business economists do not agree with the assumption of profit maximization (for example, Anthony, 1960). Furthermore, the assumption of profit maximization is inconsistent with the literature on corporate social responsibility whereby a firm engages in actions to support social good beyond the interest of the firm (for example, Wood, 1991; McWilliams and Siegel, 2001). In macroeconomics, the unrealistic assumption of wage and price flexibility has been used, in conjunction with the rational expectations hypothesis, to prove (mathematically, of course) that government intervention in the economy is destabilizing at best and hazardous at worst (for example, Lucas and Sargent, 1981; Sargent and Wallace, 1976).

Irrelevance to Policy

The most important consequence of the increasing emphasis on mathematics in economics is that economics has become increasingly irrelevant to policy makers, for at least three reasons: (1) typically, mathematical models do not address policy problems directly, because mathematical elegance is much more important than policy-related issues; (2) policy makers cannot comprehend the models; and (3) mathematical economists cannot translate equations into words – hence they cannot transmit their findings to policy makers.

If Any, Bad Policy

Mathematical models are used to justify policies that have been pre-determined by politicians on ideological grounds. In this case complexity is useful because the public can be told that a brilliant mathematical economist has worked out that this is the best policy action. Mathematical models have been used to formulate the rational expectations hypothesis and its offshoot, the policy ineffectiveness hypothesis, to justify wholesale privatization and deregulation in the early 1980s. Rationality means that the behaviour of rational individuals can be predicted by mathematical models. The conclusion that politicians wanted to hear was that markets could correct themselves without the need for government intervention. The financial counterpart of the REH, the efficient market hypothesis (EMH), was developed to justify financial deregulation.

What has been the result of these policies? One crisis after another, rising inequality and poverty. In any case, mathematical models say nothing about who bears the burden of crashes (the poor) and how many lives are eased through periods of economic turmoil by government assistance and intervention in markets. Anyone with some training in humanities understands that while smoothing by government might push up the economic cost of a downturn compared to just letting the market correct, it reduces the human cost of downturns considerably.

Divorce from Reality

According to Bergmann (1999) economics fails to advance because "modern" economists are not interested in doing any real observing. When a modern economist decides to work on some topic, he or she does not try to look around the world to see what is actually going on – rather, they retire to their offices and think about an elegant, albeit unrealistic and counterfactual, theory. Reality has no place in the analysis, particularly for those practising mathematical economics. Bergmann cites a study conducted in the 1930s by R.L. Hall and C.J. Hitch who surveyed business people and found that marginal cost and marginal revenue never crossed their minds when setting prices (Hall and Hitch, 1939). In response, "the economics profession received this news with pained condescension and strove mightily to forget it". She also refers to Alan Blinder's (1991) survey, asking business people how they decide to change their prices, suggesting that Blinder's work "may breathe new life into the aborted Hall and Hitch revolution and take us to a microeconomics that incorporates realities".

Likewise, Fox (2009) suggests that those writing in the spirit of the efficient market hypothesis "sealed off in their academic cocoons" to write papers in their mathematical jargon – as a result "they developed an internal logic quite divorced from market realities". The prime efficient marketeer, Eugene Fama, provides perhaps the best example of divorce from reality and failure to observe. Fama refuses to acknowledge the presence of bubbles in asset markets, even in the aftermath of the global financial crisis. In an interview with Hilsenrath (2004), Richard Thaler (a behavioural economist) described Fama as "the only guy on earth who doesn't think there was a bubble in Nasdaq in 2000". For Fama the market is a mechanical or electrical system that has some sort of a control feedback loop or circuit breaker – it cannot go wrong because it is self-correcting. In another interview with John Cassidy, Fama rejected the very notion of bubble, suggesting that he does not even know what a bubble means (Cassidy, 2010). In fact he said that he became so tired of seeing the word "bubble" in *The Economist* that he did not renew his subscription.

Downgrading of Academic Economics

The mathematizaton of economics has led to a downgrading of academic economics – this downgrading takes several shapes and forms. First of all, the trend has created barriers to entry in the profession, depriving the discipline from people with different perspectives who can contribute significantly by bringing in different insights. On the other hand, some brilliant economists have left the field and moved to other disciplines because they cannot read the literature or publish in leading journals. Currently the profession has a class structure whereby those who sit on the top are those who know enough mathematics to be able to publish in *Econometrica*. Economists from different classes cannot even communicate. Furthermore, the mathematization of economics has inflicted damage on other disciplines through a process of brain drain, by attracting people from physics, mathematics and engineering.

I recall that one occasion the keynote speaker in a conference made his presentation, and when it was time for Q&A, only one person (belonging to the same class) asked a question. The rest of the participants had no clue what those two were talking about. On the same occasion, I asked one of my colleagues who was sitting next to me if he understood anything – he replied by saying "yes, but only the first 45 seconds of the presentation". Would something like this happen in a conference on physics, medicine, psychology or any other discipline apart from economics (and finance)?

3.6 CONCLUDING REMARKS

Perhaps the best way to close is to recall a quote from Alfred Marshall (Sills and Merton, 2000):

> [I had] a growing feeling in the later years of my work at the subject that a good mathematical theorem dealing with economic hypotheses was very unlikely to be good economics: and I went more and more on the rules – (1) Use mathematics as a shorthand language, rather than an engine of inquiry. (2) Keep to them till you have done. (3) Translate into English. (4) Then illustrate by examples that are important in real life. (5) Burn the mathematics. (6) If you can't succeed in (4), burn (3). This last I did often.

More recently, McCloskey (1998) and Nelson (2001) argued that mathematics in economic theory serves, in McCloskey's words, primarily to deliver the message "Look at how very scientific I am". In the aftermath of the great recession, the failure of economics to protect the economy resurfaced. In 2009, Paul Krugman commented in *The New York Times* with a version of the mathiness diagnosis: "As I see it, the economics profession went astray because economists, as a group, mistook beauty, clad in impressive-looking mathematics, for truth". Krugman believes that the desire of economists to show off their mathematical prowess is the "central cause of the profession's failure" (Krugman, 2009). The mathematization of economics is neither inevitable nor indispensable – it is more like extravaganza that can be lethal.

4. The laws of economics and science

4.1 THE LAWS OF ECONOMICS: GENERAL CONSIDERATIONS

The use of econometric methods (the quantification of economics in general) has led to the illusion that there are laws in economics, laws that govern the behaviour of decision makers and market participants. Baltagi (2002) describes as "the exciting thing about econometrics" the concern "for verifying or refuting economic laws, such as purchasing power parity, the life cycle hypothesis, the quantity theory of money, etc." Then he says that "economic laws or hypotheses are testable with economic data". Baltagi, it seems, cannot tell the difference between laws and hypotheses. Laws differ from hypotheses, which are proposed before and during validation by experiment and observation. Hypotheses are not laws because they have not been verified to the same degree, but they may lead to the formulation of laws, which are universal.

Laws reflect knowledge that has been repeatedly verified and never falsified. Laws summarize and explain facts determined by experiments or by formal observation and they are tested based on their ability to predict the results of future experiments. In the *Oxford Dictionary*, a scientific law is a "statement inferred from particular facts, applicable to a defined group or class of phenomena, and expressible by the statement that a particular phenomenon always occurs if certain conditions are present". Scientific laws are some sort of conclusions based on repeated experiments and observations over many years and which have become accepted universally within the scientific community.

It is therefore ludicrous to suggest that purchasing power parity, the life cycle hypothesis and the quantity theory of money are laws. As a matter of fact not even economists call them laws. The empirical evidence on PPP is all over the place. The life cycle hypothesis is called a hypothesis and hence cannot be a law, since it has not been verified repeatedly. The quantity theory of money cannot be tested in its full version because, as we have seen before, one of its components (the velocity of circulation) is calculated as a residual from the other variables (money supply, output and the general price level, all of which are measured with significant errors).

Economists disagree on these postulates to the extent that the so-called "laws" are not universally accepted by the community of economists. The evidence on these propositions reveals instances of positive, negative and insignificant responses.

For laws to be laws, they must satisfy certain conditions: (1) validity, in the sense of no repeatable contradicting observations; (2) universality, in the sense that they hold everywhere; (3) simplicity, in the sense that a law is typically expressed in terms of a single mathematical equation; and (4) stability, in the sense of staying unchanged since discovery. Surely the "law" of purchasing power parity does not satisfy these criteria: its empirical validity is questionable and it is not universal in the sense that it can be shown to be valid for some countries under certain conditions but not always. While PPP can be expressed in a single equation, this equation may take many shapes and forms and it is not a deterministic equation but rather a stochastic testable equation. And it is not stable in any shape or form: even for a single country over the same period of time, it can be demonstrated that the estimated coefficients are time-varying, implying instability. It is also not stable in the sense of exhibiting structural breaks. The deterministic, science-like, version of PPP does not make sense as it is expressed as $S = P/P^*$, where S is the exchange rate and P/P^* is the price ratio. How can S, which is the price of one currency in terms of another, be equal to the ratio of two price indices, which are measured without units? This version of PPP is derived by aggregating the law of one price, which is about the price of one commodity in two locations – and even this law is not a law as we are going to see later.

The fact of the matter is that there are no laws in economics, not even the laws that are called laws such as Okun's law, Say's law and the law of one price. This is not a trivial issue because laws in economics may be used to guide policy, with catastrophic consequences. Karabell (2013) refers to statements such as one that attributes losing the war on drugs to the laws of economics and the other statement that says "the laws of man can be bent and broken but the laws of economics cannot". He attributes this desire for having laws in economics to the notion that "economics is a science with irrefutable laws", which appeals to economists "who have long tried to elevate the profession out of the realm of observation and description and into the realm of science". Karabell (2013) asserts that "even if there are laws of economics, we haven't been observing them for long enough to know what they actually are" and that "given the vagaries of human behavior and the mercurial nature of states, people and institutions, the notion that there's some grand mechanistic, master system that explains all and predicts everything is at best a comforting fiction and at worst a straitjacket that precludes creativity, forestalls innovation and destroys dynamism".

Yes, econometricians are responsible for belief in the laws of economics. Take, for example, the following statement of Klein (1971):

> Econometrics had its origin in the recognition of empirical regularities and the systematic attempt to generalize these regularities into "laws" of economics. In a broad sense, the use of such "laws" is to make predictions – about what might have or what will come to pass. Econometrics should give a base for economic prediction beyond experience if it is to be useful. In this broad sense it may be called the science of economic prediction.

The "science of economic prediction"? This is nonsense coming from a Nobel Prize winner. Interestingly, Klein is mostly known for the construction of large-scale macroeconometric models, which have for a long time been found to be inferior, in terms of predictive power, to simple univariate models (which have lagged dependent variables, of course).

Like Klein, Geweke et al. (2006) suggest that the early empirical work of King and others "seems to have been the discovery of 'laws' in economics, very much like those in physics and other natural sciences". This quest for economic laws was, and to a lesser extent still is, rooted in the desire to give economics the status that Newton had achieved for physics. Statements like these are no more than rhetoric, made without any reference to the meaning of the word "law". If any consolation, Geweke et al. put the word "law" in quotation marks.

4.2   SPECIFIC LAWS OF ECONOMICS

Let us look at some of the laws of economics, the laws that are actually called laws as listed in Appendix Table 4A.1. These are not really laws – they are testable hypotheses with weak theoretical foundations and a variety of conditions under which they do not hold. When these hypotheses are tested, the results are all over the place, with the evidence changing according to model specification, estimation method, measurement of variables and data sample, producing variations in the results across time and locations. In what follows we examine the theoretical foundations of and empirical evidence on some of the laws of economics.

Bowley's Law

Bowley's law (also known as the law of constant wage share) is named after Arthur Bowley, the statistician who first observed it, based on British economic data from the late 19th century and early 20th century. The law states that the wage (income earned by labour) share of total output is

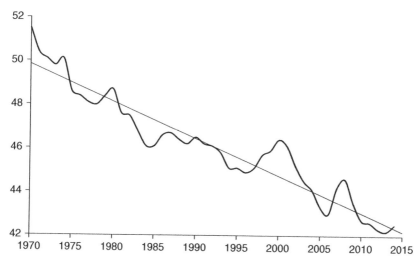

Figure 4.1   Wage share of total output in the US

constant over time. In reference to this law, which ironically sounds like Boyle's law, Krämer (2011) argues that "since the data actually reveal strong fluctuations of aggregate income shares over time, the conclusion has to be drawn that the major macroeconomic theories of growth and distribution are built around an invalid – or at least highly questionable – assumption about the real world". Contrary to this law, the long-term decline of the wage share in most countries in the last 30 years or so is acknowledged by the literature. In fact, one of the salient features of the neo-liberal era has been the ongoing redistribution of national income to profit away from wages.

The Economist (2013) acknowledges that the labour share of national income has been falling across much of the world since the 1980s, citing the Organisation for Economic Co-operation and Development (OECD), that labour captured just 62 per cent of all income in the 2000s, down from over 66 per cent in the early 1990s. Without reference to the law, *The Economist* states that "that sort of decline is not supposed to happen". In Figure 4.1 we observe that, contrary to Bowley's law, the wage share of output in the US has been in secular decline. Around the world, this trend has been the rule rather than the exception (see, for example, Guscina, 2006; Bentolila and Saint-Paul, 2003; Elsby et al., 2013; Karabournis and Neiman 2014).

Gibrat's Law

Gibrat's law implies that small and large firms grow at the same rate. Samuels (1965) suggested that "during the last decade the law has ceased to operate" and that "large firms are growing at a significantly faster proportional rate than small firms". Nassar et al. (2014) review empirical studies of Gibrat's law and find that some studies accept the law, others reject it and the rest reconcile the acceptance and rejection of the law. They also find that the law fails to hold in the manufacturing sector, but it is valid for the service sector. However, most of the empirical studies using data from developed countries reject Gibrat's law. Relander (2011) suggests that "the extensive literature has rejected the law, but various studies have found that the law is valid for certain subsamples or time periods". The conclusion derived from the literature is that the question is not whether or not Gibrat's law is valid, but rather when and with what restrictions it is valid. Hence Gibrat's law is not a law.

Gresham's Law

Gresham's law is a monetary principle stating that bad money drives out good money. For example, if two forms of commodity money are accepted by law as having similar face values, the more valuable commodity will disappear from circulation. For example, silver coins were widely circulated in Canada and the US until 1968 and 1964, respectively. In both countries coins were debased by the switch to cheaper metals, thereby inflating the new debased currency in relation to the supply of the former silver coins. The silver coins disappeared from circulation as citizens retained them to capture the steady current and future intrinsic value of the metal content over the newly inflated and therefore devalued coins, using the newer coins in daily transactions. However, this process may work in reverse. For example, Rolnick and Weber (1986) contend that bad money would drive good money to a premium rather than driving it out of circulation. Guidotti and Rodriguez (1992) point out that the experiences of dollarization may be seen as Gresham's law operating in its reverse form.

Under hyperinflation, Gresham's law definitely works in reverse. Adam Fergusson (2010) contends that in 1923 during the great inflation in the Weimar Republic, Gresham's law began to work in reverse, as the official money became so worthless that virtually nobody would take it. This was particularly serious because farmers began to hoard food. Accordingly, any currency backed by any sort of value became the circulating medium of exchange. The same happened in Zimbabwe where hyperinflation led to the replacement of the Zimbabwean dollar (bad money) with the US dollar and South African rand (good money).

The Law of Iron Wages

The law of iron wages states that in the long run real wages converge on the minimum level necessary to sustain livelihood. It has been criticized on the following grounds: (1) firms pay workers a premium over subsistence levels to make them more efficient; (2) in the theory of efficiency wages, firms pay above market clearing wages in order to incentivize employees and reduce turnover of experienced employees; and (3) workers enter and stay in a field because of the wages offered. Booming industries offer higher wages, forcing other industries to pay more in order to keep workers, so long as the supply of workers does not exceed demand. The fact that workers can strike means that wages must be high enough to dissuade them from doing so.

It is one thing to say that real wages have been stagnant and another that they converge on a subsistence level. In Figure 4.2 we observe real wages in the US during the period 1950–2015. We can see that real wages grew rapidly until about 1978, then they went down and stayed stagnant at about the 1988 level. The law of iron wages cannot be valid for the period up to 1978 because real wages were rising (and rising rapidly). It cannot be valid for the period since 1988 unless the 1988 level (which is about the current level) is the subsistence level. There is no evidence that this is the subsistence level, which means that the law is not valid for the recent period either.

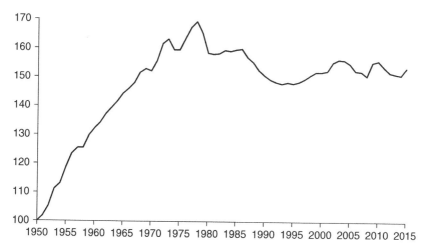

Figure 4.2   US real wages (1950 = 100)

The Law of Demand

The first thing that we learn in microeconomics is that, *ceteris paribus*, as the price of a commodity rises, the demand for the commodity declines – this is the law of demand. However, this law has many exceptions, which means that it is not universal. The first exception is Giffen goods, the demand for which rises as the price rises. For example, during the Irish potato famine of the 19th century, potatoes were considered a Giffen good. Potatoes were the largest staple in the Irish diet, so as the price rose people responded by reducing spending on luxury goods such as meat and vegetables, buying more potatoes instead. The second exception occurs when the price of the commodity is expected to change. If an increase in the price of a commodity causes households to expect the price to rise further, consumers may start purchasing greater amounts of the commodity even at a higher price. Similarly, if consumers expect the price of a commodity to decline, purchases may be postponed. The third exception is that of basic or necessary goods, the goods that people need and buy no matter how high the price (see, for example, Baxter and Moosa, 1996). An increase or a decrease in the price of such a good does not affect the quantity demanded (that is, demand is highly inelastic). The same applies to goods that command a negligible portion of a consumer's budget – for example, salt. While the law of demand implies a downward-sloping demand curve, the exceptions imply either an upward-sloping or a vertical demand curve.

The Law of One Price

The LOP is derived as a no-arbitrage condition, stating that a commodity must sell at the same price everywhere when prices are expressed in terms of one currency. This is why, for example, gold sells for the same price anywhere in the world. A violation of this law triggers commodity arbitrage whereby arbitragers make profit by buying a commodity where it is cheap and selling it where it is expensive. However, this law holds for very few commodities (such as gold bullion) and it is violated for many reasons. For example, it is violated if buyers have less than perfect information about where to find the lowest price. In this case, sellers face a trade-off between the frequency and profitability of their sales – that is, firms may be indifferent between posting a high price (thus selling infrequently, because most consumers will search for a lower one) and a low price (at which they will sell more often, but earn less profit per sale).The Balassa–Samuelson effect implies that the law of one price is not applicable to non-traded goods as they may be cheaper in some countries than others because of the relative prices of land and labour (they are typically cheaper in less developed countries). Another reason for the violation of the LOP is pricing to market, whereby producers charge different prices in different countries. For example, the cover price of *The Economist* varies considerably across countries when it is measured in the same currency.

Ardeni (1989) argues that in spite of the empirical failure of the LOP it is usually assumed that commodity prices are arbitraged perfectly, at least in the long run. He casts doubt on the validity of this proposition, describing it as "counterfactual" and suggesting that much of the empirical evidence provided to support LOP is flawed and affected by econometric shortcomings (spurious regressions, nonstationary data, inappropriate use of first differences, and so on). He demonstrates that the LOP fails and that deviations from the no-arbitrage condition are permanent. Rashid (2007) contends that the LOP is "one of the most basic laws of economics and yet it is a law observed in the breach" – in other words, it is not a law. Rogoff et al. (2001) examine annual commodity price data from England and the Netherlands over a period of 700 years and find that the magnitude, volatility and persistence of deviations from the LOP have not declined by as much as expected. This has happened despite lower transportation costs, lower trade protection and fewer wars and plagues in the modern era. The analysis is consistent with the growing evidence that commodity arbitrage remains highly imperfect.

Okun's Law

Okun's law tells us how much growth is needed to reduce unemployment by, for example, one percentage point. The law can be represented by equations in terms of deviations from the natural levels or rates of change, with an added stochastic error term reflecting the lack of precision. The available evidence provided by extensive literature shows considerable variation in the estimated value of Okun's coefficient. Okun's law enjoyed some popularity following its inception in 1962, but it is no longer taken seriously. It is unstable (Meyer and Tasci, 2012), it is dead (Gordon, 2010) and it broke down during the great recession as recoveries have become jobless (IMF, 2010). More evidence on Okun's law is presented in Chapter 10.

Say's Law

Say's law, which was introduced by the French economist Jean-Baptise Say, says that supply creates its own demand, meaning that producers should not worry about how much to produce because whatever they produce will be sold. Say (1834) further argued that the law implied that a general glut (excess supply) could not arise. If this proposition (law) were valid then Boeing and Airbus are working on a flawed business model because they do not produce unless they receive orders. Say's law has been one of the principal doctrines used to support the laissez-faire proposition that a free economy reverts to full employment, which cannot occur in the presence of government intervention.

Say's law is not a law because it is counterfactual. General gluts do occur, particularly when the economy is heading south. Market participants may choose to hold more money, thereby reducing demand but not supply. Keynes (1936) argued that Say's law was not valid and that demand, rather than supply, was the key variable that determines the overall level of economic activity. According to Keynes, demand depends on the propensity of individuals to consume and on the propensity of businesses to invest, both of which vary throughout the business cycle. There is no reason to expect enough aggregate demand to produce full employment. Some contemporary economists believe that demand creates its own supply. For example, Krugman (2015) writes:

> Not only doesn't supply create its own demand; experience since 2008 suggests, if anything, that the reverse is largely true – specifically, that inadequate demand destroys supply. Economies with persistently weak demand seem to suffer large declines in potential as well as actual output.

Blanchard and Summers (1986) point out that adverse demand shocks can lead to persistently high unemployment, therefore persistently reducing the supply of goods and services. Fatás and Summers (2015) believe that shortfalls in demand, resulting both from the global economic downturn of 2008 and 2009, and from subsequent attempts to reduce government spending, have had large negative effects on both actual and potential world economic output. A law is not a law if it tells us something that is exactly the opposite to what happens in reality.

Verdoorn's Law

Verdoorn's law, which is named after Dutch economist Petrus Johannes Verdoorn, is about the relation between output and productivity. Verdoorn put a numerical value on this relation, suggesting that "in the long run a change in the volume of production, say about 10 per cent, tends to be associated with an average increase in labour productivity of 4.5 per cent" (see, for example, Verdoorn, 1980). The model representing this law can be expressed as:

$$P_{it} = \alpha_i + \beta_i Q_{it} + \varepsilon_{it} \qquad (4.1)$$

where P and Q are labour productivity and output in the manufacturing sector, respectively, and $\beta > 0$ is Verdoorn's coefficient. Alternatively the model is expressed in terms of growth rates as follows:

$$\dot{P}_{it} = \alpha_i + \beta_i \dot{Q}_{it} + \varepsilon_{it} \qquad (4.2)$$

$$\dot{E}_{it} = \alpha_i + \beta_i \dot{Q}_{it} + \varepsilon_{it} \qquad (4.3)$$

where $\dot{P}$, $\dot{Q}$ and $\dot{E}$ are the growth rates of labour productivity, output and employment of the manufacturing sector of the economy. Like Okun's law, Verdoorn's law is represented by equations containing error terms. The laws of science, on the other hand, are written in terms of exact deterministic equations.

Castiglione (2011) investigates Verdoorn's law and finds a mixed bag of views and results: (1) Verdoorn's law is confirmed; (2) Verdoorn's law is not supported in growth rates; (3) the Verdoorn specification suffers from a failure to specify the economic process through which growth affects productivity; and (4) the direction of causality from output to productivity growth is not confirmed. Moreover, many problems are involved in testing the law: (1) the potential problem of bias due to simultaneity between the two variables; (2) the direction of causality; (3) the law ignores the contribution of capital, which can be substituted with labour, thus implying that the Verdoorn coefficient is not stable since the elasticity of capital with respect to labour is not constant; (4) whether output (employment or productivity) is endogenously or exogenously determined; and (5) the apparent paradox when measuring static or dynamic economies of scale. In fact, different values of the Verdoorn coefficient (and thus increasing returns to scale) are often obtained when estimating a linear model in static terms (variables in levels) or dynamic terms (variables in first differences). A law that tells us different things is not a law.

Wagner's Law

Wagner's law, which is named after the German economist Adolph Wagner, states that economic growth leads to increasing share of public expenditure in GDP. Like Verdoorn's law and Okun's law, Wagner's law can be represented by several specifications that are likely to give inconsistent results.

The evidence on Wagner's law is a mixed bag. Magableh (2006) found that the law has withstood the test of disproof for some empirical studies, or for some countries, but in others it is either rejected or cannot be confirmed. Likewise, Kumar et al. (2010) state that Wagner's law has been tested empirically for various countries using cross-section, time series and panel data, producing results that vary considerably from country to country with some supportive and some opposing evidence. Supportive evidence is presented by Ahsan et al. (1996), Biswal et al. (1999), Islam (2001) Kolluri et al. (2000), Sideris (2007) and Ghali (1999). No evidence for the law is found by Chow et al. (2002), Burney (2002), Courakis et al. (1993), Ansari et al. (1997) and Sinha (2007). Even the direction of causality is not clear.

In 1883 Wagner postulated that social, administrative and welfare issues increase in need and complexity as an economy develops, implying that the direction of causation is from GDP to the share of government expenditure (Musgrave and Peacock, 1958). Keynes (1936), on the other hand, postulated that fiscal stimuli are occasionally required to boost aggregate demand, particularly in times of recession, which means that the direction of causality is from government expenditure to GDP.

4.3   THE EFFICIENT MARKET HYPOTHESIS AS A LAW OF ECONOMICS

The efficient market hypothesis (or Fama's law) tells us that the market is efficient in the sense that market-determined financial prices (stock prices in particular) reflect all available information. Since information arrives randomly, it follows that financial prices move in a random and an unpredictable manner – in other words, financial prices tend to follow a random walk process. For a long time, the EMH dominated the thinking of finance academics to the extent that it was (and still is for the true believers) something like heresy to question its validity. An enthusiastic efficient marketeer, Michael Jensen, went as far as claiming that "there is no other proposition in economics which has more solid empirical evidence supporting it than the efficient market hypothesis" (Jensen, 1978).

The opponents of the EMH, and most neutral observers, believe that the hypothesis provides the intellectual underpinning for embracing financial deregulation, which is widely and justifiably believed to have been a cause of the global financial crisis. In another sense, however, the EMH is a casualty of the crisis. With the benefit of hindsight, we know that financial and housing markets were experiencing bubbles that eventually burst and that bonus recipients did not perform that well to deserve the bonuses. We also know that complex derivatives and securities were overvalued to the extent that some smart people managed (by exploiting overvaluation) to make enormous profit, which is an outcome that defies the EMH. The crisis, therefore, exposed the implausibility of the EMH, put it under scrutiny and forced economists and regulators (except the true believers, the enthusiastic efficient marketeers) to re-examine their faith in the hypothesis.

The efficient market hypothesis has played an extraordinarily big role in shaping mainstream thinking in financial economics, with significant practical implications. Since investors respond rationally to available information, as reflected in financial prices, they sell when prices are too high, and vice versa. In other words, one implication of the EMH is that assets and markets cannot be overvalued or undervalued and that market-determined prices are always at the right level. Any deviation of the price of an asset from its intrinsic value is eliminated very quickly. What does not make sense here is the rational expectations idea that every market participant believes that an asset is overvalued or otherwise (and to the same extent). This idea is ludicrous, to say the least. If they all want to sell an overvalued asset, who is going to buy? There is simply no such thing as a "representative agent" or a typical trader behaving in a standardized and predictable manner.

A related implication is that financial prices should exhibit no pattern and move randomly because information arrives in a random manner and gets reflected in prices almost instantly. Therefore the EMH lies at the heart of neoclassical thinking that the market takes care of things, restoring equilibrium on its own. This, of course, leads to the important implication that there is no need for regulation and that deregulation enhances market efficiency. For regulators, therefore, the challenge is to ensure that all investors have access to the same information, which means that regulation should be confined to accounting standards, timely publication of company news and data, disclosure of fees, and full description of financial products.

Yet another implication of the EMH is that the market cannot be outperformed consistently because available information is already reflected in financial prices. As Hilsenrath (2004) put it, "markets distil new information with lightning speed and provide the best possible estimate of the underlying value of listed companies". It is true that beating the market is not easy and that most people cannot do that, but casual observation tells us that, more often than never, markets can be outperformed. Warren Buffett's view of the EMH, as expressed by Dehnad (2009), is interesting: the EMH "advocates no due diligence when investing – just buy the market – so it is good for his [Buffett's] business". In fact it has been stated that "unless you're Warren Buffett, an index fund is where you should put your money" (Nocera, 2009). This is strange because even Buffett is not supposed to beat the market since the EMH is a "universal law" of economics.

The global financial crisis produced big winners, those who did their research properly (without econometrics) and reached the conclusion that the market for structured products would collapse. By betting on that prediction (for example, by taking short positions on credit default swaps) they made a killing. The majority who lost believed in the EMH, explicitly or implicitly, and followed herd behaviour on the grounds that there was no bubble, but there was a bubble and that bubble came to the end of its natural life. So, it is not only Warren Buffett who can outperform the market.

For a long time, the EMH was accepted as an undisputed fact of life and imposed on finance students in a vibrant process of indoctrination. Andrew Lo, a financial economist at the Sloan School of Management (MIT), says that "efficient-market theory was the norm" when he was a doctoral student at Harvard and MIT in the 1980s and that "it was drilled into us that markets are efficient". He also says that it took him five to ten years to change his views (Cassidy, 2010). Has anyone heard a physicist who initially believed in the validity of Boyle's law, then he changed his view five years later?

4.4   THE LAWS OF SCIENCE

Let us now look at some of the laws of science, which are described briefly in Appendix Table 4A.2. Unlike the laws of economics, the laws of science are formulated either after testing hypotheses under laboratory conditions or by observing and measuring the variables under investigation using instruments, as in astronomy and celestial mechanics. The laws of science are typically expressed as exact equations relating the underlying variables. In what follows, we present the equations representing some of the laws of science from the fields of (1) physics and physical chemistry, (2) geology and geophysics, (3) thermodynamics, (4) mechanics and fluid mechanics, and (5) optics, electromagnetism and radio technology.

Coulomb's Law

Coulomb's law describes the force interacting between static electrically charged particles. In its scalar form the law is expressed as:

$$F = k_e \left[\frac{q_1 q_2}{r^2} \right] \tag{4.4}$$

where k_e is Coulomb's constant, q_1 and q_2 are the signed magnitudes of the charges and r is the distance between the charges. The force of interaction between the charges is attractive if the charges have opposite signs and repulsive if they have the same signs.

Jurin's Law

The law describes the rise and fall of a liquid within a thin capillary tube. It is expressed as:

$$h = \frac{2\gamma cos\theta}{r\rho g} \tag{4.5}$$

where h is the liquid height, γ is the surface tension, θ is the contact angle of the liquid on the tube wall, ρ is the liquid density, r is the tube radius and g is the gravitational acceleration. This law is valid if the tube radius is smaller than the capillary length.

Pascal's Law

Pascal's law is represented by the equation:

$$\Delta P = \rho g(\Delta h) \tag{4.6}$$

where ΔP is the hydrostatic pressure (in Pascals), or the difference in pressure at two points within a fluid column due to the weight of the fluid, ρ is the fluid density (in kilograms per cubic metre), g is acceleration due to gravity (normally using the sea level acceleration due to Earth's gravity, in metres per second squared), and Δh is the height of fluid above the point of measurement, or the difference in elevation between the two points within the fluid column (in metres). This means that the change in pressure between two elevations is due to the weight of the fluid between the elevations or that the pressure change is caused by the change of potential energy per unit volume of the liquid due to the existence of the gravitational field.

Archie's Law

Archie's law can be represented by the equation:

$$C_t = \frac{1}{a}C_w \phi^m S_w^n \tag{4.7}$$

where ϕ denotes the porosity, C_t is the electrical conductivity of the fluid saturated rock, C_w is the electrical conductivity of the brine, S_w is the brine saturation, m is the cementation exponent of the rock (usually in the range 1.8–2.0 for sandstones), n is the saturation exponent (usually close to 2) and a is the tortuosity factor.

Birch's Law

Birch's law can be represented by the equation:

$$v_p = a(M_{avg}) + b\rho \tag{4.8}$$

where v_p is the compressional wave velocity of rocks and minerals, M_{avg} is a constant average atomic weight and ρ is density.

Avogadro's Law

Avogadro's law stipulates that for a given mass of an ideal gas, the volume and amount (moles) of the gas are directly proportional if the temperature and pressure are constant. This implies that $V \propto n$ where V is the volume of the gas and n is the amount of substance of the gas (measured in moles). Hence:

$$\frac{V}{n} = k \tag{4.9}$$

where k is a constant equal to RT/P, where R is the universal gas constant, T is the Kelvin temperature, and P is pressure. As temperature and pressure are constant, RT/P is also constant and represented as k. Alternatively, the equation can be written as:

$$\frac{V_1}{n_1} = \frac{V_2}{n_2} \tag{4.10}$$

which says that as the number of moles of gas increases, the volume of gas increases proportionately, and vice versa.

Boyle's Law

Boyle's law can be expressed as:

$$P \propto \frac{1}{V} \tag{4.11}$$

where P and V are the pressure and the volume of the gas, respectively. Alternatively it can be expressed as:

$$PV = k \tag{4.12}$$

where k is a constant. This means that the product of pressure and volume is a constant for a given mass of confined gas as long as the temperature is constant.

Charles' Law

When the pressure on a sample of a dry gas is held constant, the Kelvin temperature and volume will be directly related, such that $V \propto T$ or:

$$\frac{V}{T} = k \tag{4.13}$$

where V is the volume of the gas, T is the temperature of the gas (measured in Kelvin) and k is a constant.

Graham's Law

Graham's law stipulates that the rate of effusion of a gas is inversely proportional to the square root of the mass of its particles. It can be expressed as:

$$\frac{R_1}{R_2} = \sqrt{\frac{M_2}{M_1}} \tag{4.14}$$

where R_1 is the rate of effusion of the first gas (volume or number of moles per unit time), R_1 is the rate of effusion for the second gas, M_1 is the molar mass of gas 1 and M_2 is the molar mass of gas 2.

Darcy's Law

A simple proportional relation between the instantaneous discharge rate through a porous medium, the viscosity of the fluid and the pressure drop over a given distance. It can be expressed as:

$$Q = \frac{-kA(p_b - p_a)}{\mu L} \tag{4.15}$$

where Q is the total discharge, k is the intrinsic permeability of the medium, A is the cross-sectional area to flow, and $p_b - p_a$ is the total pressure drop, μ is viscosity and L is the length over which the pressure drop is taking place. The negative sign implies that the fluid flows from high pressure to low pressure.

Marconi's Law

If H is the height of the antenna and D is the maximum signalling distance in metres, then:

$$H = c\sqrt{D} \qquad (4.16)$$

where c is a constant. For Marconi's original apparatus, c was 0.17–0.19 for a distance of 60 kilometres.

Ohm's Law

Ohm's law can be represented by the equation:

$$I = \frac{V}{R} \qquad (4.17)$$

where I is the current going through the conductor in units of amperes, V is the voltage measured across the conductor in units of volts, and R is the resistance of the conductor in units of ohms.

The Stefan–Boltzmann Law

The Stefan–Boltzmann law can be represented by the equation

$$j = \sigma T^4 \qquad (4.18)$$

where j is the total energy radiated per unit surface area of a black body across all wavelengths per unit time (also known as the black-body radiant emissive power), T is the black body's thermodynamic temperature, and σ is the Stefan–Boltzmann constant.

4.5   THE LAWS OF SCIENCE VERSUS THE LAWS OF ECONOMICS

Despite the belief of some economists and econometricians that the laws of economics are just as valid as the laws of science, this view is becoming increasingly unacceptable, following the lessons we learned from the global financial crisis. In a comment on the internal models used by financial institutions to determine capital adequacy and measure risk, Dowd et al. (2011) argue that these models are shaky because the process governing the operations of financial markets (as social systems) are not immutable to the laws of physics. In this section it is demonstrated that the laws of economics are not really laws, let alone being as valid as the laws of science.

For a law to be law, the necessary condition is that it must be consistent with observed data universally and that it can be used for the purpose of prediction. Let us see if the laws of economics and those of science satisfy these requirements. For this purpose we examine three laws of economics: the law of one price, Okun's law and Wagner's law, and three laws of science: Boyle's law, Charles' law and Marconi's law. The laws of science are verified by using experimental data, as in Boyle's law and Charles' law, or by measurement using instruments, as in Marconi's law. The laws of economics, on the other hand, are tested by using cross-sectional, time series or pooled data.

Figure 4.3 shows the performance of the laws of economics and those of science in relation to observed data – and what a difference it turns out to be (as expected). The laws of science show a perfect fit to the data, which are generated by experiments in the cases of Boyle's law and Charles's law. No matter where the experiments are conducted the data give a perfect fit. In the case of Boyle's law the experiment involves changing the pressure on a gas while keeping the temperature constant. For Charles's law, the experiment involves changing temperature and observing what happens to the volume of gas when pressure is kept unchanged. For Marconi's law, the data are generated by measurement.

Conversely, the data used to test the laws of economics are all over the place in relation to what is predicted by the law. For example, the law of one price tells us that the same commodity should sell for the same price anywhere if the price is expressed in the same currency. If that currency is the US dollar, the LOP is represented by the equation $P_X = SP_\$$ where P_X is the price measured in terms of currency X, $P_\$$ is the price in terms of the US dollar and S is the exchange rate measured as the price of one dollar in terms of X. The law states that $S = P_X/P_\$$ which gives the exchange rate predicted by the law. If the LOP is valid then the predicted exchange rate should be equal to the observed exchange rate, in which case a scatter diagram shows that all points should fall on a 45 degree line – this is not the case as shown in Figure 4.3, which is based on the prices of Big Macs as reported by *The Economist*.

As for Wagner's law, cross-sectional data are used on 76 countries with various degrees of development. The data are on GDP (in billions of dollars) and government expenditure as a percentage of GDP. Again there are significant deviations from the line representing the relation between government expenditure as a percentage of GDP and the level of GDP. It is not that the use of log-log specification or any other specification of Wagner's law would change the results. And we will see later (in Chapter

Econometrics as a con art

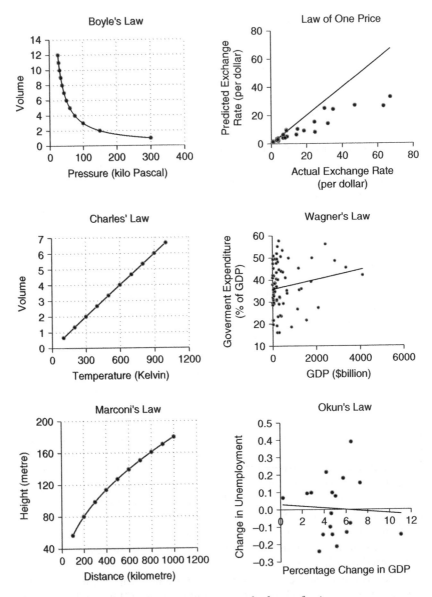

Figure 4.3   The laws of economics versus the laws of science

10) that this law does not hold on a time series basis, using various specifications, variable definitions and estimation methods.

Okun's law does not fare any better, using data for 18 countries. The relation between GDP and unemployment (which is supposed to be negative) is hardly negative and the value of Okun's coefficient is all over the place. In Chapter 10 it will be demonstrated that Okun's law is not a law, based on time series data and various model specifications. One can only reach one conclusion by looking at Figure 4.3: unlike the laws of science, the laws of economics are not laws.

4.6 CONCLUDING REMARKS

Econometrics is not a science because economics is not a science. Modelling the response of the exchange rate to a change in interest rates is not as precise as modelling the path of a projectile. The laws of science are used to develop technology but the laws of economics are verified by econometric methods with the prior objective of proving a pre-conceived belief. It is therefore ludicrous to talk about the laws of economics and how "sciency" econometric methods are. Economics, as a social science, cannot discover eternal laws – rather, it has to deal with ever-changing and inherently complex phenomena (Horn, 2009). Guisan (2001) argues that we must not forget that economics and econometrics are social sciences, where mathematics is just an instrument that should be used in a flexible way to solve social questions and to obtain solutions to important problems, giving priority to the relevance from the economics point of view and not to mathematical sophistication.

Unlike economists and econometricians, scientists are more humble in reporting their findings. This is how Ritholtz (2009) explains the humility of science:

> Let's start with the basics. Hard "science" – Physics, Biology, Chemistry, and all variants thereto – begins humbly. They try to describe the universe around us by creating theories, and then testing them. These theorems are always preliminary. Even when testing validates them, Science is always prepared – even eager – to replace them with newer theories that are proven to be even more valid.

For Ritholtz (2009), scientists begin with the admission that they know nothing and seek to learn through experiments and logic to find accurate explanations. Unlike economists, scientists do not assume or presume while embarking on an ongoing search for better explanations, more proof, further verification, and a quest for the truth. Economists, on the other hand, begin with a few basic assumptions, many of which are outrageous,

to say the least. Ritholtz (2009) suggests that "economics has had a justifiable inferiority complex versus real sciences", which economists have
attempted to overcome by "throwing lots of smart mathematicians at its
practice, in an attempt to make the social art seem more 'sciency' and thus
more credible". This practice has created an illusion of precision that does
not exist even in natural science. Economists and econometricians working
on risk models believe that they can calculate the capital that precludes the
possibility of insolvency with a confidence level of 99.9 per cent. This is
pure arrogance, to say the least.

Let us not forget that scientists talk about the law of gravity and the
laws of thermodynamics, but they never refer to the theory of continental
drift or the big bang as laws. Economists (at least some of them) have the
extraordinary courage (perhaps arrogance) to refer to purchasing power
parity as a law.

APPENDIX

Table 4A.1   The laws of economics

Law	Description
Baxter's Law	A monopoly in a regulated industry can extend into, and dominate, a non-regulated industry.
Bowley's Law	The proportion of gross national product from labour is constant.
Engel's Law	As income rises, the proportion of income spent on food falls even if actual expenditure on food rises.
Gibrat's Law	The proportional rate of growth of a firm is independent of its absolute size.
Gresham's Law	Bad money drives out good money.
Hotelling's Law	In many markets it is rational for producers to make their products as similar as possible.
Iron Law of Wages	In the long run real wages tend towards the minimum wage necessary to sustain the life of the worker.
Law of Demand	All else being equal, as the price of a product goes up, the quantity demanded falls, and vice versa.
Law of One Price	A good must sell for the same price in all locations when prices are expressed in a common currency.
Okun's Law	For every percentage point that unemployment rate falls (rises) in excess of the natural unemployment rate, real output rises (falls) by approximately 3%.
Say's Law	Aggregate production necessarily creates an equal quantity of aggregate demand. In other words, supply creates its own demand.
Wagner's Law	Public expenditure rises constantly, which means that the development of an industrial economy is accompanied by a growing share of public expenditure in aggregate output.

Table 4A.2   The laws of science

Law	Field	Description
Ampère's Law	Physics	The law relates magnetic fields to electric currents that produce them. Ampère's law determines the magnetic field associated with a given current, or the current associated with a given magnetic field, provided that the electric field does not change over time.
Archie's Law	Geology	The law relates the electrical conductivity of a sedimentary rock to its porosity and brine saturation.
Avogadro's Law	Thermodynamics	The law relates the volume of a gas to the amount of substance of gas present. Avogadro's law states that equal volumes of all gases, at the same temperature and pressure, have the same number of molecules. For a given mass of an ideal gas, the volume and amount (moles) of the gas are directly proportional if the temperature and pressure are constant.
Beer–Lambert Law	Optics	The law relates the attenuation of light to the properties of the material through which the light is travelling.
Biot–Savart Law	Electromagnetics, Fluid Dynamics	It relates the magnetic field to the magnitude, direction, length and proximity of the electric current.
Birch's Law	Geophysics	A linear relation of the compressional wave velocity of rocks and minerals with given average atomic weight and density.
Boyle's Law	Thermodynamics	A law that describes how the pressure of a gas tends to increase as the volume of a gas decreases. The absolute pressure exerted by a given mass of an ideal gas is inversely proportional to the volume it occupies if the temperature and amount of gas remain unchanged within a closed system.
Byerlee's Law	Geophysics	The law is used to determine the shear stress required to slide one rock over another.
Charles' Law	Thermodynamics	When the pressure on a sample of a dry gas is held constant, the Kelvin temperature and volume will be directly related.
Coulomb's Law	Physics	A law that describes the force interacting between static electrically charged particles.
Darcy's Law	Fluid Mechanics	A law that describes the flow of a fluid through a porous medium.
Dermott's Law	Celestial Mechanics	An empirical formula for the orbital period of major satellites orbiting planets in the Solar System.

Faraday's Law of Induction	Electromagnetism	A basic law of electromagnetism predicting how a magnetic field interacts with an electric circuit to produce an electromotive force – a phenomenon called electromagnetic induction. It is the fundamental operating principle of transformers, inductors, and many types of electrical motors, generators and solenoids.
Graham's Law	Thermodynamics	The rate of effusion of a gas is inversely proportional to the square root of the mass of its particles.
Hooke's Law	Physics	The force needed to extend or compress a spring by some distance is proportional to that distance.
Jurin's Law	Physics	A law that describes the rise and fall of a liquid within a thin capillary tube.
Lenz's Law	Physics	An induced current flows in a direction such that it opposes the change which produced it.
Marconi's Law	Radio Technology	The relation between height of antennas and the maximum signalling distance of radio transmissions.
Newton's Laws of Motion	Mechanics	Three physical laws that describe the relation between a body, the forces acting upon it, and its motion in response to those forces.
Ohm's Law	Electronics	The current through a conductor between two points is directly proportional to the voltage across the two points.
Pascal's Law	Physics	The pressure exerted anywhere in a confined incompressible fluid is transmitted equally in all directions throughout the fluid such that the pressure variations (initial differences) remain the same.
Raoult's Law	Physical Chemistry	The partial vapour pressure of each component of an ideal mixture of liquids is equal to the vapour pressure of the pure component multiplied by its mole fraction in the mixture.
Stefan–Boltzmann Law	Thermodynamics	The total energy radiated per unit surface area of a black body across all wavelengths per unit time is directly proportional to the fourth power of the black body's thermodynamic temperature.

5. Econometric analysis: loopholes and shortcomings

5.1 INTRODUCTION

Apart from the true believers, economists in general have lost faith in econometrics, and for a variety of reasons. Econometrics is criticized on the basis of its usefulness as a discipline and the perceived widespread methodological shortcomings of econometric analysis. Econometrics must be evaluated as a tool that is used by economists to advance knowledge, with the ultimate objective of making sound policy decisions, but there is no evidence that there has been such a contribution. A regression of the number of papers published in major econometrics journals, or the number of estimation and testing methods and models, on a measure of our understanding of the economy and financial markets is likely to produce insignificant results, except perhaps when correlation is negative. The proliferation of econometric techniques has been disproportional to our understanding of the economy, which defies the purpose for which econometrics was invented in the first place.

For the true believers, any economist who disputes issues like the excessive quantification of economic theory is no longer capable of reading much of the literature (or contributing to it at this level). Those economists who know (in addition to economics) sociology, law, history, logic and philosophy (including Adam Smith) are not good enough as economists because they do not have an advanced knowledge of quantitative methods. In this chapter we identify some loopholes and shortcomings of econometric analysis. Chapter 6 is devoted to the criticism of econometrics advanced by influential economists and econometricians, including Edward Leamer, J.M. Keynes, Robert Lucas and economists who subscribe to the Austrian school of thought.

5.2 QUANTITATIVE MODELS IN ECONOMICS AND FINANCE

There is a widespread view that quantitative models have not only failed to predict the global financial crisis, but may have contributed to the advent of the crisis. They failed to predict the crisis because they are divorced from reality and contributed to its advent because they led to the adoption of wrong policies on the part of the government (regulatory authorities) and complacency on the part of financial institutions exposed to financial risk. As *The Economist* (2015) put it, both financiers and economists still get the blame for the 2007–2009 financial crisis: the first group for causing it and the second for not predicting it. As it turns out, the two issues are related. The economists failed to understand the importance of finance while financiers put too much faith in the models produced by economists.

Divorce from Reality

One lesson that we have not learned from the global financial crisis is that quantitative models do not work because they do not provide an adequate representation of the behaviour of market participants. For example, Blommestein (2009) identifies two important underlying reasons why academic finance models systematically fail to account for real-world phenomena: (1) treating economics not as a social science but as a branch of applied mathematics inspired by the methodology of physics; and (2) using economic models as if the empirical content of economic theories is not very low (and it is low, thanks mainly to econometrics and econometricians). According to Farmer and Foley (2009) empirical statistical models that are fitted to past data forecast a few quarters ahead as long as things stay more or less the same, but fail in the face of big change. Horn (2009) argues that "we seem to be witnessing the dismantling of an approach that, at least in its shallow mainstream version, has to make a series of absurd assumptions in order to reach any conclusion – with both the assumptions and the conclusions being astonishingly out of touch with reality". The assumptions are typically formulated to achieve one objective: model elegance.

Colander et al. (2009) trace the deeper roots of the failure of quantitative models to the profession's insistence on constructing models that, by design, disregard the key elements driving outcomes in real-world markets. The economics profession has failed in communicating the limitations, weaknesses, and even dangers of quantitative models to the public, perhaps because of the belief that quantitative models are perfect (beauty is in the eyes of the beholder). Economists have largely developed and come to rely on models that disregard key factors (including heterogeneity of decision rules, revisions of forecasting strategies, and changes in the social context) that drive outcomes in asset markets. It is obvious, even to the casual observer, that these models fail to account for the actual evolution of the real-world economy. The implicit view behind standard models is that markets and economies are inherently stable and that they only get off track temporarily. This is the neoclassical view of the world, which is rather amenable to quantification.

The Aftermath of the Crisis

In the wake of the global financial crisis many people have come to wonder why economists have not been able to predict mishaps, despite the availability of conspicuous indicators. Some economists respond to this legitimate line of wondering, with typical arrogance. For example, Levine (2012) argues that "it is a fundamental principle that there can be no reliable way of predicting a crisis", which is strange because some people, who are not at the same level of sophistication as Levine, did actually predict the crisis. Syll (2012a) describes the response of Levine as "a proof of a rather arrogant and insulting attitude". He also suggests that "it is an enormous waste of intellectual power to build these kinds of models based on useless theories". Interestingly, not even Robert Lucas, who developed the line of reasoning followed by Levine, lives in the same state of denial as Levine. In an interview with Kevin Hoover (http://econ.duke.edu/~kdh9/), Lucas was asked if he would accept any of the blame for providing the intellectual justification for deregulation. He replied as follows:

> You know, people had no trouble having financial meltdowns in their economies before all this stuff we've been talking about came on board. We didn't help, though; there's no question about that. We may have focused attention on the wrong things, I don't know.

Nouriel Roubini, who is not an econometrician, warned of a looming crisis as early as September 2006 when he declared in a meeting at the International Monetary Fund that he expected a bleak sequence of events: a housing bust, mortgage defaults, a collapsing market for mortgage-backed securities, declining consumer confidence and deep recession (Mihm, 2008). The participants at the IMF meeting were sceptical, even dismissive. When Anirvan Banerji delivered his response to Roubini's talk, he noted that Roubini's predictions were not based on mathematical models and dismissed his hunches as those of a "career naysayer". According to *The Guardian*, Roubini was ridiculed for predicting a collapse of the housing market and worldwide recession (Brockes, 2009). Robert Shiller wrote an article a year before the collapse of Lehman Brothers in which he predicted that a slowing US housing market would cause the housing bubble to burst, leading to financial collapse (Shiller, 2007). Nassim Taleb, author of *The Black Swan*, spent years warning against the breakdown of the banking system in particular and the economy in general. According to David Brooks of the *New York Times*, "Taleb not only has an explanation for what's happening, he saw it coming" (Brooks, 2008). The economists relying on quantitative models failed to predict the crisis because their models told them that a crisis on the scale witnessed in 2008 can only happen once every few billion years.

Flaherty et al. (2013) refer to three model-related lessons that we should have learned from the crisis. The first lesson is that traditional risk management methods are rooted in history – and history does not always repeat itself exactly. What has not happened in the past may very well happen in the future. The second lesson is that models are not well-suited to handle new complex instruments. The so-called financial innovation has introduced complex instruments, complicating risk management. It is ironic that while the new derivatives were supposed to be used to manage risk, they have become the main source of risk. One must not forget to say that those "financial innovators" and "financial engineers" used quantitative models to design the Frankenstein instruments that turned out to be toxic assets that destroyed lives and bankrupted countries. The third lesson is that investors take too much comfort in standard risk metrics and discount the probability of adverse tail events.

The Failure of Risk Models

The models used by financial institutions failed miserably in predicting the losses incurred by them as a result of the global financial crisis. These models, which are invariably based on the concept of value at risk (VaR), created some sort of complacency as they predicted that losses of the magnitudes actually endured by financial institutions could only happen once every few million years. Flaherty et al. (2013) contend that investors likely felt secure that an industry standard risk metric such as VaR, widely adopted and considered to be a downside risk measure, must provide a reasonable estimate of potential downside. In reality, VaR and similar risk metrics are better suited for normal environments because they assume normal markets.

When the crisis was surfacing in the second half of 2007, David Viniar, the CFO of Goldman Sachs, declared that Goldman was experiencing "25-standard deviation moves, several days in a row" (Dowd et al., 2008). Bonner (2007) finds this claim to be preposterous because, he argues, these events are supposed to happen once every 100,000 years, concluding "either that or Goldman's models were wrong". Bonner's argument is valid, except that he got the number wrong. Dowd et al. (2008) demonstrate that a 25-sigma event would happen, according to models assuming normally distributed returns, once every 1.309×10^{135} years. In reality, however, extreme events (the so-called low-frequency, high-severity events) are quite common. The need to recapitalize banks after the onslaught of the crisis reveals that the internal models of many banks performed poorly and greatly underestimated exposure to risk, which reflects the difficulties associated with accounting for low-frequency, high-severity losses.

"Sophisticated" risk models can be hazardous because they create a sense of complacency (the attitude of "we know the risk and we are ready for it because we have a powerful model"). However, these models can be completely inadequate. For example, *The Economist* (2008) argues that internal models "can be seriously flawed". Doerig (2003) is sceptical about the existence of one "catch-all model with a credible outcome" (hence, "more sizzle than steak", as he puts it). Wood (2008) raises the question whether or not the industry's models are any good, citing a high-profile quant as saying that "a lot of them [the models] are disastrous" and that "modeling is currently in terribly, terribly bad shape" (most likely, it will be so for a long time to come). Wood also points out that "practitioners and regulators alike will argue that models do what they say on the tin", but in private "they're more willing to admit to doubt and frustration". Furthermore, Wood cites Richard Pike, product director with software vendor Ci3 in Dublin, as saying that "many of the industry's risk managers claim to be happy with the numbers their models produce but if you ask them to guarantee that it's correct then, no – they can't".

These models fail because they ignore history and human nature, and this is why Kaufman (2009) argues that business schools should teach students financial history before risk modelling. *The Economist* (2012) examines the models used by the hedge fund LTCM in the 1990s, which predicted the impossibility of divergence between the yields on bonds issued by countries like Russia and the US, and the models (used by AIG among others) that predicted the impossibility of a simultaneous collapse of house prices across the US. In both cases, it is pointed out, "financial firms quickly found themselves racking up daily losses that the computer said should occur only once in millions of years".

As financial assets became increasingly complex and harder to value, investors were reassured because both the credit rating agencies and bank regulators (who came to rely on them) accepted as valid the prediction of complex mathematical models that (theoretically, of course) risk was much smaller than what it turned out to be. George Soros commented that "the super-boom got out of hand when the new products became so complicated that the authorities could no longer calculate the risks and started relying on the risk management methods of the banks themselves" (Soros, 2008). Mortgage risks were underestimated by every institution in the chain from originators to investors by underweighting the possibility of falling house prices based on the historical trends of the past 50 years. Limitations of default and prepayment models (the core of pricing models) led to overvaluation of mortgage and asset-backed products and their derivatives by originators, securitizers, broker-dealers, rating agencies, insurance underwriters and investors (Samuelson, 2011; Kourlas, 2012).

Likewise, Smith (2010) suggests that the financial models used for risk management underestimate tail risk and they are based on the implausible and dangerous assumption that correlations between different types of exposure and assets are stable and that markets are continuous (always liquid). It remains to say that internal models are typically developed by academics who are happy to receive consultancy fees and conduct experiments on these models using other people's money, but they will never bet their superannuations on the predictions of their models. This is why Taleb (2009) calls for the marginalization of the economics and business school establishments and for abolishing the Nobel Prize in economics.

The Views of a Brilliant Economist

A brilliant economist, Kevin Dowd, contends that "in the last two decades or so, there have been major problems with financial modeling, not least because faulty financial models were a big contributor to the recent financial crisis" (Dowd, 2014). He defines a risk model as "a computer algorithm that projects possible future financial outcomes and perhaps their associated probabilities". Risk models are used to manage risk, guide investment decisions, and give a sense of potential exposure to future losses. Furthermore they are used to determine capital requirements, such that if the risk model is wrong, the risk estimates can be too low, which means that the underlying bank is undercapitalized and more vulnerable to failure. Dowd (2014) views a risk model as a "black box based on calibrated data that spews out loss risk forecasts or loss projections, usually known as risk measures", then he identifies three sources of the problems associated with using models to estimate risk: (1) the black box or model itself; (2) the model's input – that is, the data used to calibrate it; and (3) the model's output, the risk measure. Some of the problems identified by Dowd are (1) inability to identify the true loss distribution; (2) unavailability of reliable data to calculate the probability of default, correlation and events like a housing market collapse; and (3) inadequacy of the most common risk measure, value at risk.

When it comes to the inadequacy of the models used as the basis of risk management in financial institutions, no one puts it better than Dowd

(2009) who argues that these models are based on implausible assumptions. This is what he says:

> They assume that financial risks follow Gaussian distributions (and so ignore "fat tails" which really matter); they assume that correlations are constant (and ignore the fact that correlations tend to radicalize in crises and so destroy the portfolio diversification on which a risk management strategy might be predicted); and they make assumptions about market liquidity that break down when they are most needed.

Dowd adds that risk models are focused far too much on normal market conditions, which do not matter, at the expense of ignoring the abnormal conditions that do. Dowd et al. (2011) argue that internal models offer a very shaky foundation for either capital adequacy or good risk management – one reason being that the processes governing the operations of financial markets (as social systems) are not immutable to the laws of physics.

Dowd (2014) is also sceptical of the models used by regulators to conduct "stress tests" for the purpose of determining regulatory capital, arguing that while stress tests were intended to make the financial system safe, they have instead created a "potential for a new systemic financial crisis". Specifically, he argues that markets are not "mathematizable", which gives rise to several problems with stress testing. According to Dowd, the Fed's regulatory stress tests are problematical because they (1) ignore well-established weaknesses in risk modelling and violate the core principles of good stress testing; (2) expose the whole financial system to the weaknesses in the Fed's models and greatly boost systemic risk; (3) impose a huge and growing regulatory burden; (4) are undermined by political factors; (5) fail to address the major risks identified by independent experts; and (6) fail to embody lessons to be learned from the failures of other regulatory stress tests. The solution, according to Dowd (2014), is to "establish a simple, conservative capital standard for banks based on reliable capital ratios instead of unreliable models".

5.3   LOOPHOLES AND SHORTCOMINGS

Econometrics is criticized on several grounds, which are discussed briefly in this section. This is followed by criticisms of econometrics as applied to microeconomic and social policies and macroeconomics.

Sensitivity of the Empirical Results

The results of empirical work in economics and finance are sensitive to model specification, definitions of variables, sample period, estimation method, and data transformation. Hence econometric testing can be used to prove almost anything because the researcher (by manipulating the underlying model) is bound to find some results that support a preconceived belief or an agenda of some sort. The use of atheoretical models makes the task of obtaining the desired results even easier, as the researcher will not be constrained by a particular theory-based specification. The search for "good" results makes it tantalizing to indulge in data mining, involving the estimation of thousands of regression equations and reporting the most appealing one or more.

If the analysis is performed for policy purposes, it can lead to faulty policy prescriptions. Those economists who act as hired guns for politicians and special interests use empirical work to support the agendas of their masters. For example, the gun lobby in the US is willing to pay anything for empirical results showing that more guns lead to less crime, which has been proved (for example, Lott and Mustard, 1997). In corporate finance, manipulating the underlying model can be used to prove either of the two competing theories of capital structure (for example, Moosa, 2012).

Insensitivity of the Empirical Results

The empirical results may be insensitive to the estimation method and model specification, which casts doubt on the usefulness of "sophisticated" econometric estimation methods. For example, Moosa (2003, 2011a) and Maharaj et al. (2008) demonstrate that the use of estimation methods of various degrees of sophistication does not make any difference for the estimation of the hedge ratio and hedging effectiveness, because what matters is correlation. The results of a similar exercise will be presented in Chapter 10.

Unexplainable Cross-Sectional Differences

When a particular hypothesis is tested using time series data across countries, regions or subjects, the results are typically all over the place without any clear explanation for cross-sectional differences. For example, Bahmani-Oskooee and Alse (1994) found a mixed bag of results when they tested for the J-curve effect for 19 developed and 22 less developed countries. The same thing applies to the estimation of Okun's coefficient (for example, Moosa, 1997). This point will be illustrated in Chapter 10.

Dubious Tests and Procedures

Econometrics provides estimation and testing methods that enable a researcher to prove almost anything and to make any model look good. A prominent example of a test that enables anyone to prove anything is the Johansen test for cointegration, which (fortunately) has gone the way of the dinosaurs. This test over-rejects the null of cointegration and produces results that are sensitive to the specification of the underlying model, particularly the lag length. Given confirmation and publication biases – that is, the desire to produce results that do not reject the underlying hypothesis so that the results can be published – this procedure has become a useful tool for producing desirable but misleading results. It provided a relief from the Engle–Granger residual-based test that is difficult to pass, but then cointegration is supposed to be a rare occurrence.

As for procedures that make any model look good, try the Cochrane–Orcutt correction for serial correlation. By using this procedure to estimate a regression equation, the results change dramatically from those produced by using OLS: an R^2 of 0.99, and a DW statistic close to 2 – that is, perfect results. As an example, a regression of the Canadian dollar/US dollar exchange rate on the pound/dollar rate produces R^2 of 0.146 and a DW statistic of 0.078. When the same equation is estimated by the Cochrane–Orcutt method, R^2 jumps to 0.94 and the DW statistic goes up to 1.80. While Mizon (1995) has warned against correction for serial correlation, it is still business as usual. The "versatility" of the Johansen test will be illustrated in Chapter 9.

Correlation versus Causation

A major problem associated with empirical work is deriving inference on the basis of correlation as if it were causation. Econometricians came up with an answer when Clive Granger devised a test for causality based on temporal ordering – something causing something else because the first something occurs before the second something. Subsequently, many variants of the Granger causality test appeared, allowing economists to test the same hypotheses over and over again without reaching any conclusion. The notion of causality is ludicrous, a fallacy that is sometimes described as *post hoc ergo propter hoc*, which is Latin for "after this, therefore because of this". The development of causality testing follows from the desire to make economics physics-like. In physics we know that force causes motion: when a shopping trolley is pushed, it moves to the front and when it is pulled it moves backwards. There is no question that the pushing and pulling (force) causes motion, and not vice versa. In economics we depend on the misleading causality testing to find out whether inflation and the current account cause the exchange rate or vice versa. Of course we can prove anything we want by changing the lag structure of the underlying VAR. And in all of this, economists do not bother presenting a narrative as to why X causes Y – we simply have to trust the results of the Granger causality test or those produced by its disciples.

Spurious Correlation

When two variables are correlated it is most likely that they are related spuriously. For example, Beard et al. (2011) look at the effect of on-budget regulatory agency spending on private sector employment in the US and find that reducing the total budget of all US federal regulatory agencies by 5 per cent produces 1.2 million more private sector jobs each year. They argue that firing one regulatory agency staff member creates 98 jobs in the private sector. These results sound ridiculous, most likely the product of extensive data mining motivated by an ideological anti-regulation stance. I wonder why this great discovery has not been called the "Beard et al. law", since the number 98 seems to be as precise as the number 32 that represents acceleration under gravity.

Naturally, Beard et al. do not tell us anything about the mechanism whereby the firing of a regulator leads to job creation. This is an example of spurious correlation, resulting from the interpretation of a multiple regression equation. Once again, econometricians have come to the rescue by providing two tests for spurious correlation that do not work: one is based on a comparison between R^2 and DW and the other is based on cointegration (see, for example, Moosa, 2016a). In reality it is common sense, not econometrics, that tells us whether correlation is spurious or genuine – so, it is unfortunate that we have decided to ditch common sense in favour of econometrics.

Hypothesis Testing versus Prediction

Unlike science, model validation in econometrics depends on testing rather than predictive power, which is why Goertzel (2002) criticizes econometrics for the lack of predictive testing. Look, for example, at the corporate finance literature, in which we typically find a regression equation going over three lines because it contains some 15 explanatory variables. Several versions of the model are estimated and only the best results are reported, including the t statistics, the coefficients and maybe (only maybe) some diagnostic tests. Nothing is said about the ability of the model to make predictions. Actually, validating the model by evaluating its predictive power is more common in time series analysis. This is where economists brag about the power of their models to do a good job in out-of-sample forecasting – these models are typically dynamic. It has been demonstrated that using any form of dynamics introduces a lagged dependent variable, which is a con job (Moosa and Burns, 2014a).

Kling (2011) opposes the use of lagged dependent variables in the "most accurate forecasting models" and argues that the resulting equations often have structural properties that are not desired by the model builders. Including a lagged dependent variable serves to vitiate the model's structure. On the other hand, failure to include a lagged dependent variable tends to cause large prediction errors. The use of "add factors" can be viewed as an attempt to keep the modellers' preferred equations while judgmentally including the information in the lagged dependent variable so as to make a somewhat accurate prediction. However, the "accurate" predictions derived from dynamic models are not really accurate, as we are going to see in Chapter 11.

The Significance Level

A regression equation containing 15 explanatory variables or so is typically estimated with a menu of stars to indicate the significance level (* for 10 per cent, ** for 5 per cent and *** for 1 per cent), but we are not told what to consider to be statistically significant. How about going half a star for 20 per cent or six stars for 0.5 per cent? Gelman and Stern (2006) raise many issues with statistical significance, including the following: (1) statistical significance is not the same as practical importance, (2) dichotomization into significant and insignificant results encourages the dismissal of observed differences in favour of the null hypothesis of no difference, and (3) any particular threshold for declaring significance is arbitrary. However, they place emphasis on an additional problem involving an error of interpretation: changes in statistical significance are often not themselves statistically significant. Instead of making the commonplace observation that any particular threshold is arbitrary, only a small change is required to move an estimate from a 5.1 per cent significance level to 4.9 per cent, thus moving it into statistical significance.

On 7 March 2016 the American Statistical Association (ASA) released a "Statement on Statistical Significance and P-Values" with six principles underlying the proper use and interpretation of the p-value. These principles are as follows: (1) p-values can indicate how incompatible the data are with a specified statistical model; (2) p-values do not measure the probability that the studied hypothesis is true, or the probability that the data were produced by random chance alone; (3) scientific conclusions and business or policy decisions should not be based only on whether a p-value passes a specific threshold; (4) proper inference requires full reporting and transparency; (5) a p-value, or statistical significance, does not measure the size of an effect or the importance of a result; and (6) by itself, a p-value does not provide a good measure of evidence regarding a model or hypothesis.

The choice of the significance level has been recognized in the finance literature. With respect to studies aimed at explaining variation in a cross section of expected returns (in the spirit of the CAPM and the Fama–French models), Harvey et al. (2015) consider the relevant studies to involve extensive data mining, arguing that "it does not make any economic or statistical sense to use the usual significance criteria for a newly discovered factor" (that is, a t-ratio greater than 2). The one-million-dollar question is the following: what hurdle should be used for current research? They suggest that a newly discovered factor needs to clear a much higher hurdle, with a t-ratio greater than 3. Accordingly, they argue that "most claimed research findings in financial economics are likely false".

Likewise, Kim (2016), Kim and Choi (2016), and Kim and Ji (2015) observe the use of conventional significance level without due consideration given to factors such as the power of the test and sample size, which makes them sceptical of "research credibility and integrity". Kim (2016) evaluates the statistical significance reported in two studies of the effect of weather on stock returns (which sounds like a joke, unless spurious correlation is not a joke) and concludes that the results are biased against the null hypothesis of no effect. Kim and Choi (2016) examine significance with respect to unit root tests and conclude that the use of a conventional level of significance is not optimal due to the low power of the test. Kim and Ji (2015) survey the significance levels used in recent papers published in the top finance journals and conclude that low significance levels are used because of publication bias in favour of significance.

Magnus (1999) raises another point pertaining to the significance level, arguing against the exclusion of variables that have insignificant coefficients as judged by the t statistic because the exclusion of these variables may have adverse implications for the estimates of other coefficients. This is perhaps why Frisch (1933b) talked about a "new type of significance" when he wrote:

> In this field we need, I believe, a new type of significance analysis, which is not based on mechanical application of standard errors computed according to some more or less plausible statistical mathematical formulae, but is based on a thoroughgoing comparative study of the various possible types of assumptions regarding the economic-theoretical set up, and of the consequences which these assumptions entail for the interpretation of the observational data.

We all know that current practices in econometrics are far away from what Frisch recommended more than 90 years ago.

Omitted and Unmeasurable Variables

The problem of omitted variables is particularly relevant when a model is not theory-based, particularly models estimated from cross-sectional data. Take for example the determinants of foreign direct investment inflows, which are numerous (see, for example, Moosa, 2002; Moosa and Cardak, 2006). A typical model would have FDI inflows as the dependent variable and a large number of explanatory variables, which are related to the dependent variable by various unrelated hypotheses. In the absence of a theoretical model there is no guarantee that all of the relevant explanatory variables are included in the model. Sometimes, an explanatory variable is excluded deliberately because it cannot be measured. When a relevant explanatory variable is excluded from the model, the results will be biased in the sense that the model compensates for the missing variable by over- or underestimating the effect of one of the other variables.

For bias to be present, two conditions must be satisfied: (1) the omitted variable must be a determinant of the dependent variable (that is, it would produce a significant coefficient when it is included in the model); and (2) it must be correlated with another explanatory variable in the equation. When this problem is present, the error term will be correlated with the regressors, which is a violation of one of the assumptions required to obtain the best, linear and unbiased estimators (the result would be biased and inconsistent). While it is claimed that some econometric methods can deal with this problem, the model remains theoretically misspecified when it excludes a relevant explanatory variable.

5.4 ECONOMETRICS AS APPLIED TO MICROECONOMIC AND SOCIAL POLICIES

Goertzel (2002) criticizes the use of econometric modelling to evaluate the impact of social policies, given that multiple regression cannot be used to distinguish between correlation and causation. Some of the studies that use econometric modelling to make microeconomic and policy recommendations have produced results telling us the following (all are based on US data): (1) every time a prisoner is executed, eight future murders are deterred; (2) a 1 per cent increase in the percentage of a state's citizens carrying concealed guns causes a 3.3 per cent decline in the murder rate; (3) 10–20 per cent of the decline in crime in the 1990s was caused by an increase in abortions in the 1970s; (4) the murder rate would have increased by 250 per cent since 1974 if it were not for the building of new prisons; and (5) the welfare reform of the 1990s would force 1,100,000 children into poverty. Also recall what deserves to be called the "Beard et al. law", postulating that firing one regulator leads to the creation of 98 new private sector jobs.

According to Goertzel (2002), "if you were misled by any of these studies, you may have fallen for a pernicious form of junk science", the use of econometric modelling to evaluate the impact of social policies. He goes on to describe these studies as "superficially impressive", "produced by reputable social scientists from prestigious institutions", "often published in peer reviewed scientific journals", and "filled with statistical calculations too complex for anyone but another specialist to untangle". These studies are supposed to give precise numerical "facts" that are often quoted in policy debates, but the "facts" turn out to be fiction sooner or later. He goes on to say the following: "often before the ink is dry on one apparently definitive study, another appears with equally precise and imposing, but completely different, facts" and that "despite their numerical precision, these facts have no more validity than the visions of soothsayers".

These studies have serious implications in the sense that the results provide justification for draconian policies. They imply that capital punishment is moral despite the possibility of a miscarriage of justice. They imply that carrying concealed guns should be encouraged despite the horrendous murder rate in the US. They imply that there is nothing wrong with the US providing accommodation for 25 per cent of the world prison population, more on a per capita basis than what is found in the so-called rogue and terrorist states (naturally, without suggesting, for example, that the motivation for mass incarceration is the desire to benefit the private prison industry). And they imply that the fate of children should be left to the almighty market. Empirical studies based on multiple regression analysis have been used, or can be used, to justify evils like slavery and war as well as the right-wing obsession with deregulation.

Although the results of these studies are fragile and purpose-designed, they are believed as "facts" because the starting point is that they are the right policies to follow. Even if other studies produce contrasting evidence, the original results remain the basis of policy formulation. For example, Lott and Mustard (1997) reach the conclusion that carrying concealed guns is a deterrent to crime, which is music to the ears of the gun lobby, but not to the ears of Piers Morgan and sensible people in general. Even better, carrying concealed guns deters violent crime without causing any increase in accidental death. When sensible people oppose these conclusions, Lott (2000) accuses them of "putting ideology ahead of science" (which science, and who is putting ideology first?). Zimring and Hawkins (1997) have the following to say in this respect:

> Just as Messrs. Lott and Mustard can, with one model of the determinants of homicide, produce statistical residuals suggesting that "shall issue" laws reduce homicide, we expect that a determined econometrician can produce a treatment of the same historical periods with different models and opposite effects. Econometric modeling is a double-edged sword in its capacity to facilitate statistical findings to warm the hearts of true believers of any stripe.

They (Zimring and Hawkins) were right. Black and Nagin (1998) published a study showing that if they changed the statistical model slightly, or applied it to different segments of the data, Lott and Mustard's findings disappeared. They found that when Florida was removed from the sample there was "no detectable impact of the right-to-carry laws on the rate of murder and rape". They concluded that "inference based on the Lott and Mustard model is inappropriate, and their results cannot be used responsibly to formulate public policy". This criticism of econometrics is about the sensitivity analysis of empirical results to model specification and other factors.

Goertzel (2002) attributes the failure of multiple regression analysis to (1) the assumption of linearity; (2) the assumption of normally distributed variables; (3) not knowing the direction of causality; and (4) the lack of predictive testing. He suggests that the most reliable work is based on simpler statistical techniques that do not require so much adjustment and standardization of the data. Simplicity has the great advantage that the work can be read and used by people who have not devoted years of their lives to learning obscure econometric techniques. Studies that make extensive use of graphics, such as those of Sellin (1959) and Blumstein and Wallman (2000), have been much more successful and informative than studies relying on multiple regression, although the former look "less sophisticated".

5.5   ECONOMETRICS AS APPLIED TO MACROECONOMICS

Summers (1991) has criticized econometric formalism as applied to macroeconomics, arguing that "the empirical facts of which we are most confident and which provide the most secure basis for theory are those that require the least sophisticated statistical analysis to perceive". He examines some highly praised macroeconometric studies (Hansen and Singleton, 1982, 1983; Bernanke, 1986), arguing that while these papers make a brilliant use of econometric methods, they do not prove anything that future theory can build on. Noting that in the natural sciences, "investigators rush to check out the validity of claims made by rival laboratories and then build on them", Summers points out that this rarely happens in economics, which he attributes to the fact that "the results [of econometric studies] are rarely an important input to theory creation or the evolution of professional opinion more generally". Summers describes successful empirical research as follows:

> Successful empirical research has been characterized by attempts to gauge the strength of associations rather than to estimate structural parameters, verbal characterizations of how causal relations might operate rather than explicit mathematical models, and the skilful use of carefully chosen natural experiments rather than sophisticated statistical technique to achieve identification.

Summers, therefore, criticizes the use of econometrics in macroeconomics on the grounds that it involves confusion between causation and correlation, the use of mathematical equations in preference to verbal exposition, and the use of statistics rather than experiments.

Another economist who is rather critical of the use of econometrics in macroeconomics is Arnold Kling (2011) who argues that "macroeconometric models are built on astonishingly precarious grounds and yet are used by policy makers to project precision and certainty". In particular he is critical of the use of lagged dependent variables, add factors, and other techniques to make their models more "accurate" at the expense of integrity. The reason for the unscientific nature of macroeconometric models is that, unlike the objects of controlled experimentation, real-world events are often unique and non-repeatable. He tells the following story to point out the fragility of macroeconometric models:

> Ten days prior to President Obama's inauguration in 2009, two of his economists, Christina Romer and Jared Bernstein (2009), published a memorandum analyzing the effects of fiscal stimulus proposals. In the introduction to the memo, the authors caution, our estimates of economic relationships and rules of thumb are derived from historical experience and so will not apply exactly in any given episode. Furthermore, the uncertainty is surely higher than normal now because the current recession is unusual both in its fundamental causes and its severity. However, the rest of the memo conveys certainty and precision.

Kling (2011) further argues that macroeconometric models of the sort used by Romer and Bernstein to project the impact of a fiscal stimulus are "pure fabrications" and that the model's confrontation with the data produces awkward or surprising results, in which case the modeller adjusts the a priori structure and re-estimates the model in a process that goes through

many iterations. This assessment pertains to the point of torturing the data
until the desirable results are obtained.

Kling (2011) also refers to the sensitivity of the results to model specification and similar factors, arguing that an almost limitless number of
factors could affect key macroeconomic variables, and that there are
several potential specifications for the variable representing that factor. He
refers to linear versus nonlinear specifications, detrended versus trended
data and current versus lagged data. Then he argues that a quarterly data
set covering 20 years does not provide 80 but rather fewer observations
because of time aggregation arising from the effect of an observation in
any one quarter on the observation in the following quarter, which is why
the lagged dependent variable is such a powerful predictor. With a limited
number of observations, and a wide range of plausible control variables
(taking into account alternative specifications), there is not even a remote
resemblance to a quasi-experiment. In Chapter 11, it will be demonstrated
that the lagged dependent variable is a "powerful predictor" only in the
sense that a random walk is so.

5.6   CONCLUDING REMARKS

Econometrics is criticized because of the sensitivity of empirical results
to a large number of factors such as model specification and estimation
methods. In Chapter 7 it will be demonstrated, by using cross-sectional
data, that the results are so sensitive that we can prove the validity of
either of two competing theories. The same point is illustrated by using
time series data in Chapters 8, 9 and 10. In some situations, the results are
insensitive to model specification and estimation methods that it makes
one wonder why not stick to basics. This point is illustrated in Chapter 10
with respect to the estimation of the hedge ratio.

Another problem with econometric analysis is the unexplainable cross-
sectional differences when a time series study is conducted on a large
number of country-specific samples. It is rather difficult to explain why
the results for Somalia are similar to those for Sweden and that the latter
are different from those for Finland. The ability of researchers to obtain
the desired results is enhanced by the availability of dubious tests and
procedures that make it possible to prove that any number of variables (no
matter what they are) form a long-run relation. There are also procedures
that allow researchers to convert poor diagnostics and goodness of fit
results to perfect ones.

Econometricians tell us that it is easy to distinguish between correlation and causation and identify spurious correlation through econometric

testing, but this is at best wishful thinking. Some results on this issue are presented in Chapters 8 and 9. Econometric causation is not really causation and only common sense tells us whether a relation is spurious or genuine. Econometric forecasting is as bad as econometric causation. There is also the problem of choosing the significance level, because any hypothesis can be rejected or otherwise by choosing an "appropriate" significance level. Last, but not least, there is the problem of unmeasurable and expectational variables, which also makes the results sensitive to how they are measured.

While these criticisms are not adequate to construct a list of "50 Reasons why Econometrics is Useless", they are adequate to deprive econometrics of any credibility that it may have had at one time. Econometrics is indeed "junk science" and the "science of hubris" as suggested by two enlightened, non-conforming economists.

6. Criticism of econometrics: Keynes, Leamer, Lucas and the Austrians

6.1 INTRODUCTION

In Chapter 5 a collection of arguments was presented to support the proposition that econometric modelling can be used to prove almost anything, hence the expression "junk science". These arguments are valid in the sense that any down-to-earth economist doing empirical work must wonder if there is any value in the work they do. The response of the true believers is that down-to-earth economists do not understand the underlying mathematical and statistical theory, hence they do not do a good job of econometric analysis. I have often heard the argument that econometric work should be done only by an econometrician. In reality, down-to-earth economists do not have to understand asymptotic theory to realize that there is little value in econometric analysis. Only very few of us know how the internal combustion engine works, but we all know that cars are useful because they take us to faraway places in comfort.

A large number of brilliant economists who contributed to our understanding of how the economy works refused to use econometrics and concentrated on the use of diagrams and descriptive text. One example is the great Joan Robinson who did not use formal equations but rather favoured diagrams and graphs backed up by clear verbal descriptions and discussions – in other words, she had no reason to hide behind sophisticated mathematics. In recognition of the importance of her work, she was invited in 1949 (by Jan Koopmans, a leading econometrician of his time) to be on the board of the Econometric Society, but she declined on the grounds that she did not want to be part of something that produced things she (and the vast majority of economists at that time, and even now) could not read (Crawford, 2016). Another eminent economist, Ronald Coase, is often cited as having said that if you torture the data you will get the results you want. Leonard (2014) argues that you do not have to be Ronald Coase to realize that. He writes:

> You don't have to be a Nobel Prize winning economist, like Ronald Coase, to understand the implications of "working over" data to reveal the most desirable outcome. The on-going problem that occurs when data is collected,

manipulated, and distributed in a non-systematic way to broad sets of users. You lose objectivity, consistency and any ability to look at historical data with any level of reasonable confidence. It's a problem.

It is indeed a problem, particularly when confirmation bias is prevalent and ideology is the starting point. Another criticism is based on a point that we have already dealt with, as the role of economic theory (and intuition and common sense) has paled into insignificance as econometrics has become the end itself as opposed to the means to an end. McCloskey (1985) argues that in published econometric work, economists tend to rely excessively on statistical techniques and often fail to use economic reasoning for including or excluding variables.

It is not only down-to-earth economists who criticize econometrics as criticism has come from intellectuals whose knowledge of mathematics and statistics is undisputable. These intellectuals include J.M. Keynes, Edward Leamer and Robert Lucas. Criticism has also come from economists believing that knowledge of mathematics and statistics is not a necessary or sufficient condition for someone to be a good economist. This is in particular the attitude taken by the Austrian school towards the quantification of economics. In this chapter the views of these intellectuals are exposed.

6.2 KEYNES'S CRITICISM OF ECONOMETRICS

Detailed accounts of Keynes's criticism of econometrics can be found in Garrone and Marchionatti (2004) and Patinkin (1976). The criticism is centred on the work that Jan Tinbergen (1939a, 1939b) submitted as a two-volume report to the League of Nations (Keynes, 1939, 1940). The report was on the statistical testing of business cycle theories, which was aimed at providing general economic forecasts and guide government policies to control business cycles. The first volume of the report, on which Keynes chose to focus, contained an explanation of the method of econometric testing, while the second volume was an application to business cycles in the US during the period 1919–1932. Keynes (1940) was rather harsh in evaluating Tinbergen's work, as he said the following:

> No one could be more frank, more painstaking, more free of subjective bias or parti pris than Professor Tinbergen. There is no one, therefore, so far as human qualities go, whom it would be safer to trust with black magic. That there is anyone I would trust with it at the present stage or that this brand of statistical alchemy is ripe to become a branch of science, I am not yet persuaded. But Newton, Boyle and Locke all played with alchemy. So let him continue.

Keynes's criticism of econometrics was initially rejected and his conception of economics was considered old-fashioned. Samuelson (1946) maintained that Keynes was technically incompetent. Klein (1951) called Keynes's review of the work of Tinbergen as "one of his sorriest professional performances". Stone (1978) suggested that Keynes had little or no awareness of the economic literature and attributed his harsh criticism of econometrics to "his temperamental characteristics". Stigler et al. (1995) suggested that "Keynes' long reign at the *Economic Journal* probably discouraged its publication of econometric work, of which he was a sceptic, again a subsidy to *Econometrica*, and his policies also helped the *Review of Economic Studies*". Well, it is unfortunate that the *Economic Journal* has followed these two journals by starting to publish incomprehensible little-value papers, just to look as good and as "cool" as the journals that took the lead in this direction.

Since the end of the 1970s, new contributions have recognized the relevance and soundness of Keynes's criticism. It was Patinkin (1976) who first found it "somewhat depressing to see how many of [Keynes's criticisms to the use of correlation analysis to estimate equations] are, in practice, still of relevance today". Hendry (1980) wrote that "[Keynes's] objections make an excellent list of what might be called problems of the linear regression model". Pesaran and Smith (1985) recognized that Keynes was right on both the technical and logical arguments. Rowley (1988) maintained that "Keynes' criticisms have been diluted, forgotten or mis-stated rather than absorbed into the prevalent orthodoxy". He regretted that "we have waited too long for econometric methodology to come of age and address its logical bases". McAleer (1994) and Dharmapala and McAleer (1996) suggest that some of Keynes's criticisms of Tinbergen's econometric methodology "remain relevant to this day" and that his implicit research programme "subsequently led to the development of numerous econometric techniques that are now widely used in applied econometrics". Likewise, Keuzenkamp (2000) maintains that Keynes's sceptical attitude remains substantially justified. In conclusion, it is now recognized that Keynes's criticism of Tinbergen was sound in many respects.

Keynes (1940) raised the issue of unmeasurable variables as he wondered what place was left for expectations, for the state of confidence relating to the future and for non-numerical factors, such as inventions, politics, labour troubles, wars and financial crises. He also commented on the related problem of testing theories when different econometric specifications can be derived from a theory by saying the following:

> The seventy translators of the Septuagint were shut up in seventy separate rooms with the Hebrew text and brought out with them, when they emerged,

seventy identical translations. Would the same miracle be vouchsafed if seventy multiple correlators were shut up with the same statistical material? And anyhow, I suppose, if each had a different economist perched on his a priori, that would make a difference to the outcome.

Keynes raised the problem of spurious correlation by suggesting that "if we are using factors which are not wholly independent, we lay ourselves open to the . . . complications of 'spurious' correlation".Then he drew attention to the problem of simultaneity by writing the following:

> What happens if the phenomenon under investigation itself reacts on the factors by which we are explaining it? When he investigates the fluctuations of investment, Tinbergen makes them dependent on the fluctuations of profit. But what happens if the fluctuations of profit partly depend (as, indeed, they clearly do) on the fluctuations of investments? Professor Tinbergen mentions the difficulty in a general way in a footnote. . . where he says . . . that "one has to be careful". But is he? . . . In practice Professor Tinbergen seems to be entirely indifferent whether or not his basic factors are independent of one another.

Keynes raised issues of technical importance concerning functional forms, time lags and trends. He maintained the implausibility of the widespread assumption of linearity and called for the examination of alternative functional forms. About the general problem of dynamic specification, Keynes accused Tinbergen of scarce rigour in treating time lag and trends in an ad hoc manner by choosing them by trial and error. This is what he said in this respect:

> Professor Tinbergen . . . invents them [time lags] for himself. This he seems to do by some sort of trial-and-error method. That is to say, he fidgets about until he finds a time lag which does not fit in too badly with the theory he is testing and with the general presuppositions of his method. . . . The introduction of a trend factor is even more tricky and even less discussed. . . . In the case of fluctuations in investment, "trends", Professor Tinbergen explains, have been calculated as nine-year moving averages for pre-war periods . . . and as rectilinear trends for post-war periods.

What Keynes effectively said was that a model can always be found to fit historical data and tells a good story, but it proves nothing. He questioned the manipulation of data to "make possible to fit an explanation to any fact" (Keynes, 1939). He also expressed scepticism concerning the assumptions of structural instability, casting doubt on the assumption of the constancy of the parameters.

Pesaran and Smith (1985) re-estimated some of Tinbergen's relations by OLS using the original undetrended series to find out the effect of detrending on Tinbergen's results. They found that "the un-detrended OLS results suffer from a significant degree of residual autocorrelation which sheds considerable doubt on the size and the statistical significance of the estimated regression coefficients". They concluded that the presence of residual autocorrelation can be due to the factors stressed by Keynes: omitted variables, functional form misspecification, structural change and a host of other factors, "all of which are highlighted in Keynes' review".

Keuzenkamp (1995) credits Keynes for more than identifying the problem of misspecification as suggested by Patinkin (1976), Pesaran and Smith (1985) and McAleer (1994). He argues that "Keynes' critique is not primarily one of mis-specification" and that "it is neither based on an objection to econometrics and probabilistic inference in general, nor does it follow from an outdated misunderstanding of the crucial issues at stake". He actually makes a distinction between Tinbergen, who is described as a very pragmatic research worker, and Keynes who was "preoccupied with the logical conditions for probabilistic inference, as may be clear from his earlier work". Keuzenkamp concludes that "the fact that econometric modelling of investment has turned out to be a notoriously difficult issue in applied econometrics, even today, suggests that Keynes' objections were not altogether misguided".

Another economist who defends Keynes and his criticism of econometrics is Syll (2012b, 2012c, 2012d) who is particularly concerned with the (outrageous) allegation that Keynes did not know what he was talking about. This is what he has to say:

> Unfortunately, economists often hold the view that Keynes's criticism of econometrics is the conclusions of a sadly misinformed and misguided intellectual who disliked and did not understand much of it. This is really a gross misapprehension. To be careful and cautious is not the same as to dislike. And as any perusal of the mathematical statistical and philosophical works of people like for example Nancy Cartwright, Chris Chatfield, Hugo Keuzenkamp or Aris Spanos would show, the same critique is more or less put forward by respected authorities today. (Syll, 2012b)

Syll argues strongly against the "common knowledge" that Keynes misunderstood the crucial issues at stake in the development of econometrics. Keynes actually knew them all too well, but he was not satisfied with the validity and philosophical underpinning of the assumptions made for applying econometric methods. Keynes was right about everything that he said or wrote about. He was right about the hazard of treating Germany too harshly in the aftermath of the First World War. He was right about the implausibility of a US-dollar based international monetary system. And he was right in his criticism of econometrics.

6.3   THE LEAMER CRITIQUE

In the early 1980s, a brilliant statistician by the name of Edward Leamer urged those who conducted empirical work in economics to "take the con out of econometrics" (Leamer, 1983), suggesting that "hardly anyone takes data analysis seriously". Leamer diagnosed the empirical work of his contemporaries as suffering from a distressing lack of robustness to changes in key assumptions – assumptions he called "whimsical" because one seemed as good as another. The remedy he proposed was sensitivity analysis whereby the results can be shown to be robust, or otherwise, with respect to changes in specification or functional form. Leamer also argued for an intuitive approach called "extreme bounds analysis", which involves the reporting of a range of estimates of the coefficient on the variable of interest. The procedure overcomes data mining and the tendency to report the preferred model.

The Response of Angrist and Pischke

Angrist and Pischke (2010) sympathize with Leamer's (1983) view that much of the applied econometrics of the 1970s and early 1980s lacked credibility. To make his point, and to illustrate the value of extreme bounds analysis, Leamer picked an inquiry into whether capital punishment deters murder. This issue had been analysed in a series of papers by Isaac Ehrlich, who employed time series data (Ehrlich, 1975a) and cross-sectional data (Ehrlich, 1977b). He concluded that the death penalty had a substantial deterrent effect. Leamer (1983) did not try to replicate Ehrlich's work, but reported on an independent time series investigation of the deterrence hypothesis using extreme bounds analysis, forcefully arguing that the evidence for deterrence is fragile at best, a view that is disputed by Ehrlich and Liu (1999).

Ehrlich's work has been criticized harshly by a number of economists in addition to Leamer, most notably Bowers and Pierce (1975) and Passell and Taylor (1977). His results appeared to be sensitive to changes in functional form, the inclusion of additional control variables, and to changes in the sample. The finding of a significant deterrent effect seems to depend on observations from the 1960s, when the murder rate was high, an observation that the critics attribute to factors other than the sharp decline in the number of executions during that period. Ehrlich (1975b, 1977a) disputes the critics' claims about functional form and argues that the 1960s provided useful variation in executions that should be retained.

Angrist and Pischke (2010) argue that Ehrlich's critics failed to identify the most obvious flaw in his analysis. Indeed, Ehrlich was aware of the possibility that the murder rate might affect the number of executions, and vice versa, and that his results might be biased by omitted variables. Ehrlich sought to address problems of reverse causality and omitted variables bias by using instrumental variables in a two-stage least squares procedure. He treated the probabilities of arrest, conviction, and execution as endogenous in a simultaneous-equations set-up. His instrumental variables were lagged expenditure on policing, total government expenditure, population, and the fraction of non-white population. Naturally, Ehrlich did not explain why these are good instruments, or even how and why these variables are correlated with the right-hand-side endogenous variables. For all we know, he could have tried different instruments that gave him results that did not support what he wanted to prove, so he did not report them.

Angrist and Pischke (2010) recognize Ehrlich's work on capital punishment as being typical of applied work in the period about which Leamer (1983) was writing. They make the following interesting observations: (1) most studies of that time used fairly short time series samples with strong trends common to both dependent and independent variables; (2) the use of panel data to control for year and fixed effects was still rare; and (3) the use of instrumental variables to uncover causal relationships was typically mechanical, with little discussion of why the instruments affected the endogenous variables of interest or why they constitute a "good experiment". However, they contend that "Ehrlich was ahead of many of his contemporaries in that he recognized the need for something other than naive regression analysis". The main problem with Ehrlich's work, according to them, was the "lack of a credible research design", as he failed to isolate a source of variation in execution rates that is likely to reveal causal effects on homicide rates.

Angrist and Pischke (2010) argue that there is less con in econometrics today. This is what they say:

> Improvements in empirical work have come from many directions. Better data and more robust estimation methods are part of the story, as is a reduced emphasis on econometric considerations that are not central to a causal interpretation of the main findings. But the primary force driving the credibility revolution has been a vigorous push for better and more clearly articulated research designs.

As far as the data issue is concerned, Ehrlich (1975a) analysed a time series of 35 annual observations, which was not unusual for that time period. In contrast, Donohue and Wolfers (2005) investigate capital punishment using a panel of US states from 1934 to 2000, with many more years and richer within-state variation due to the panel structure of the data. It is, however, unlikely that the use of panel data reduces the con in econometrics as identified by Leamer – on the contrary, the opposite may be true. Yes, the use of panel data means larger samples but the results derived from panel regressions hardly tell us anything useful. Panel regressions can still be used to indulge in data mining and produce the desired results, which is a con job.

Angrist and Pischke (2010) refer to what they call "fewer distractions" – the distractions being serious econometric problems that Keynes was concerned with. They argue that Bowers and Pierce (1975) devoted considerable attention to Ehrlich's (1975a) use of the log transformation, as well as his choice of sample period. Likewise, Passell and Taylor (1977) were distracted by the use of F-tests for temporal homogeneity and log specifications. Therefore, according to them, Ehrlich's critics did not "hit this nail on the head" by not concentrating on instrument validity and omitted variables bias. While there is no doubt that these are important issues, model specification and sample selection are equally important because they can be used to do a con job. Concern about these issues does not represent "dogmatic understanding of regression analysis".

For Angrist and Pischke (2010), a "less dogmatic understanding of regression analysis" lies in better research design, particularly in applied microeconometrics. They refer to "design-based" studies in that they give the research design underlying any sort of study the attention it would command in a real experiment. The econometric methods that feature most prominently in quasi-experimental studies are instrumental variables, regression discontinuity methods, and differences-in-differences-style policy analysis. They refer to regression discontinuity research design and fuzzy regression discontinuity design. Paralleling the growth in quasi-experimental design, they argue, the number and scope of real experiments has increased dramatically, with a concomitant increase in the quality of experimental design, data collection, and statistical analysis. Economists, they observe, are increasingly running their own experiments as well as processing the data from experiments run by others. However, experiments in economics can never be the same as experiments in physics, at least because the objects (humans) have emotions, biases and are prone to telling lies. Horwitz (2012) asserts that despite the pretensions of many mainstream economists, their empirical studies (including newer work in experimental economics) do not have quite the same scientific power as experiments in the natural sciences do. The design rhetoric of Angrist and Pischke (measured by the number of times they use the d-word) does not take the con out of econometrics.

But where does this leave macroeconomics? According to Angrist and Pischke (2010) some sort of experiments are possible in macroeconomics. They refer to "many macroeconomists" who have abandoned traditional empirical work entirely, focusing instead on "computational experiments", as described by Kydland and Prescott (1996). In a computational experiment, researchers choose a question, build a (theoretical) model of the economy, "calibrate" the model so that its behaviour mimics the real economy along some key statistical dimensions, and then run a computational experiment by changing model parameters (for example, tax rates or the money supply rule) to address the original question. The last two decades have seen countless studies that follow this procedure, often in a dynamic stochastic general equilibrium framework. Kling (2011), on the other hand, believes that rhetoric about experiments is motivated by aspiration to scientific rigour, because "the gold standard for scientific rigor is the controlled experiment". Since economists cannot conduct controlled experiments, as in physics, they use statistical techniques, primarily regression analysis, but obsession with the desire to conduct experiments led them to devise the term "natural experiment", such as the division of Germany after the Second World War into a Communist East and a non-Communist West. Even if we accept the proposition that economists running experiments are doing as good a job as physicists, these are still a tiny minority because it is easier and cheaper to use published data to conduct empirical work and because it is rarely possible to conduct an experiment to test an economic hypothesis.

Angrist and Pischke (2010) talk about the "credibility revolution" in econometrics, although they limit the scope of this revolution to empirical microeconomics. Macroeconomic research does not to lend itself to the newer design-oriented approaches to empirical work. They suggest that Leamer was correct in his diagnosis but not necessarily in his prescription. They argue that the "credibility revolution" experienced in empirical microeconomics since Leamer's critique is primarily due to a greater focus on research design, not on the sensitivity analysis prescribed by Leamer.

The design-based defence of econometrics is shared by Nevo and Whinston (2010) who contend that "applied work today, compared to 25 years ago, is based on more careful design, including both actual and 'natural', or 'quasi-', experiments, yielding more credible estimates". They claim that empirical work has also changed in at least two other significant ways since the publication of Leamer's (1983) article. First, econometric methods have advanced on many dimensions that allow for more robust inference, such as nonparametric and semiparametric estimation (Powell, 1994), robust standard errors (White, 1980), and identification based on minimal assumptions (Manski, 2003) – these methods, they claim, are aimed at improving the credibility and robustness of data analysis (but how?). A second major development, according to them, has been in the improvement and increased use in data analysis of what are commonly called "structural methods" – that is, the use of models based on economic theory. They reach the conclusion that better and larger data sets, more powerful computers, improved modelling methods, faster computational techniques, and new econometric methods have allowed researchers to make significant improvements.

It is strange that Nevo and Whinston (2010) refer to White's standard errors as a major development since Leamer's article. This is like Hillary Clinton telling Edmund Hillary that she was named after him following his ascent to Mount Everest (White's standard errors came before the Leamer critique and Hillary was born before the other Hillary reached the top of the world). We have seen that the trend has been to use less and less economic theory to build econometric models. Larger data sets, more powerful computers and faster computational techniques are exactly what is needed to indulge in data mining on a massive scale. The proliferation of econometric methods has served no purpose whatsoever – just recall how much we have benefited from the extravaganza of ARCH and its disciples. Then what is the difference between "improved modelling methods" and "new econometric methods". This is simply hollow rhetoric in defence of econometrics. If anything, there is more con in econometrics now than in Leamer's time.

The Response of McAleer et al.

The most prominent response to the Leamer critique in defence of econometrics is that of McAleer, Pagan and Volker (1985) who put forward some proposals to take the con out of econometrics. At the time of writing in the mid-1980s, they did not deny that applied econometrics was not "in the most robust of health", but they describe Leamer's critique to be "entertaining or perceptive" (not serious or to be taken seriously). They describe extreme bounds analysis as the "medicine to cure an ailing patient". And that is right – nothing can cure an ailing patient like econometrics, not even "better research design" and "more powerful estimation methods".

McAleer et al. argue against EBA on the grounds that extreme bounds are generated by the imposition of highly arbitrary, and generally unknown, restrictions between the parameters of a model, arguing that it is "something of a mystery" why such bounds should be of interest. They further demonstrate that "the methodology is flawed on other grounds" because "EBA demands a general, adequate model from which the bounds may be derived, and a consensus over which variables are critical to a relationship". Then they move on to describe their own diagnosis and prescription, which are founded on "the belief that many of the difficulties applied econometrics currently faces originate in the very poor attempts currently

made to accurately describe the process whereby a model was selected, and
to ascertain its adequacy".

With these considerations in mind they propose a three-stage approach
to modelling, involving the selection and subsequent simplification of a
general model and a rigorous evaluation of any preferred model. They
apply these criteria to the money demand example in Cooley and LeRoy
(1981) and find that their specification was to fail even the simplest of the
criteria, making "any conclusions drawn from it highly suspect". In a sharp
contrast to this failure, they demonstrate that the application of a modelling strategy beginning with a general model and progressively constraining
the parameter space led to a representation that passed all items of the
checklist. Still they admit that their prescription provides "the necessary
rather than sufficient conditions for taking the con out of econometrics". In
truth nothing can take the con of econometrics and claims like those made
by McAleer et al. show that econometricians are in a terrible state of denial.

The Reply of Cooley and LeRoy

Cooley and LeRoy did reply to McAleer et al. in a subsequent issue of the
American Economic Review, in which case I will leave it to the reader to
see that reply (Cooley and LeRoy, 1986). However, I will go through the
Cooley and LeRoy (1981) paper, which McAleer et al. commented on, as
it provides a good and justifiable criticism of econometrics. They start by
reiterating a major difference between economics and natural science theories, which are validated by controlled experiments, and economics where
the data are characteristically generated by "measurement of uncontrolled
systems". In economics, they contend, theories take the form of restrictions on the models assumed to generate the data, and statistical methods
replace experimental controls in testing these restrictions.

The difficulty as identified by Cooley and LeRoy is that in economics
(particularly macroeconomics) the theory used to derive tests ordinarily
does not generate a complete specification of which variables are to be
held constant when statistical tests are performed on the relation between
the dependent variable and explanatory variables of primary interest.
Accordingly, which is the idea put forward by Leamer, "there will be a set
of often very different candidate regression-based tests, each of which has
equal status with the others since each is based on a different projection of
the same underlying multivariate model". They conclude that if a theory
does not generate a complete specification of the regression model, the
results must be robust over the permissible alternative specifications, which
motivated Leamer's suggestion of the use of sensitivity analysis. They add
the following:

If the restrictions indicated by the theory are satisfied in some projections, but not in others that have an equal claim to represent implications of the theory, one cannot conclude that the theory has been confirmed. The fact that the observable implications of valid theories must obtain over a broad (but usually incompletely specified) set of regressions rather than for a single regression introduces a large and unavoidable element of imprecision into hypothesis testing in macroeconomics.

Applying these ideas to the demand for money function, which is a macroeconomic application, they suggest that (1) the negative interest elasticity of money demand reported in the literature represents prior beliefs much more than sample information; and (2) the treatment of simultaneity in the literature is totally inadequate. Thus they cast serious doubt on the validity of the estimates of a money demand equation and present a final conclusion that is rather devastating for econometrics:

> We believe that no progress can be made in estimating such structural macroeconomic equations as that for the demand for money until we rid ourselves of the habits of data mining, of building in priors through selective reporting, and of casually adopting what Christopher Sims has called "incredible" identifying assumptions to dispose of simultaneity problems.

The final conclusion of Cooley and LeRoy (1981) says it all, but it made them the target of attack by econometricians in a state of denial. Leamer was right in claiming that there was con in econometrics. If anything, there is more con in econometrics now than in the 1980s, facilitated by the very tools that some econometricians claim to be the means whereby con can be taken out of econometrics.

6.4   THE LUCAS CRITIQUE

Robert Lucas (1976) criticized the use of econometric models of the macroeconomy to predict the consequences and implications of economic policy, arguing that the structural relations observed in models estimated from historical data break down if decision makers adjust their preferences to reflect policy changes. Lucas argued that policy conclusions drawn from econometric models were invalid as economic actors tend to alter their expectations and adjust their behaviour accordingly. Hence, the argument goes, a good macroeconometric model should incorporate microfoundations to account for the effects of policy changes, with equations describing economic representative agents responding to economic changes based on rational expectations of the future.

The Lucas critique implies that econometric models cannot be considered as structural in the sense of being invariant with respect to changes in government policy variables. Because the parameters of econometric models are not structural (that is, not policy-invariant), they would necessarily change whenever changes are introduced to policy (the rules of the game). This means that policy conclusions would be misleading. Lucas summarizes his critique as follows:

> Given that the structure of an econometric model consists of optimal decision rules of economic agents, and that optimal decision rules vary systematically with changes in the structure of series relevant to the decision maker, it follows that any change in policy will systematically alter the structure of econometric models.

Econometricians acknowledge the Lucas critique. For example, Pesaran (1990) describes the critique as follows:

> The message of the REH for econometrics was clear. By postulating that economic agents form their expectations endogenously on the basis of the true model of the economy and a correct understanding of the processes generating exogenous variables of the model, including government policy, the REH raised serious doubts about the invariance of the structural parameters of the mainstream macroeconometric models in face of changes in government policy.

However, Pesaran (1990) considers the Lucas critique to be just like any other econometric problem that can be dealt with by developing "more sophisticated" econometric methods that make it possible to produce more reliable results. It is ironic that econometric methods give rise to problems that are dealt with by developing new methods. It sounds like a vicious circle.

The Lucas critique has been tested empirically, with varying results. Lubik and Surico (2006) argue that evidence for the inapplicability of the Lucas critique is due to problems with the size of the underlying econometric tests. They use a structural model of the US economy as a data generating process to illustrate these issues both conceptually and by means of Monte Carlo analysis. Their empirical findings confirm that the Lucas critique is relevant to the shift in US monetary policy behaviour in the early 1980s. It sounds as if the development of econometric methods that deal with the Lucas critique as an econometric problem may take the form of a test that fails to detect its effects. This again sounds like a con job.

A word of warning. When Lucas formulated his critique, which is valid, he was not motivated by the desire to expose weaknesses in econometrics. Rather, his main motivation was to demonstrate that government intervention in the economy was to be avoided because it is destabilizing and that a better course of action would be to leave it all to the almighty market. The hidden agenda was to encourage deregulation, laissez-faire economics, or what Al-Nakeeb (2016) calls "parasitic economics". Still, saying the right thing to serve a hidden agenda is better than saying the wrong thing for the same reason.

6.5 THE AUSTRIAN SCHOOL CRITICISM OF ECONOMETRICS

One reason, perhaps the main reason, why Austrian economists do not get more publications in mainstream journals is that they rarely use mathematics or econometrics, which they reject as a matter of principle. They reject econometrics on the grounds that while statistical methods are appropriate for natural sciences, where factors can be isolated in laboratory conditions, the actions of humans are too complex for such a treatment because humans are not passive and non-adaptive subjects.

According to Austrian economists, deduction is preferred to induction for the purpose of interpreting economic developments because if performed correctly, it leads to certain conclusions and inferences that must be true if the underlying assumptions are accurate. Deduction is a kind of reasoning from the general to the specific, such that a conclusion necessarily follows the stated premises – that is, if the premises are accepted as true, it follows that the conclusion is also true. Induction, on the other hand, is a kind of reasoning from the specific or individual to the general, which means that even if all the premises are true, the conclusion can be false. Austrian economists believe that induction does not assure certainty like deduction, as real world economic data are inherently ambiguous and subject to a multitude of influences that cannot be separated or quantified. Therefore, they argue that econometricians have no way of verifying cause and effect in real world economic events, since economic data can be correlated to multiple potential chains of causation. This is once more the issue of distinguishing between correlation and causation.

Ludwig von Mises, a leading Austrian economist, is highly critical of empirical work in economics. This is how he puts forward his arguments against econometrics (von Mises, 1998):

> It is true the empiricists reject [a priori] theory; they pretend that they aim to learn only from historical experience. However, they contradict their own principles as soon as they pass beyond the unadulterated recording of individual single prices and begin to construct series and to compute averages. . . . Nobody is so bold as to maintain that a rise of *a* per cent in the supply of any commodity must always – in every country and at any time – result in a fall of *b* per cent in

its price. But as no quantitative economist ever ventured to define precisely on the ground of statistical experience the special conditions producing a definite deviation from the ratio $a : b$, the futility of his endeavors is manifest.

Austrian economists reject statistical methods and artificially constructed experiments, advocating instead to isolate the logical processes of human action via "praxeology". The Austrian praxeological approach is based on the heavy use of logical deduction from what is perceived to be self-evident axioms – this is the one area where Austrian economists differ most significantly from other schools of economic thought. Although Austrian economists do not discount induction, they contend that it does not assure certainty like deduction.

Von Mises (1998) argued that statistical analysis can never be a source of economic theory and that theory is prior to the gathering and analysis of data. In a comment on this view, Murphy (2002) contends that although the student of Austrian economics may share von Mises's opinions about the dubiousness of econometrics, the fact is that he or she must take classes and exams in this field in order to receive a degree from most programmes in the US. It is the tyranny of the status quo.

6.6   CONCLUDING REMARKS

Econometrics has been criticized left, right and centre, and justifiably so. A middle of the road stance is that econometrics has its limitations but it is still useful. This is the stance taken by Pesaran (1990) who attributes the limitations of econometrics to incompleteness of economic theory and the non-experimental nature of economic data. But the very fact that economic data is non-experimental casts a big shadow of doubt on the soundness of applying statistical methods to observations of data collected from various sources with significant measurement errors. It is not obvious how incompleteness of economic theory is bad for econometrics, when econometric methods are supposedly designed to test economic theories. In any case, econometrics has been moving away from economic theory.

Pesaran goes on to say that "these limitations should not distract us from recognizing the fundamental role that econometrics has come to play in the development of economics as a scientific discipline". If anything, this is a failure of econometrics, because economics is not a science. The belief that economics is a science and the resulting policy prescriptions have been taking us from one crisis to another. Econometrics-ridden economics leads to complacency, the feeling of safety because the econometric model says that bad things will not happen. Pesaran also says that while it may not be possible to reject conclusively economic theories by means of econometric methods, this does not mean that nothing useful can be learned from attempts at testing particular formulations of a given theory against rival alternatives. A look at the literature dealing with any theory (for example, purchasing power parity) leads to the conclusion that nothing useful can be learned by testing a given theory, because the results are all over the place and because any result (supportive, unsupportive or neutral) can be produced.

In what seems to be a comment directed at the Leamer critique, Pesaran (1990) plays down the fact that econometric modelling is inevitably subject to the problem of specification searches, arguing that this problem does not make the whole activity pointless. If specification searches lead to data mining and the production of the desired results, the activity must be pointless – even hazardous when policy actions are taken on the basis of such results. While Pesaran claims that "econometric models are important tools for forecasting and policy analysis", there is no evidence that we have learned much about the economy from these models. Are we more knowledgeable of how the economy and financial markets work after over thirty years of ARCH/GARCH and cointegration?

Pesaran predicts that it is unlikely that econometric methods will be discarded in the future, a proposition that I agree with, not because econometric methods are useful or indispensible, but because they represent an established and profitable industry. The challenge, according to Pesaran, is "to recognize their limitations and to work towards turning them into more reliable and effective tools" because "there seem to be no viable alternatives" – this means another 50 years of ARCH/GARCH. As to "no alternative", I would just like to remind everyone that the brilliant work of Adam Smith, Karl Marx, J.M. Keynes, Joan Robinson, Ludwig von Mises, J.K. Galbraith and Hayman Minsky was done without econometrics. There is certainly a viable alternative, which is the next 50 years without new ARCH/GARCH models.

7.   Stir-fry regressions as a con job

7.1   INTRODUCTION

In 1983 Edward Leamer published his provocative article "Let us Take the Con out of Econometrics", in which he justifiably criticized a (mal-) practice – that of estimating 1000 regressions and reporting the one or the few that they like (Leamer, 1983). More than thirty years later, this practice is still highly popular – in fact it has become more widespread because of the growth in the power of computing and the prevalence of the publish or perish culture. It is particularly widespread in corporate finance where testable models are assembled by combining various hypotheses to come up with a cross-sectional regression equation that has no corresponding theoretical model. The regression equation is subsequently twisted and turned until it produces the results that make a dream come true. Typically, the researcher aims at producing results that tell a good story to sell, corroborate the results reported in a paper published by a journal editor or a potential referee, or to support an ideological preconceived belief.

The problem with cross-sectional regressions is that theory is not adequately explicit about the variables that should appear in the "true" model as determined by theory (if there is theory at all). This would be the case if, for example, the final model specification is derived by solving a theoretical optimization problem. In the absence of a theoretical model, the regression equation (empirical model) is constructed haphazardly, by specifying the dependent variable, y, to be a function of several explanatory variables, x_i, where $i = 1, \ldots, n$. The results invariably turn out to be difficult to interpret – for example, x_1 is significant when the regression includes x_2 and x_3 but not when x_4 is included. So, which combination of all available x_j's is to be chosen?

It is a common practice to report the most "appealing" or convenient regression or regressions after extensive search and data mining (given that the "true" model is unknown). While scientific research should be based on a quest for the truth, this practice is motivated by the urge to obtain the desirable results. Gilbert (1986) casts significant doubt on the validity of the practice of assigning 999 regressions to the waste bin, because they do not produce the anticipated results. Because of this problem, Leamer

(1983) suggested that "econometricians confine themselves to publishing mappings from prior to posterior distributions rather than actually making statements about the economy".

Leamer and Leonard (1983) argued strongly against the conventional reporting of empirical results, stating that "the reported results are widely regarded to overstate the precision of the estimates, and probably to distort them as well". They further argued that the conventional econometric methodology (or "technology" as they called it) "generates inference only if a precisely defined model were available, and which can be used to explore the sensitivity of inferences only to discrete changes in assumptions". According to Leamer and Leonard (1983), this "deflects econometric theory from the traditional task of identifying the unique inferences implied by a specific model to the task of determining the range of inferences generated by a range of models". Hussain and Brookins (2001) point out that the usual practice of reporting a preferred model with its diagnostic tests need not be sufficient to convey the degree of reliability of the determinants (explanatory variables).

A regression equation constructed by lumping together a large number of variables that represent unrelated hypotheses is what I cynically refer to as a "stir-fry regression". In a previous paper (Moosa, 2012) it was demonstrated that stir-fry regressions constitute a con job because they can be used to prove almost anything. Specifically, the paper demonstrates that (1) the sign and significance of an estimated coefficient change with the selected set of explanatory variables; (2) adding more explanatory variables to the regression equation changes the sign and significance of a coefficient on a variable that is already included in the equation; (3) it is possible to change coefficients from significantly positive to significantly negative and vice versa; (4) obtaining the desirable results can be achieved by introducing various forms of nonlinearities (predominantly partial and selective logarithmic transformation); and (5) it is possible, by changing model specification, to support either of two competing theories. In this chapter a similar exercise is conducted by using data on 614 US shareholding companies.

7.2   STIR FRY AND ECONOMETRICS

These days, stir-fry regressions are encountered frequently in conference and seminar presentations. The presenter would typically start with a regression equation that goes over three or more lines because it has many explanatory variables written in words, not symbols, resulting from a combination of a diversified set of variables. Eventually the presenter shows a table of results containing five or six versions of the original equation with different combinations of the variables and a menu of one, two or three stars to imply statistical significance at the 1 per cent, 5 per cent and 10 per cent levels, respectively. To most people this is an acceptable practice whereby the researcher contributes to human knowledge. The post-presentation discussion revolves typically around some trivial issues, and it is rarely the case that model specification is challenged in the spirit of Keynes and Leamer.

Whenever I witness a presentation of this sort, I react by wondering what we are supposed to believe, since the results are contradictory. The coefficient on a particular variable may turn out to be significantly positive in some reported regressions, significantly negative in others and statistically insignificant in the remaining ones. Then what significance level are we supposed to use to distinguish between significant and insignificant coefficients (***, ** or *)? Sometimes the presenter would say that a particular coefficient is insignificant but correctly signed in accordance with the underlying hypothesis. This of course is nonsense because "insignificant" means insignificantly different from zero – that is, it is statistically zero, in which case the sign does not matter.

Alternatively the presenter would show one regression equation, out of the hundreds of equations tried, the equation that tells a nice story that supports the underlying hypothesis. The specification would typically involve selective log transformation and perhaps some square and/or square roots, indicating a massive scale of data mining. My reaction in this case would be as follows: "give me your data and I will turn your results upside down, changing significantly positive coefficients into significantly negative, and vice versa". In the process I made a lot of enemies. Young academics would typically complain that everyone does that, and that if they did not do it, they would not be able to publish. I would react by telling them to do it and get published because otherwise they would lose their jobs at worst and denied promotion at best, courtesy of the culture of publish or perish. However, I would also say that by following this approach they should not convince themselves and others that they are contributing something to human knowledge. It is a game that academics play to keep their jobs and get promoted. Do you see the connection between the rise of stir-fry regressions and the culture of publish or perish?

Let us now see what stir fry and cross-sectional regressions have in common. The two processes, that of preparing a stir fry and estimating a cross-sectional regression with a large number of explanatory variables, allow a large set of possibilities so that the desirable outcome is bound to be obtained. The desirable outcome is a tasty dish in the process of preparing a stir fry (which is fine) and (in the case of empirical work) results that tell a good story – a story that makes the paper more publishable, typically confirming the underlying hypothesis. So, let us examine the possibilities offered by stir fry and stir-fry regressions.

A stir fry can be prepared with prawns, chicken, lamb or beef. These kinds of meat have several varieties but it suffices to use two varieties: small or big for prawns, leg or breast for chicken, Australian or New Zealand for lamb, and tenderloin or sirloin for beef. The second component of a stir fry is vegetables, which can be any of the following and more: carrots, spring onions, chillies, green peppers, red peppers, baby corn, peas, and broad beans. Then we have the sauces, including, amongst others, light soy, dark soy, plum sauce, sesame oil, oyster sauce and black bean sauce. We assume that the stir fry is prepared by using one kind of meat, four kinds of vegetables and two sauces. The cook can try various combinations until he or she converges on the right recipe, the recipe that produces a product that is nice for their palate. Given the number of ingredients that can be used to prepare the stir fry, the number of possibilities is 8400 ($8 \times C_4^8 \times C_2^6$).

If the number of possibilities for preparing a stir fry looks great, wait until you see the number of possibilities for estimating a stir-fry regression equation containing 15 explanatory variables. For n explanatory variables, the equation looks like this:

$$Y_i = \alpha_0 + \sum_{j=1}^{n} \alpha_j X_{ji} + \varepsilon_i \qquad (7.1)$$

If all of the available explanatory variables appear in the final equation, then $n = 15$ but this equation may not give the desirable results. We assume that the final equation contains at least five variables, which means that n may assume values ranging between 5 and 15. If $n = 8$, such that $i = 1,2,\ldots,8$, then the number of possible regression equations is 6435 (C_8^{15}), which gives the researcher a wide range of possibilities that is bound to contain an equation telling a nice (but not necessarily a true) story. This is not the end of it, however. As is typically the case in empirical economics and finance, the variables may be defined or measured in more than one way. Let us make the humble assumption that each of the variables (including the dependent variable) is defined or measured in two different ways, either of which can be used in the regression equations. For the equation containing n explanatory variables this means 2^{n+1}. For example, when $n = 5$, the number of possibilities becomes $C_5^{15} \times 2^6 = 192,192$.

Then comes the introduction of nonlinearities by converting some variables into logarithmic values, which is done haphazardly and without any justification. Logarithmic transformation is typically (and wrongly) used to scale the variables, and this is why it is applied only to large numbers such as sales, GDP, total assets, and so on. This of course does not make sense because variables can be scaled by measuring them in units of one million rather than one or by converting them into indices. Selective logarithmic transformation amounts to the introduction of selective nonlinearity. Even by the rules of econometrics, logarithmic specification is used only if the regression equation is derived theoretically (as, for example, in purchasing power parity) or by testing linear versus log-linear specifications.

Let us for the purpose of our exercise assume that the logarithmic transformation can only be applied to a limited number of the variables, which give another eight possibilities in each case. Assume also the squares of some of the variables can be used, which gives another eight possibilities in each case. The overall number of possibilities when five explanatory variables appear in the regression equation is over 12 million and the number of possibilities corresponding to the number of explanatory variables are shown in Figure 7.1. The grand total obtained from the overall possibilities is displayed in Figure 7.2: it is a staggering 1.8 billion. Some of these specifications are as follows where lower case letters imply logarithms.

$$Y_i = \alpha_0 + \sum_{j=1}^{15} \alpha_j X_{ji} + \varepsilon_i \tag{7.2}$$

$$Y_i = \alpha_0 + \sum_{j=1}^{7} \alpha_j X_{ji} + \alpha_8 x_{8i} + \alpha_{10} X_{10i} + \varepsilon_i \tag{7.3}$$

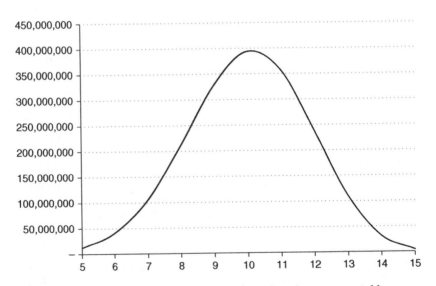

Figure 7.1 Possibilities with a fixed number of explanatory variables

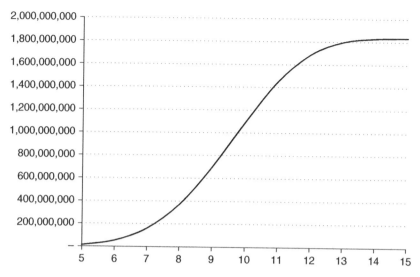

Figure 7.2   The grand total of possibilities

$$y_i = \alpha_0 + \sum_{j=1}^{4} \alpha_j X_{ji} + \alpha_8 x_{8i} + \alpha_{12} X_{12i}^2 + \varepsilon_i \qquad (7.4)$$

$$y_i = \alpha_0 + \alpha_2 x_{2i} + \alpha_5 X_{5i} + \alpha_7 x_{7i} + \alpha_{12} X_{12i}^2 + \alpha_{14} X_{15i} + \varepsilon_i \qquad (7.5)$$

With the computer power available today, there is no better time to experiment with these specifications until we hit the jackpot and get a paper that a referee would like. But this is not all, because sometimes the so-called "interaction variables" are used to make data mining even more versatile. These variables are constructed as the product of two individual variables or the product of a dummy variable and one of the explanatory variables. A typical table of results would look like Table 7.1, reporting five regression equations containing a unique selection of variables for each equation. I am not sure why more than one regression equation is presented but I reckon that it is to show the "balance of the evidence". Alternatively only one equation is presented to avoid embarrassment. It is an insult to scientific research to present results that look like those displayed in Table 7.1.

7.3   STIR-FRY REGRESSIONS IN STUDIES OF THE CAPITAL STRUCTURE

Studies of the capital structure are typically based on a cross-sectional regression of the form:

Table 7.1   A typical results table from stir-fry regressions

Variable	1	2	3	4	5
C	+(***)	0	−(*)	+(***)	+(**)
X_1	−(**)	−(*)		0	+(***)
X_2	+(**)		−(***)		
X_3	+(*)	+(***)	0	−(*)	
$\log(X_4)$	0	−(*)		+(***)	+(*)
X_5	+(***)	0		0	−(***)
$\log(X_6)$	+(**)	0	−(***)	−(***)	0
X^2_7	0	−(***)		−(***)	+(*)
X_8	−(**)	+(***)	−(*)		−(*)
X_9	−(***)		−(*)	+(***)	
$X_8{}^*X_9$	+(*)	0	+(***)	−(***)	+(**)
X_{10}	0	−(***)		−(***)	+(*)
X_{11}	−(***)	0	+(***)		−(***)
$X_{10}X_{11}$	+(*)		+(***)	0	
$D_{10}X_{11}$	−(**)		+(**)	+(**)	
$D_{11}X_{11}$	0	0	0	−(**)	
R^2	0.09	0.07	0.08	0.12	0.06

Notes: + significantly positive; − significantly negative; 0 insignificant; * significant at the 10% level; ** significant at the 5% level; *** significant at the 1% level.

$$LEV_i = \alpha_0 + \sum_{j=1}^{n} \alpha_j X_{ji} + \varepsilon_i \qquad (7.6)$$

where *LEV* is the leverage ratio and X_{ji} is explanatory variable j for company i. The problem of the sensitivity of the estimated coefficients with respect to model specification arises in studies of the capital structure because no single theoretical model is available to determine an explicit set of explanatory variables to include in any empirical model. For example, Fauver and McDonald (2015) list 28 explanatory variables in their Appendix 1 and report five regression equations, three of which are for developed countries, with the customary ***, ** and *.

Because they use a large number of explanatory variables they erroneously refer to their equations as "multivariate regressions" (instead of the correct term "multiple regressions"). The variables include Individualism, Risk Aversion, Top Quintile of Total Assets*Individualism, Bottom Quintile of Total Assets*Individualism, Firm Governance Score, Firm-Level Governance Score*Individualism, Firm-Level Governance Score*Risk Aversion, log(ROE), CES, log(Total

Assets), Cash/Total Assets, Income Tax/Total Assets, Religious Fervor, Private Credit/GDP, Market Cap/GDP, Country Governance, Emerging Market, Top Quintile of CES*Risk Aversion, and Bottom Quintile of CES*Risk Aversion and Constant. It is strange that they use the log of ROE, which is a fraction, when typically the logarithmic transformation is reserved for large numbers such as assets and sales. This must have been driven by data mining. Despite the extremely large number of explanatory variables, the explanatory power of their equations is 0.36 at best and 0.09 at worst. Yet, they feel confident enough to derive inference from their results.

Huang and Ritter (2005) correctly argue that no single theory of capital structure is capable of explaining the time-series and cross-sectional patterns that have been documented. Likewise, Frydenberg (2008) points out that neither the pecking order theory, nor the trade-off theory provides a complete description of empirical observations or explain why some firms prefer equity while others prefer debt. Titman and Wessels (1988) and Harris and Raviv (1991) argue along similar lines, pointing out that the choice of explanatory variables in the analysis of cross-sectional variation in capital structure is fraught with difficulty. The consequence is that researchers are tempted to try various combinations of the explanatory variables (defined in many ways) and report the results they like. This is why some firm-specific factors that are reported as important for capital structure may not be so – they only appear to be so because of a model specification that contains a particular combination of potential explanatory variables with specific definitions (Moosa et al., 2011).

Studying capital structure of Chinese companies, Li et al. (2009) use a sample of 417,068 firm-year observations over the period 2000–2004. They test the importance of nine explanatory variables: size, profitability, tangibility, asset maturity, industry concentration, industry leverage, state ownership, foreign ownership and marketization (classified into firm characteristics, ownership variables and institutional variables). The results show that state ownership is positively associated with leverage (long-term debt), while foreign ownership is negatively associated with all measures of leverage. Other conclusions are derived on the effect of firm-specific factors. The Li et al. (2009) study provides the best illustration of the problem addressed in this chapter. Five different model specifications are estimated: a full specification (all variables), firm characteristics only, ownership variables only, institutional variables only, and ownership/institutional variables. The diversity and inconsistency of the results can be demonstrated with just a few examples out of many:

1. For total leverage, industry concentration is highly significant in the full specification but not so in the specification that has firm characteristics only.
2. For short-term debt, size is highly significant in the full specification but not so in the specification that has firm characteristics only. The same goes for industry concentration. Marketization is insignificant when only institutional variables are included in the model but becomes significant when ownership variables are added.
3. In a model designed to explain the probability of having long-term debt, asset maturity is significant when only firm characteristics are used but not so in the full specification. It is exactly the other way round for industry concentration.
4. When the equations are estimated with fixed effects, industry concentration, state ownership and marketization are highly significant when the model includes ownership and institutional variables only, but not so in any of the other model specifications.

The same problem can be observed in Liu et al. (2009) who present three different models: (1) with a constant and six explanatory variables (2) without a constant and six explanatory variables; and (3) without a constant and four explanatory variables. The results turn out to be a mixed bag: size is significant only if the constant term is taken out, while profitability is significant only in the second regression.

Evidence on the determination of capital structure is definitely a mixed bag across the board. Prasad et al. (2001) survey a large volume of literature on capital structure, concluding that the evidence on trade-off versus pecking order theories remains inconclusive. Booth et al. (2001) argue that it is difficult to distinguish between trade-off and pecking order models because the variables used in one model are also relevant in the other model. Lopez-Iturriaga and Rodriguez-Sanz (2008) examine capital structure in an international framework and find that size, asset tangibility and growth opportunities have a "relevant but differential effect across different international systems". Their results suggest that "the legal and institutional system of each country does not only affect firms capital structure but also creates the conditions to explain a differential effect of the common determinants of firms' financial choices".

This, however, does not mean that the results are uniform for a single country. Take, for example, the numerous studies of capital structure in China. The results are all over the place as can be seen in Table 7.2, which shows some contradictory results with respect to the sign and significance of the coefficients on various explanatory variables. For example, two of

Table 7.2   A summary of capital structure studies of Chinese firms

Study	Data Sample	Reported Results
Huang and Song (2002)	More than 1000 listed companies up to 2000	Size + Profitability – Fixed assets + Non-debt tax shields +
Chen (2004)	88 publicly listed firms 1995–2000	Size – Profitability – Tangibility + Growth opportunities +
Hongyan (2008)	722 observations (202 firms over the period 2004–2007)	Size + Liquidity + – Profitability – Growth opportunities +
Shen (2008)	1089 listed companies, 1991–2000	Size – Tangibility 0 Profit – Tax rate + Growth + Capital intensity + Product diversification + Asset specificity – Risk 0 Duration 0
Bhabra et al. (2008)	Listed companies on the Shanghai and Shenzhen Stock Exchanges during the period 1992–2001 (number of companies increased from 54 in 1992 to 1154 in 2001)	Size + Tangibility + Profitability – Growth options –
Li et al. (2009)	417,068 firm-year observations over the period 2000–2004	State ownership + Foreign ownership – Firm-specific factors + –
Liu et al. (2009)	92 IT companies	Size + Profitability – Growth opportunities – Liquidity – Growth – Profit growth –
Qian et al. (2009)	650 publicly listed firms, 1999–2004	Size + Profitability – Tangibility + Growth – Volatility – State shareholding + Non-tax debt shields –

Notes: + significantly positive; – significantly negative; + – significantly positive or negative; 0 insignificant.

the reported studies reveal a negative effect of size, when it is universally accepted that size affects leverage positively.

So, what are we supposed to believe and how can we derive robust inference from these results? The answer is that since we do not know what to believe, we cannot derive robust inference. With this kind of result we cannot identify the factors determining capital structure with any degree of robustness. The best answer to the question "what determines capital structure" should be "anything and nothing". It is, therefore, clear that the literature (on China and in general) does not offer a consistent theoretical framework for guiding empirical work on capital structure, because no single model specifies a full list of the explanatory variables.

7.4   AN ILLUSTRATION

The sensitivity of the results to the selection of explanatory variables, definitions of variables and logarithmic transformation implies that it is always possible to obtain the desired results. For the purpose of illustration, a cross-sectional data set is used covering observations on the determinants of capital structure for 614 US shareholding companies obtained from Datastream. The determinants of capital structure are taken to be size (*SIZ*), liquidity (*LIQ*), profitability (*PRF*), tangibility (*TAN*), growth opportunities (*GOP*), the payout ratio (*POR*), stock price performance (*SPP*), the age of the firm (*AGE*), and income variability (*VAR*). The dependent variable is taken to be the leverage ratio, defined and measured in six different ways (*LEV1. . . LEV6*). Two definitions each are used for two explanatory variables: *SIZ* (*SIZ1* and *SIZ2*) and *PRF* (*PRF1* and *PRF2*). All of the definitions are exhibited in Table 7.3.

Sensitivity to Model Specification

The initial step is to demonstrate how the results change with the choice of explanatory variables, variable definition and logarithmic transformation. Table 7.4 displays the correlation coefficients between various definitions of the leverage ratio and the explanatory variables. We can see that only when *LEV1* and *LEV3* are used, do we find significantly positive correlation between the leverage ratio and growth opportunities and significantly negative correlation with profitability. Tangibility is positively related to the leverage ratio for *LEV2*, *LEV4* and *LEV6*, but not for the others.

The next step is to estimate 47 equations from a set of numerous

Table 7.3   Definitions of variables

Variable	Definition
LEV1	At book value, the ratio of total liabilities to total assets
LEV2	At market value, the leverage ratio is calculated by adjusting total assets by subtracting the book value and adding the market value of equity
LEV3	At book value, the ratio of debt to total assets
LEV4	At market value, the leverage ratio is calculated by adjusting total assets by subtracting the book value and adding the market value of equity
LEV5	At book value, the ratio of debt to capital where capital is the sum of debt and equity
LEV6	At market value, the leverage ratio is calculated by replacing the book value of equity in the denominator with the market value
SIZ1	Sales
SIZ2	Total assets
LIQ	The current ratio (current assets to current liabilities)
PRF1	Earnings before interest, taxes, depreciation and amortization (EBITDA) divided by total assets
PRF2	Return on assets (ROA)
TAN	Ratio of fixed assets to total assets
GOP	Market value of total assets divided by book value of total assets
POR	Ratio of dividends to net income
SPP	Ratio of net income to common equity
AGE	Number of years since incorporation
VAR	Standard deviation of net operating income

Table 7.4   Correlation with measures of leverage

	LEV1	LEV2	LEV3	LEV4	LEV5	LEV6
SIZ1	−0.12	0.16	−0.12	0.19	0.14	0.15
SIZ2	−0.04	0.14	−0.02	0.18	0.08	0.16
LIQ	−0.18	−0.37	−0.19	−0.19	−0.03	−0.27
PRF1	−0.55	0.11	−0.68	0.09	0.20	0.07
PRF2	−0.70	0.09	−0.79	0.07	0.23	0.04
TAN	0.01	0.26	0.07	0.35	0.09	0.30
GOP	0.71	−0.14	0.32	−0.09	−0.06	−0.08
POR	−0.04	−0.02	−0.03	0.02	0.01	−0.03
SPP	0.03	0.00	0.08	−0.01	−0.02	−0.01
AGE	−0.10	0.21	−0.11	0.13	0.05	0.10
VAR	−0.08	0.06	−0.06	0.09	0.09	0.05

possibilities. The starting point is the equation that contains all of the explanatory variables:

$$LEV = \alpha_0 + \alpha_1 SIZ + \alpha_2 LIQ + \alpha_3 PRF + \alpha_4 TAN + \alpha_5 GOP + \alpha_6 POR +$$
$$\alpha_7 SPP + \alpha_8 AGE + \alpha_9 VAR + \zeta \qquad\qquad (7.7)$$

For a given definition of the leverage ratio, size and profitability, six regression equations are estimated with a subset of the explanatory variables. The process is repeated for the six possible definitions of the leverage ratio, which gives 36 equations. Then six equations are estimated with the same variable combinations by using the first definition of the leverage ratio and the alternative definitions of size and profitability. This is followed by four equations in which size and age appear as logarithms. In the last equation (number 47) the leverage ratio appears in logarithmic form. The t statistics of the coefficients on the explanatory variables are shown in Figure 7.3, where the two horizontal lines represent the critical value of the t statistic (the range −2 to +2). The estimated coefficients are all over the place. The coefficients on *SIZ*, *PRF*, *TAN*, *GOP* and *AGE* turn out to be significantly positive, significantly negative or insignificant. The coefficients on *LIQ*, *POR*, *SPP* and *VAR* turn out to be either significantly negative or insignificant.

Sensitivity to Sample Selection

The second point to demonstrate is the sensitivity of the results to sample selection. For this purpose, equation (7.7) is estimated using the same definitions of variables without logarithmic transformation for the whole sample and five sub-samples chosen in an arbitrary manner. The results are presented in Table 7.5, showing less sensitivity to the sample than to model specification, definitions of variables and logarithmic transformation. Although we cannot see a coefficient changing from significantly positive to significantly negative and vice versa, some coefficients change from significantly positive or significantly negative to insignificant. There are, of course, other possibilities that may do just that. With 614 observations, the sample can be constructed in numerous ways, some of which are bound to give the desired results. And it is always possible to try variations of variable selection, definitions and logarithmic transformations by using sub-samples.

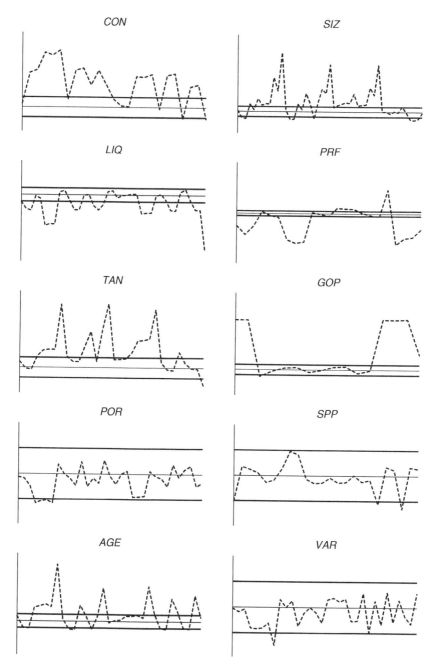

Figure 7.3 The t-statistics of the constant term and explanatory variables

Table 7.5   Estimates of equation (7.7) with various samples

	1–614	1–200	201–400	401–614	1–300	301–614
CON	0.70	−1.62	0.82	1.10	−0.06	1.26
SIZ	0.35	0.99	0.53	0.51	1.69	0.46
LIQ	−2.15	0.09	−1.07	−0.87	−0.46	−1.07
PRF	−10.09	5.53	−1.27	3.86	5.84	1.64
TAN	1.19	0.60	0.55	1.70	−0.02	1.83
GOP	19.53	3.71	−0.24	2.27	3.88	0.31
POR	−0.29	0.05	0.32	−0.26	−0.06	−0.07
SPP	−2.02	−2.16	0.64	0.04	−2.22	0.78
AGE	1.44	2.03	−1.03	−1.28	0.86	−1.29
VAR	−0.01	0.06	0.51	0.39	−0.07	0.81

Trade-Off versus Pecking Order

The last task is to demonstrate that it is possible, with the help of stir-fry regressions, to support either of two competing theories. This proposition is illustrated by "running a match" between two competing theories of the capital structure: the trade-off theory and the pecking order theory. According to the trade-off theory, a firm sets a target debt level and moves towards it gradually. As its name implies, the trade-off theory explains observed capital structures in terms of a trade-off between the costs and benefits of debt. The theory postulates that firms raise their debt level to the extent that the marginal tax advantages of additional borrowing are offset by the increase in the cost of financial bankruptcy.

The pecking order theory, which was pioneered by Myers and Majluf (1984), suggests that firms do not have a leverage target and that they focus on information costs and signalling effects. They demonstrate that firms prefer to finance projects from internally generated cash flows – namely, retained earnings and depreciation expenses. When this source of funds is exhausted, they move on to debt. Additional equity is issued only when debt is not sufficient to meet financing needs. This hierarchy is justified by differences in financing costs: issuing additional equity is the most expensive source of financing as it involves information asymmetries between managers, existing shareholders and potentially new shareholders. In view of the fixed payments associated with debt financing, it is less sensitive to information asymmetries, while internally generated resources do not produce issuing costs.

In designing a "match" between the two theories, the winner is the theory that achieves a higher score by predicting correctly the sign and

Table 7.6   Significance of coefficients and theory scores

	LIQ	PRF	TAN	GOP	SPP	VAR	TO	PO
1	–	–	0	+	–	–	3.5	10
2	–	0	+	–	0	–	8.5	4.5
3	0	–	+	0	0	0	4.5	5.5
4	–	0	+	0	0	–	6.0	5.5
5	0	+	0	0	0	0	5.5	3.0
6	–	0	+	0	0	–	7.0	5.5
7	–	0	+	+	0	–	6.0	7.0
8	0	–	0	0	0	0	3.0	5.5
9	–	0	+	+	0	0	4.5	7.0
10	0	+	0	0	0	0	5.5	3.0

Note: – significantly negative; + significantly positive; 0 insignificant; TO trade-off theory; PO pecking order theory.

significance of the estimated coefficients in the underlying regression. The trade-off theory predicts that *PRF* and *TAN* affect the leverage ratio positively whereas *GOP* and *VAR* affect it negatively. On the other hand, the pecking order theory predicts a negative influence for *PRF*, *LIQ* and *SPP* and a positive influence for *GOP*. If the underlying coefficient is significant and correctly signed the theory scores 2.5 points, otherwise one point is given for an insignificant coefficient and zero for a coefficient that is significant but incorrectly signed.

For the purpose of running the match, equation (7.7), which contains all of the explanatory variables, is estimated using various definitions of the variables. Overall, 10 equations are estimated, producing the results presented in Table 7.6 (only the t statistics of the relevant variables are reported). If I am in favour of the pecking order theory, I would report the first equation, which produces significantly negative coefficients on *PRF*, *LIQ* and *SPP*, and a significantly positive coefficient on GOP (perfect results for those who like the pecking order theory). Alternatively if I want to prove that the trade-off theory is better, I will report the second equation, which produces a significantly positive coefficient on *TAN*, significantly negative coefficients on *GOP* and *VAR* – almost a perfect result except for the insignificant coefficient on *PRF*. Figure 7.4 shows the score difference, where a positive value supports the trade-off theory, and vice versa. It turns out that the trade-off theory beats the pecking order theory on five occasions while the opposite is true on the other five occasions. This con job enables the researcher to prove anything.

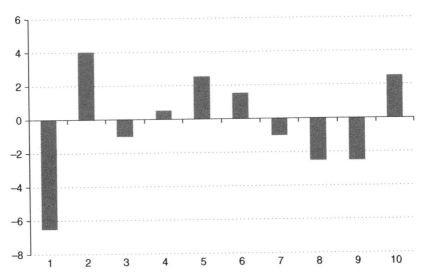

Figure 7.4   Trade-off theory versus pecking order theory (score difference)

7.5   CONCLUDING REMARKS

The empirical exercise undertaken in this chapter demonstrates the hazard of using stir-fry regression, although the hazard can be convenience if one is after publishing a paper or supporting a point of view rather than going on a quest for the truth in the spirit of scientific research and the desire to contribute to human knowledge. An examination of the literature in economics and finance shows how popular stir-fry regressions are.

You do not need to read a paper to realize that the results are based on stir-fry regressions, just a glance would do. You would recognize a paper with stir-fry regressions by its characteristics. You will see a list of hypotheses relating the dependent variable to a large number of explanatory variables. Then you find a single-equation empirical model extending over three lines with the variables written in words rather than symbols. Turn to the results page and you will find a long table with stars indicating the level of significance and columns labelled 1, 2, 3. . ., or something like that, indicating model specification. You will also find some variables expressed in logarithmic terms and perhaps others appearing in squares. Interaction variables will be observed, obtained by multiplying two of the explanatory variables or multiplying a dummy variable by one of the explanatory variables. Such a table would be the product of painstaking work involving extensive data mining.

Stir-fry regressions provided the motivation for the Leamer critique of econometrics. As a remedy, Leamer suggested extreme bounds analysis to measure the sensitivity of the estimated coefficients to model specification. Not many economists are even aware of this technique, because it is inconvenient – it is the antithesis of stir-fry regressions. So, stir-fry regressions prevail, which is fine if the objective is to publish in order for academic economists to keep their jobs and get promoted (to hell with contribution to human knowledge). The real hazard of stir-fry regressions is when the results are used to prescribe economic and social policies because they can be used to prove that the death penalty and human trafficking are useful, the underground economy is good, gun control causes more murders, and that global warming is not man-made, even that it does not exist. This is why policy makers should not take seriously studies based on stir-fry regressions. This conclusion is valid for other econometric techniques as we are going to see in the following chapters.

8. Cointegration analysis: principles and fallacies

8.1 INTRODUCTION

In the second half of the 1980s, specifically following the publication of the "seminal" paper of Engle and Granger (1987), the world of academic finance and economics experienced a "revolution" similar to that experienced by the world of music and dancing as a result of the introduction of rock and roll and twist. Engle and Granger formalized their work on cointegration and error correction, leading to the modification of the causality test of Granger (1969) to take into account the possibility of cointegration. The introduction of these techniques has created a thriving industry with a rapidly growing output of papers written by academics testing theories in economics and finance that were previously tested by using straightforward regression analysis.

Tens of thousands of papers and thousands of PhDs later, it is about time to ask whether or not the cointegration "revolution" has changed our lives and led to discoveries that enhance our understanding of the working of the economy and financial markets, which is presumably the objective of scientific research. One would tend to imagine that, since this work was awarded the Nobel Prize, it must be valued the same way as the discovery of Penicillin, which was awarded the same prize. However, it seems to me that while cointegration analysis has provided the means for finance and economics academics to get their promotion and students to obtain their PhDs, the technique has contributed almost nothing to the advancement of knowledge.

My story with cointegration started in 1991 when I took the heroic decision to move from investment banking to academia, where I had to publish to keep my job and get promoted. The first thing I did was to get myself acquainted with cointegration, since I had graduated long before the invention (or discovery) of cointegration. In particular the Johansen test of cointegration was in its heyday in the early 1990s, so I made sure that I knew how to execute the test. Subsequently, I wrote a paper in which I tested the monetary model of exchange rates by using the Johansen test (Moosa, 1994). Naturally, I was happy that the results supported the model as a "long-run equilibrium condition", showing more than one significant cointegrating vectors. I submitted the paper to a journal and received a request for revise and resubmit. The reviewer described my results as "interesting but tantalizing" and wondered why I had not reported the estimated coefficients of the cointegrating vectors. In my reply, I had to tell the truth, that the estimates of the coefficients made no sense, implausible relative to what is implied by the theory. So, I had to say that the Johansen test tended to produce implausible estimates of the coefficients of the cointegrating vectors. Luckily for me the paper was accepted, but I have hardly used this test since then, and particularly as a result of the devastating critique of Michael Wickens (1996). In fact I even refuse to teach it or allow my graduate students to use it in their research.

With the passage of time, I became increasingly uncomfortable with cointegration, both through my research and teaching. I would tell students that unit root tests are used to find out whether a variable is stationary or not and that looking at a time series graph of the underlying variable or its autocorrelation function does not constitute a formal test. It turns out, however, that looking at a graph is more informative than the results of unit root testing. The students would wonder why a variable that looks stationary, such as the interest rate differential, is indicated to be integrated of order 2 according to the unit root test. In reply, I would say "go by the graph". I would tell the students about Granger's representation theorem, that cointegration implies and is implied by the presence of a valid error correction model, but that turns out not to be true, which is typically justified in terms of the "low power" of the Dickey–Fuller test. Students are typically puzzled as to why the Dickey–Fuller test does not reject the null of no cointegration more often than never while the Johansen test invariably rejects the null (and if it does not at first, just change the lag length and enjoy the rejection of the null). Students also find that two variables that are related by a definitional relation, such as the spot exchange rate and the forward exchange rate that is compatible with covered interest parity, turn out not to be cointegrated, which is bizarre.

The biggest myth about cointegration that we teach students is that cointegration can be used to distinguish between spurious relations and genuine ones – that cointegration can be used as a test for spurious correlation. This is a dangerous proposition because it implies that we should forget about common sense and believe cointegration. For example, if the cointegration test results show that people who eat more margarine are more prone to divorce because the consumption of margarine is cointegrated with the divorce rate, then we should believe the test and forget about common sense by refusing to accept this proposition as nonsense. All of these problems are illustrated in this chapter.

8.2   COINTEGRATION, ERROR CORRECTION AND CAUSALITY

Cointegration implies that a linear combination of two (or more) variables is stationary although the variables themselves are nonstationary in the sense that they tend to "wander around" over time. When variables are cointegrated, they are said to be tied up by long-run equilibrium relations. This means that while it is possible to deviate from the long-run condition in the short run, these deviations tend to disappear with the passage of time as a result of the tendency to move back to the equilibrium condition (the phenomenon of mean reversion).

A simple two-variable cointegrating regression (normally includes a constant term) may be written as:

$$y_t = \alpha + \beta x_t + \varepsilon_t \qquad (8.1)$$

For x_t and y_t to be cointegrated, the necessary condition is that $x_t \sim I(1)$ and $y_t \sim I(1)$, whereas the sufficient condition is that $\varepsilon_t \sim I(0)$. This is what we were told by Engle and Granger (1987), but later we were told that a cointegrating system may comprise I(1) and I(0) but not I(2) variables.

The Residual-Based Test

The null hypothesis that $\varepsilon_t \sim I(1)$ is tested by applying the Dickey–Fuller (DF) test to the residuals of the cointegrating regression (the test is called augmented Dickey–Fuller, ADF, when lagged dependent variables appear in the DF regression of the residuals). This is the residual-based test for cointegration, which has been criticized on the following grounds. First, conflicting results are likely to be obtained from the DF and ADF tests (depending on the lag length), which may be attributed to the low power of the test in small samples. Second, extending the method to the multivariate case produces weak and biased results (Gonzalo, 1994), and there is no way to tell whether this linear combination is an independent vector or a linear combination of independent vectors. Third, the results are not invariant or robust with respect to the direction of normalization – that is, the choice of the variable on the left-hand side of the cointegrating regression. Dickey et al. (1991) argue that while the test is asymptotically invariant to the direction of normalization, the results may be very sensitive to it in finite samples. Finally, there is a substantial finite sample bias (for example, Banerjee et al., 1986), and there is also the problem of implicit common factor restriction (for example, Kremers et al., 1992). Apart from that, two serious shortcomings of the residual-based test are: (1) the Dickey–Fuller test is based on a simple AR(1) representation, which means that the underlying model is mis-specified in the sense that it should contain a moving average compo-nent; and (2) the test is rather weak in distinguishing between unit root and near-unit root processes.

Engle and Granger (1987) suggested seven different tests for the station-arity of the residual of a cointegrating regression, two of which are the DF and ADF tests. Another test is the Durbin–Watson statistic for the cointe-grating regression (equation 8.1). In this case, the test statistic is called the cointegrating regression Durbin–Watson (CRDW) statistic, and it has dif-ferent critical values from those of the conventional DW statistic used as a test for serial correlation. Instead of looking for a value of 2 to indicate the absence of serial correlation, the critical values of the CRDW statistic are 0.386 and 0.511 at the 5 per cent and the 1 per cent significance levels, respectively. We will find out that the CRDW and DF/ADF tests tend to produce inconsistent results.

The Advent of the Johansen Test

In the late 1980s the Johansen (1988) test for cointegration took the world of academic economics and finance by storm. This test quickly became a "crowd pleaser" since it allowed anyone to prove anything they wanted to prove: all it takes to obtain the results that you want is a simple modi-fication to the specification of the underlying model, particularly the lag length. The test is based on a vector autoregressive representation that allows the estimation of the cointegration matrix. Subsequently, two test statistics can be calculated to determine the number of significant cointegrating vectors: the maximum eigenvalue test and the trace test. Given confirmation bias, a researcher who gets a finding of no cointegra-tion by using the DF/ADF test would resort to the Johansen test, which would definitely reject the null (producing a finding of cointegration) and confirm the validity of the underlying theory or model.

The claim to fame of the Johansen test is that, unlike the Engle–Granger test, it produces results that are invariant with respect to the direction of normalization – this is because all variables are explicitly endogenous, which means that there is no need to pick the left-hand side variable in an arbitrary manner. Another perceived advantage of the Johansen test is that it provides estimates of all of the cointegrating vectors that exist within a set of variables and offers test statistics for their number. It has also been put forward that: (1) the Johansen test fully captures the underlying time series properties of the data; (2) it is more discerning in its ability to reject a false null hypothesis; (3) it is based on a fully specified statistical model;

and (4) it has the important advantage of using all of the information in the data set, thereby increasing estimation efficiency.

This seems to be a superb list of credentials for the Johansen test but what about its shortcomings? I have always argued that this test is dodgy because it can, at the touch of a button, be used to prove the researcher's underlying beliefs. This is convenient because the majority of empirical research in economics and finance is directed at proving preconceived ideas and producing "good" results, rather than going on a quest for the truth. In this sense, the test is also dangerous, because it can be used to support faulty policy actions and financial decisions. Imagine that you want to prove that privatization is good under any circumstances to please a policy maker who believes that for ideological reasons, or that you fancy the proposition that international diversification pays off. Not a problem, you will get the results you want, thanks to the Johansen test.

The Johansen test suffers from major problems. One important short-coming is that it does not allow the identification of separate functional relations in a structural simultaneous equation model (for example, Moosa 1994). If, by applying the method to a set of variables, two cointegrating vectors are obtained, these vectors cannot be identified as specific structural equations. As a matter of fact, no one knows what the cointegrating vectors are: structural equations, reduced-form equations or a combination thereof (for example, Wickens, 1996). Moreover, Reimers (1991) asserts that the test over-rejects the null hypothesis of no cointegration when it is true, hence providing the ammunition for those wanting to prove preconceived ideas. Hjalmarsson and Österholm (2007) use Monte Carlo simulations to show that "in a system with near-integrated variables, the probability of reaching an erroneous conclusion regarding the cointegrating rank of the system is generally substantially higher than the nominal size", which means that "the risk of concluding that completely unrelated series are cointegrated is therefore non-negligible". And, as stated earlier, the test invariably produces implausible point estimates of the coefficients of the cointegrating vectors, hence a researcher may get 178.6 for the estimate of a demand elasticity that is supposed to be around unity.

Economics and finance academics are in love with the Johansen test because it invariably rejects the null of no cointegration. This is why one of the proclaimed virtues of this test is that it is "discerning" in its ability to reject a "false" null hypothesis, which is really odd. If we know that the null hypothesis is false, why do we test it to start with? And does this mean that a good test rejects the null more often than a bad test? What if the null is not false and it gets rejected? What has happened to the distinction between Type I and Type II errors? I recall having a conversation with a friend who had just used the Johansen test in his work. When I expressed

hostility towards the test because it invariably rejects the null of no cointegration, he told me that he had failed to reject the null even by using the
Johansen test. I was truly flabbergasted, telling him that what he did was
unheard of. The fact of the matter is that the null of no cointegration
should not be rejected too often because cointegration is supposed to be a
rare occurrence.

The Bounds Test

Yet another test for cointegration is the bounds test of Pesaran and Shin
(1995, 1996) and Pesaran et al. (2001), which is designed to find out if a
long-run relation is present in a group of time series, some of which may be
stationary while others are not (see also Pesaran and Pesaran, 2009). Also
known as the ARDL approach to cointegration, the test has a number of
features: (1) it can be used with a mixture of I(0) and I(1) variables; (2)
it involves a single-equation set-up, making it simple to implement and
interpret; and (3) different variables can be assigned different lag-lengths as
they enter the model. At one time we were told that a necessary but not sufficient condition for cointegration is that the variables must be integrated
of the same order, typically I(1). Now we are told that cointegration can be
found in a system comprising I(1) and I(0) variables. Two test statistics are
used in conjunction with this test (F and W), each of which has upper and
lower critical values. A finding of cointegration is established when the test
statistics are above the upper limit.

Error Correction Models

Once any of the tests shows that cointegration is present, the corresponding
dynamic relation should be represented by an error correction model, which
combines short-term dynamics (as represented by first differences) and
deviations from the long-run equilibrium relation (as represented by the
error correction term). The error correction model corresponding to (8.1) is

$$\Delta y_t = \sum_{i=1}^{k} \alpha_i \Delta y_{t-i} + \sum_{i=0}^{k} \beta_i \Delta x_{t-i} + \phi \varepsilon_{t-1} + u_t \qquad (8.2)$$

where the coefficient on the error correction term measures the speed of
adjustment towards the long-run relation or the rate at which the deviation
is eliminated. For a valid error correction model, the coefficient on the
error correction term (ϕ) must be significantly negative.

Granger's representation theorem (Engle and Granger, 1987) states that
cointegration implies and is implied by a valid error correction model.
With respect to equations (8.1) and (8.2), if $\varepsilon_t \sim I(0)$, then ϕ should be

significantly negative and vice versa. This means that it is possible to identify cointegration by finding a valid error correction model, in which case
the null of no cointegration is $H_0 : \phi = 0$ against the alternative $H_1 : \phi < 0$.
The t test is preferred to the conventional residual-based approach (using
the DF as the test statistic). Kremers et al. (1992) contend that a cointegration test involving the application of the DF unit root test (or similar
tests) to the residuals of the cointegrating regression may not reject the null
hypothesis of no cointegration when the coefficient on the error correction
term may be statistically significant. They suggest that this conflict arises
because of the implied common factor restriction that is imposed when the
DF statistic is used to test for cointegration. If this restriction is invalid, the
DF test remains consistent but it loses power relative to cointegration tests
that do not impose a common factor restriction, such as the test based on
the coefficient of the EC term.

One issue with the cointegration test based on the significance of ϕ is
what critical values are used to determine significance. In the error correction model represented by equation (8.2) all of the variables are stationary
because they are either the first differences of I(1) variables or the lagged
residual of the cointegrating regression, which is stationary under cointegration. Hence, one would tend to think that ϕ is statistically significant if
its t statistic is greater in absolute terms than the 5 per cent critical value
of the t distribution, which is around 2. After all, a significantly negative ϕ
implies mean reversion. It is not clear, therefore, why higher critical values
of the t statistic should be used with this test. Just to make things easier, a
critical value of 2 is used in the illustration presented later, not that it would
make any difference to the inevitable conclusion that the results of various
cointegration tests produce inconsistent results.

From Cointegration to Causality

Causality testing was popularized by Granger (1969). While the test was
initially based on a straight first difference model, the advent of cointegration analysis led to a rethink of causality testing. If the variables are cointegrated then the test should be based on an error correction model because
the first difference model would be misspecified. If this is the case, causality should be detected in at least one direction, from x to y or vice versa.
The model used to test for causality in the presence of cointegration is:

$$\Delta y_t = \sum_{i=1}^{k} \alpha_i \Delta y_{t-i} + \sum_{i=1}^{k} \beta_i \Delta x_{t-i} + \phi \varepsilon_{t-1} + u_t \qquad (8.3)$$

which is the same as equation (8.2) except that the contemporaneous term
Δx_t is deleted. This is because causality in economics and finance is not

really causality (as it is in physics). It is effectively temporal ordering –
something causes something else because the first something occurs
before the other. Therefore, the results of causality testing mean nothing.
Furthermore, for x to be judged to affect y, x must be exogenous, which
is hardly the case in most applications (for example, purchasing power
parity). Yet another problem is that the test results are sensitive to the
choice of the lag structure (the value of k), which induces scope for
manipulating the model to obtain the desired results. Last, but not least, if
the variables are related contemporaneously (and they are likely to be so,
particularly with low-frequency data), equation (8.3) must be misspecified.

8.3   CORRELATION AND COINTEGRATION

There seems to be some confusion about the difference between cointegration and correlation, which has been brought about by the advent of
cointegration analysis. It has been suggested that cointegration tells a
different story from that told by correlation. For example, Chan (2006)
distinguishes between the two concepts by using the co-movements of two
theoretically constructed stock prices. He argues that the two prices are
correlated if they rise and fall "in synchrony", whereas they are cointegrated if they do not "wander off in opposite directions for very long
without coming back to a mean distance eventually". By "synchrony", it
is meant that prices rise and fall together on a daily, weekly or monthly
basis. It follows, therefore, that the spread between two cointegrated prices
is mean reverting while the spread between two perfectly correlated prices
is constant. But this is misleading because "synchrony" implies perfect
correlation, which can never be the case in practice. This also means that
perfectly or highly correlated prices are necessarily cointegrated because a
constant spread is by definition stationary. Does this also mean that negatively correlated variables cannot be cointegrated as Chan (2006) argues
explicitly?

Alexander (1999) contends that "high correlation does not necessarily
imply high cointegration in prices" (not sure what "high cointegration"
means). She shows a graph of the German mark and Dutch guilder over
the period 1975–1985, arguing that "they appear to be cointegrated". Then
she adds a very small daily incremental return to the guilder, suggesting
that "the series are still highly correlated but not cointegrated". However,
this addition of incremental return affects both cointegration and correlation, to the extent that the more the two variables drift apart the less
correlated they become.

Prices or Returns

A completely different but nonsensical distinction between correlation
and cointegration is that correlation is about co-movement of stationary
variables whereas cointegration is about the co-movement of nonstationary variables. So, it is correlation of stock returns but cointegration of
stock prices. The underlying rationale is that the variance and covariance
for nonstationary variables are not well defined, which means that the
correlation of nonstationary variables is meaningless. In an answer to
a question posted on the website of Quantitative Finance (http://quant.
stackexchange.com), it is claimed that correlation between two I(1) variables depends on time, which is "not nice". However, the argument goes,
"if for example we have highly correlated stationary processes knowing
the fact that the correlation does not depend on time we can forecast
one process with high accuracy knowing the values of the other". This is
bizarre, because there is no reason why correlation between nonstationary series is time-invariant while it is time-variant between nonstationary
series.

It is also nonsense to claim that we can only talk about correlation
of returns, not correlation of prices. In the hedging literature, the hedge
ratio is calculated from a model expressed in first differences (returns) or
the levels of prices, where hedging effectiveness depends on correlation
between returns in the first case and prices in the second. The choice of
the model depends on whether the objective of the hedger is to stabilize
the price of or the return on the unhedged position. In most practical
applications, the objective of the hedger is to stabilize prices rather than
percentage changes in prices. For example, airlines use futures contracts to
stabilize the price of jet fuel; farmers hedge to stabilize the prices of their
crops, and import–export firms hedge to stabilize the streams of import
expenditure and export earnings, which depend on the levels of exchange
rates. In Chapter 10 it will be demonstrated that correlation matters more
than cointegration for hedging effectiveness. In any case, high correlation
in prices implies high correlation in returns (percentage changes). What is
called a fact of knowing that correlation of returns does not depend on
time is in fact not a fact, but rather an empirical issue. Whether or not correlation depends on time can be determined on a case-by-case basis and
only by examining the data.

The Role of the Time Horizon

Yet another explanation for the difference between correlation and cointegration can be found on http://gekkoquant.com. According to this view:

Correlation – If two stocks are correlated then if stock A has an upday then stock B will have an upday. . . . Cointegration – If two stocks are cointegrated then it is possible to form a stationary pair from some linear combination of stock A and B.

This is nonsense for at least two reasons. The first is that this description implies that correlation can only be positive (upday and upday). Does this mean that correlation is found in daily data only? The second reason is that if two series are highly correlated the difference between them will not only be stationary but also constant – this is "super-cointegration" if such a term exists. This distinction means that two correlated stock prices move together over one day (presumably between opening and closing). In other words, the condition for correlation between P_A and P_B is that when $P_{A,C} - P_{A,O} > 0$ then $P_{B,C} - P_{B,O} > 0$ where C and O indicate the closing and opening prices respectively. Cointegration, on the other hand, means that $\alpha P_A + \beta P_B \sim I(0)$, even though prices can go in opposite directions. If, for example, $\alpha = 1$ and $\beta = -1$, the condition for cointegration becomes $P_A - P_B \sim I(0)$, which means that the difference between the two prices should be a stationary mean-reverting process. If prices wander away from each other, the difference becomes bigger over time and for mean reversion this difference must be narrowed, which requires the two prices to move in the same direction. It follows that the process of mean reversion requires correlation. The question that no one seems to ask is whether or not two highly correlated series are not cointegrated – that is, whether or not correlation is incompatible with cointegration.

Correlation, according to this view, is present when two prices end up over a period of time, which may be one day, as some would suggest, and one week or one month, according to others. Even if the underlying time period is one day, price movements may be unrelated on an intra-day basis. Figure 8.1 shows the movements of two highly correlated and two uncorrelated series over a period of time that can be a day, a week or a month. The uncorrelated series are both up by the end of the period, satisfying the condition that when $P_{A,C} - P_{A,O} > 0$ then $P_{B,C} - P_{B,O} > 0$. In the case of the highly correlated series, one of them closes up while the other closes down. Thus correlation is not about whether or not they both close up at the end of the period but rather about how they move throughout the period, be it a day, a week or a month. And when they move together, or even in opposite directions (that is, whether they are correlated positively or negatively), they will produce a stationary linear combination, which means that they are cointegrated. In Figure 8.2, we observe correlation between the percentage changes in the series shown in Figure 8.1: high correlation in levels implies high correlation in first differences. We

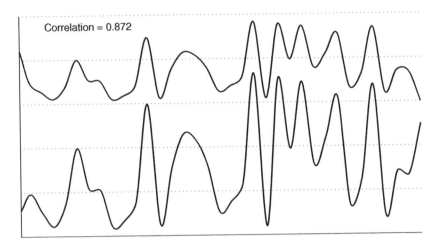

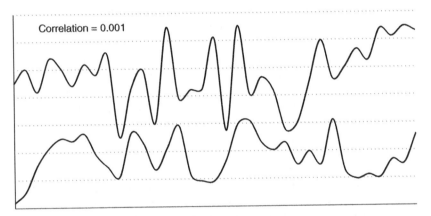

Figure 8.1   Highly correlated and uncorrelated series

cannot talk about correlation in returns only as if it is not related to correlation in prices.

More Twists

Another twist to the difference between correlation and cointegration is
that correlated stock prices move in the same direction most of the time
but the magnitude of the moves is unknown, which means that the spread
can keep growing and growing, showing no sign of mean reversion. In the
case of cointegration, on the other hand, the spread is "fixed" and if it

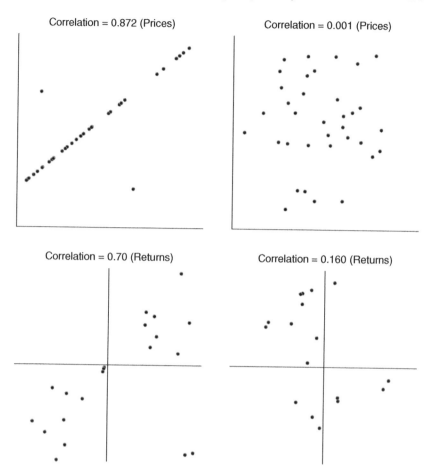

Figure 8.2   Correlation in levels and percentage changes

deviates from the "fixing" then it will mean revert. It is not clear what is meant by "the magnitude of moves is unknown", most likely that prices drift apart by an unknown amount. Does this mean that if two prices are highly correlated, they can drift from each other without bounds? The question that should be asked here is the following: is it possible for two highly correlated variables not to be cointegrated, and vice versa? If the answer to this question is in the negative, then this means that correlation is correlated with cointegration. This is an easily implementable testable hypothesis.

Yet another distinction between correlation and cointegration is the following. Correlation is used to check for the linear relation (or linear interdependence) between two variables while cointegration is used to check for the existence of a long-run relation between two or more variables. Whoever wrote this did not bother to think if it made any sense because it does not. The comparison here is between "linear" and "long-term", but the long-term relation (the "attractor") is typically taken to be linear as in equation (8.1). Comparison should be between linear and nonlinear or between short-term and long-term.

Results Based on Simulated Data

The propositions presented in this section about the distinction between correlation and cointegration can be examined empirically by using down-to-earth statistics. In this chapter we use simulated series while actual time series of economic and financial variables will be used in Chapter 9. It has already been demonstrated, by using simulated time series, that a particular description of the difference between correlation and cointegration is not valid and that correlation in levels is related to correlation in percentage changes. In what follows we examine the implied proposition that negatively correlated series cannot be cointegrated and that correlation is not related to cointegration.

The distinction between cointegration and correlation as described by Chan (2006) and Alexander (1999) seems to suggest that two negatively correlated variables cannot be cointegrated because they do not move "in synchrony", they drift apart from each other, and they move in opposite directions. Moosa (2011b) uses two time series that are negatively correlated by construction (the correlation coefficient is -0.99). The two variables drift apart, hence they cannot be cointegrated according to the descriptions of cointegration put forward by Chan and Alexander. Yet, by running a cointegrating regression and applying the Dickey–Fuller test to the residuals of the regression, the results show that ADF = -5.59, which is statistically significant. Hence, two variables that drift apart from each other are cointegrated. There is no need to repeat this exercise here.

Now we deal with the question if two highly correlated series are not cointegrated, and vice versa. For this purpose time series are generated with correlations ranging between 0.01 and 0.99. Regressions are run pair-wise to calculate the coefficient of determination (R^2), the Dickey–Fuller statistic (ADF) and the cointegrating regression Durbin–Watson statistic (CRDW). The results are presented graphically in Figure 8.3, which comprises scatter diagrams of the ADF on R^2 and CRDW on R^2. The horizontal lines represent the 5 per cent critical value of the ADF (without the negative sign) and the 1 per cent critical

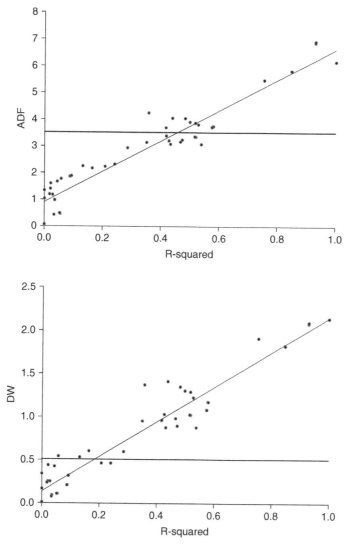

Figure 8.3   Correlation versus cointegration

value of the CRDW. Obviously, the higher the R^2 the more likely that the two variables are cointegrated. In terms of the ADF, we cannot see cointegration between two variables with a correlation of less than 0.61. Correlation and cointegration are correlated. It is not obvious what value is provided by cointegration over and above what is provided by correlation. It is correlation versus causation, not correlation versus cointegration.

8.4   COINTEGRATION AS A TEST FOR SPURIOUS CORRELATION

In the previous section it was stated that artificial distinction between cointegration and correlation is sometimes proclaimed on the grounds that cointegration is about the comovements of variables in levels (prices) whereas correlation is about comovements of variables in first differences or percentage changes (returns). If that were true, there would be no such thing as spurious correlation which is correlation between two I(1) variables that are not related by a genuine relation.

One of the proclaimed contributions of the "cointegration revolution" to the arsenal of tools used by economists to conduct empirical research is that cointegration testing can be used to reveal spurious correlation – that is, cointegration allows us to distinguish between spurious relations and genuine ones. Burns (1997) defines a spurious relation as a "situation in which measures of two or more variables are statistically related but are not in fact causally linked". It follows from this definition that what matters is causation versus correlation, not correlation versus cointegration.

Spurious correlation is believed to have been a reason for the development of cointegration analysis. The underlying proposition is that if two integrated variables are highly correlated, this correlation is spurious unless the two variables are cointegrated. However, one would tend to think that distinguishing between a spurious relation and a genuine one should be based on common sense, intuition and theory, not on test statistics. A problem that arises here is the following: if common sense tells us that a relation between two variables is obviously spurious but the two variables are cointegrated, do we believe common sense or econometrics? If cointegration testing is as good as it is portrayed to be in detecting spurious correlation, it should be consistent with common sense.

Let $y_{1,t} = \varphi_1 y_{1,t-1} + \varepsilon_{1,t}$ and $y_{2,t} = \varphi_2 y_{2,t-1} + \varepsilon_{2,t}$ where $\varepsilon_{1,t} \sim N(0,\sigma^2_{\varepsilon 1})$ and $\varepsilon_{2,t} \sim N(0,\sigma^2_{\varepsilon 2})$ such that $\varepsilon_{1,t}$ and $\varepsilon_{2,t}$ are independent. When $\varphi_1 = \varphi_2 = 1$, both $y_{1,t}$ and $y_{2,t}$ are random walk processes. If this is the case, the null $\beta_1 = 0$ in the regression $y_{1,t} = \beta_0 + \beta_1 y_{2,t} + \zeta_t$ is unlikely to be rejected even if no causal relation exists. If cointegration precludes spurious relations, this means that if $y_{1,t} \sim I(1)$ and $y_{2,t} \sim I(1)$, then a genuine relation is indicated by the stationarity of the residual of the cointegrating regression. In other words, if $\zeta_t \sim I(0)$ the relation is genuine and if $\zeta_t \sim I(1)$, the relation is spurious even if $y_{1,t}$ and $y_{2,t}$ are highly correlated.

The ability of cointegration to reveal spurious relations seems to be accepted without scrutiny. For example, Stroe-Kunold and Werner (2009) suggest that "cointegration tests are instruments to detect spurious correlations between integrated time series". They demonstrate that the Dickey–Fuller and Johansen tests provide a "much more accurate alternative for the identification of spurious relations compared to the rather imprecise method of utilizing the R^2 and DW statistics". They go further to argue that cointegration provides "precise methods of distinguishing between spurious and meaningful relations even if the dependency between the processes [that is, correlation] is very low". Lin and Brannigan (2003) suggest that "cointegration models can be regarded as remedies to the problems of 'spurious regression' arising from nonstationary time series". They go as far as arguing that spurious regression and cointegration are opposite concepts as cointegration implies a meaningful relation between integrated time series.

One of the few economists who challenged the cointegration orthodoxy is Guisan (2001) as she argues that "cointegration tests fail very often to recognize causal relations and, on the other hand, that approach does not always avoid the peril of accepting as causal relations those that really are spurious". She demonstrates the inadequacy and limitations of cointegration by examining the relation between private consumption expenditure and gross domestic product in 25 OECD countries over the period 1961–1997. Her results confirm the limitations of cointegration tests, showing that UK consumption is not related to its GDP but rather to the GDPs of 23 other OECD countries. Cointegration, therefore, can lead to a rejection of genuine relations and the acceptance of spurious ones.

To test this proposition, Moosa (2016a) examines cases of highly-correlated variables that are spuriously related as dictated by common sense. He concludes that if cointegration, as it is claimed, is a reliable test for spurious correlation, then the results tell us the following: (1) margarine is bad for marital life; (2) ski resorts must design their beds in such a way as to make it easier for guests to die by becoming entangled in bed sheets because that will boost their revenue; (3) to boost revenue, arcades must campaign so that Australia does not reduce the price of uranium exported to the US; (4) motorcycle riders must, for their own safety, refrain from eating sour cream and encourage other people to do so; (5) to reduce suicide, US universities must discourage graduate students from doing PhDs in mathematics and encourage them to convert to marketing or something else; and (6) another way to reduce suicide is for the US government to close down NASA. The results show that cointegration is not a reliable test for spurious correlation, which can only be identified by common sense (or more formally by theoretical reasoning). Furthermore,

Moosa demonstrates that cointegration testing may not pick up a genuine relation as implied by theory, using for this purpose the theory of the term structure of interest rates (long-term and short-term US interest rates are not cointegrated).

Some Results

In this exercise four cases of conspicuous spurious correlation are examined to find out if the underlying variables are cointegrated. In two cases correlation is positive while in the other two cases correlation is negative, as shown in Figure 8.4. Five cointegration tests are used: ADF, CRDW, $t(\phi)$,

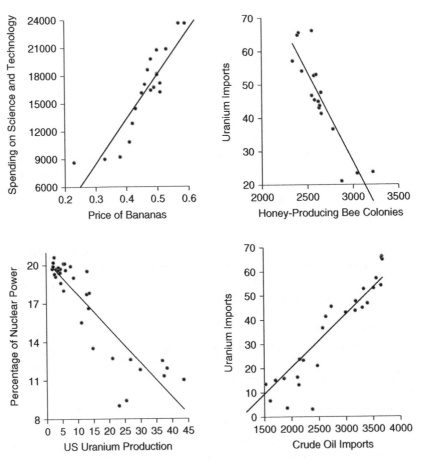

Figure 8.4   Four cases of spurious correlation

Table 8.1   Cointegration testing of spurious relations

Variable 1	Variable 2	Corr.	ADF	CRDW	$t(\phi)$	F	W
Price of Bananas	Spending on Science and Technology	0.91	−3.06	1.13*	−4.58*	11.85*	23.71*
Honey-Producing Bee Colonies	Uranium Imports	0.91	−2.55	0.90*	−2.52*	2.24	4.49
US Uranium Production	Percentage of Nuclear Power	0.89	−4.60*	0.58*	−2.17*	1.43	2.86
Crude Oil Imports	Uranium Imports	0.92	−3.28	0.76*	−2.76*	4.93	9.86

Note: * Significant at the 5% level.

F and W. Since these cases are obviously of spurious correlation, no test should indicate the rejection of the null of no cointegration. The Johansen test is not used because it always rejects the null of no cointegration. The four cases and the test statistics are shown in Table 8.1, where at least two test statistics reject the null of no cointegration. An interesting policy conclusion that can be derived from these results is that to boost the number of honey-producing bee colonies, the imports of uranium must be cut back. It is wiser in this case to follow common sense rather than the results of cointegration testing.

8.5   LINEAR VERSUS NONLINEAR ATTRACTORS

Equation (8.1), which represents the cointegrating regression (also called the long-run equilibrium condition or the attractor), is obviously linear. Failure to find cointegration may be due to the assumption of a linear attractor when the attractor is nonlinear. This is like trying to fit a straight line to data generated from an experiment to test Boyle's law where the pressure exerted on a gas is changed to record the effect on the volume of gas. A straight line does not fit very well. Naturally the comparison here is inappropriate because the observations obtained from an experiment are recorded after controlling other factors such as temperature. In economics and finance, observations on the association of two variables are not the result of one of the variables affecting the other but rather all other factors exerting an influence. Let us, for the sake of argument, suspend disbelief and assume that economics is like physics. In Figure 8.5, we observe a set

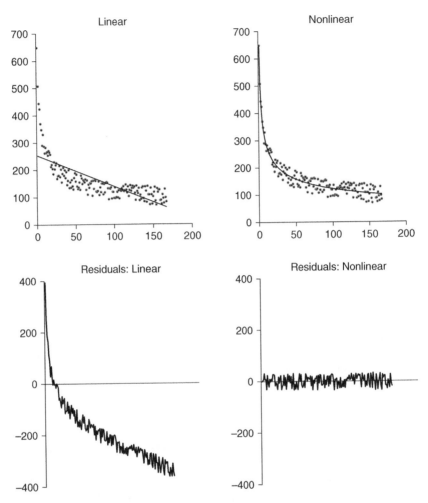

Figure 8.5   Residuals resulting from linear and nonlinear attractors

of simulated data relating two variables, with both linear and nonlinear attractors. Only when a nonlinear attractor is used do we get stationary residuals. Hence the two variables are cointegrated with a nonlinear attractor.

Moosa and Ma (2017) use simulated data to demonstrate that as we move from a linear attractor to a polynomial of higher order, the residuals become increasingly more stationary. In theory, a polynomial of sufficiently high order can be fit perfectly to a particular set of points. Before reaching the stage of a perfect fit we could have a polynomial of a sufficiently high order that can be fit to produce stationary residuals. It is therefore always possible to find a nonlinear attractor that produces stationary residuals and hence cointegration. It is true that the critical values of the Dickey–Fuller and other cointegration test statistics may not be valid in this case, but a visual inspection of the residuals tells us that as the order of the polynomial becomes greater, the residuals become more stationary. In this case, we may get cointegration without correlation, but what is the benefit of that? If a polynomial of a sufficiently high order gives stationary residuals while a polynomial of higher order gives zero residuals (perfect fit), we should choose the perfect fit in preference to cointegration. In econometrics we seem to pay more attention to cointegration than to the goodness of fit. In physics they do not even use the concept of cointegration but they care about a good or perfect fit. While econometricians pay attention to stationary residuals, physicists are only satisfied by zero residuals – this is when a law is called a law.

Consider Figure 8.6, which is basically a scatter plot of two variables with a correlation coefficient of -0.06. The linear attractor looks like a horizontal line with the equation $y = 10.81$ – in fact there is no attractor as x is independent of y. The null of no cointegration cannot be rejected with an insignificant ADF. Try, on the other hand, a nonlinear attractor in the form of a polynomial of order 6. In this case the null of no cointegration is rejected with an ADF of -6.24. Yes, it may be that the critical value of the ADF is not valid here but when a polynomial of order 6 is used, the residuals become smaller and more stationary – it is therefore a better attractor. In the extreme case, a polynomial of order 21 fits perfectly, passing through every point. Zero residuals are perfectly stationary residuals. If anything, econometricians should be like physicists, looking for goodness of fit or small residuals rather than stationary but big residuals.

8.6 CONCLUSION

Since the mid-1980s we have been told, and we have been telling our students, that cointegration analysis has been developed to save humanity from the faulty analysis of the previous hundred years resulting from inference based on regressions involving nonstationary variables. The first thing we were told, which we have been telling students, is that cointegration testing can be used to distinguish between spurious and genuine correlation. We have since pledged allegiance to cointegration to the extent that we started believing that margarine causes divorce and NASA causes suicide. We have surrendered our ability to think logically to obey the results produced by cointegration: if a cointegration test says that a

Linear

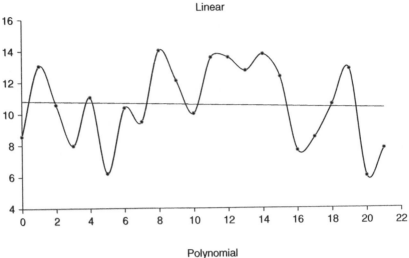

Polynomial

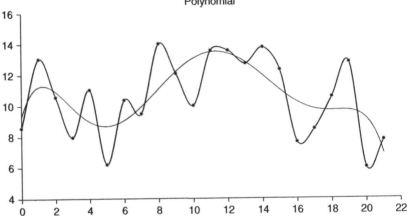

Figure 8.6   Linear and polynomial attractors

relation is not spurious, then it is not spurious, even if logic and common sense tell us otherwise.

We have been indoctrinated by the establishment that cointegration is a revolution that supersedes correlation, when in fact cointegration tells us nothing over and above what we know from correlation. The fact of the matter is that correlation does not tell us anything about causation, but cointegration fares no better than correlation when it comes to detecting the direction of causation. Econometric causality testing is a joke because if something happens before something else that does not mean that it causes it. Adjusting the causality test to take account of cointegration makes no difference. We seem to have overlooked the fact that instead of talking about correlation versus causation, we got into the habit of talking about correlation versus cointegration. In economics, causality and the direction thereof can only be determined logically in terms of economic theory, not by putting numbers in a computer and believing whatever the computer tells us, as instructed by software written by econometricians.

The true believers have been telling us that cointegration is different from correlation, which is why we should not talk about price correlation – it has to be return correlation and price cointegration. Obsession with making a distinction between correlation and cointegration has produced some bizarre propositions. We have also been told that cointegration implies and is implied by error correction but this is a source of embarrassment in the classroom when you try to show that by using actual data. The justification coming from the true believers is that the test has a low power, and this is why a valid error correction representation does not have a corresponding valid cointegrating regression.

The alternative cointegration tests available for use give totally different results, hence anything can be proved. If anything, cointegration has led to the proliferation of publications that are not worthy of the ink and paper used to print them. If you say something bad about cointegration in a paper, you will get a swift rejection. I recall that once I wrote a paper about the econometrics of the environmental Kuznets curve, the relation between environmental degradation and income per capita. In that paper I argued that the case for cointegration was overstated (and that is all I said), only to receive a rejection very quickly. It was obvious to me that the referee must have been a cointegration enthusiast, who said that the author (that is me) does not understand cointegration. Well, I suppose that anyone who is capable of solving a partial differential equation has no problem understanding cointegration.

9. Cointegration analysis: applications and illustrations

9.1 INTRODUCTION

Cointegration analysis has been used extensively in economics and finance. Harris (1995) argues that "cointegration has become an essential tool for applied economists wanting to estimate time series models" because "without some form of testing for cointegration, nonstationary variables can lead to spurious regressions". In Chapter 8 it was demonstrated that it is hazardous to use cointegration as a test for spurious correlation. For that purpose, simulated time series, as well as variables that are obviously spuriously correlated, were used to show that cointegration testing cannot be used to distinguish between spurious relations and genuine ones.

In this chapter economic and financial time series are used to demonstrate the unreliability of cointegration analysis and examine, with reference to economic data, some of the propositions put forward in Chapter 8 about the difference between cointegration and correlation. The specific issues and hypotheses dealt with in this chapter include market integration, pairs trading, purchasing power parity, covered interest parity and cointegrating relations in macroeconomics.

9.2 MARKET INTEGRATION AND RELATED ISSUES

Cointegration and causality have been used to investigate market interdependence and integration by, inter alia, Taylor and Tonks (1989), Mathur and Subrahmanyam (1990), Eun and Shin (1989), and Malliaris and Urrutia (1992). For example, Taylor and Tonks (1989) used cointegration analysis to examine the effect of the 1979 abolition of the UK exchange controls on the degree of integration of the British market with other markets (Germany, the Netherlands, Japan and the US). The results show that UK stock prices became cointegrated with other prices in the post-1979 period, which reduced the scope for diversification. Mathur and Subrahamanyam (1990) used causality testing to find out if the Nordic markets (of Denmark, Norway, Finland and Sweden) are integrated with that of the US. The results reveal that the US market affects the Danish market only and that the Norwegian, Danish and Finnish markets do not affect any of the other markets (naturally, no explanation is suggested for differences in the results). It is invariably the case that when several countries, currencies or whatever are examined using cointegration analysis, the results turn out to be all over the place. Typically, the results would show that A and B are cointegrated but A and C are not, and no one knows why because no one presents an explanation why. Theoretical and institutional considerations are ignored because all that matters is whether or not cointegration is found.

Eun and Shin (1989) estimated a nine-market VAR and detected a considerable amount of multilateral interaction and significant effect of US "innovations" on other markets. However, they also found that no single foreign market could explain the US market movements adequately. Malliaris and Urrutia (1992) investigated the lead-lag relations among six markets in diverse time zones for the period before, during and after the October 1987 crash. They concluded that the crash was probably an international crisis and that it might have begun simultaneously in all national stock markets. The implication of these results is that international diversification does not work when long positions are taken on a group of integrated markets, as shown by the results of cointegration.

Cointegration and Market Integration

The idea behind testing for cointegration between the stock prices of two countries is simple. The establishment of cointegration implies that the stock markets of the two countries are integrated (not in the econometric sense of the word), which means that international diversification involving these two markets is not effective in the sense that it does not reduce risk. Two flaws can be detected in this line of reasoning. First, the underlying assumption is that stock prices are positively correlated, which means that taking long positions on the two markets does not produce risk reduction. However, even if this is the case, diversification can be implemented by taking a short position on one market and a long position on the other. The second flaw is that the effectiveness of hedging depends on correlation, not on cointegration, which is contrary to the argument put forward by Alexander (1999).

Moosa (2011b) presents an illustration based on quarterly stock price data from a diverse set of countries over the period 2001–2010. He tests the relation between each one of these markets and that of the US by subjecting the stock price time series to the following tests: the residual-based test (ADF), the Johansen test with two different lag lengths, the test based on the error correction term and causality testing from the US market to another market and vice versa. The illustration shows the following:

1. Judged by the ADF statistic and the Johansen test (with four lags), none of the markets is integrated with that of the US. By changing the lag length in the magical Johansen procedure to 12, all of the markets become integrated.
2. The test based on the t statistic of the coefficient on the error correction term shows that only four markets are integrated with that of the US: UK, New Zealand, South Africa and Kuwait.
3. Judged by the ADF statistic, the results tell us that there is no cointegration in any case, but the coefficient on the error correction term is significant in four cases, although Granger's representation theorem stipulates that it should be significant in none. The cointegrating regressions were run both ways, but that did not change the results.
4. As far as causality is concerned, the results show that the Singapore stock prices, which are not cointegrated with US stock prices, cause them – which is fine, because cointegration does not necessarily preclude causation. The problem is to explain why, out of all of these markets, only the Singapore market has an effect on the US market.
5. The only other case of causality is that the US market has an effect on that of South Africa but not on any of the others (again, why South Africa?). Out of the four cases that exhibit cointegration, the only case that produces unidirectional causality is that of South Africa. So much for the implications of cointegration for causality.
6. Hedging is effective (international diversification is useful) in two cases only: the UK and Canada, one of which shows cointegration while the other does not, according to the error correction test. Why these two markets? Because they exhibit the highest correlation with returns on the US market. Therefore, a simple concept like correlation leads to the right inference but the "sophisticated" tests of cointegration produce messy results that may lead to faulty financial decisions. The claim that what matters for hedging is cointegration, not correlation, is unfounded.

The finding that no market is cointegrated with the US market may be disappointing for those who want to show that markets should be integrated in the age of globalization. Based on the results of Moosa (2011b), if I accepted the proposition that cointegration has implications for the benefits or otherwise of international diversification, and if I wanted to prove a preconceived idea, I would do the following. I would report the results

of the ADF test if I thought that there was scope for international diversification, but I would report the results of the Johansen test with lag 12 if
I thought that international diversification was not effective. If I held the
view of sometimes/sometimes not and perhaps/perhaps not, I would report
the results based on the error correction test. But then how would I explain
the finding that the markets of Kuwait, South Africa and New Zealand are
integrated with the US market but those of Japan, Canada and Singapore
are not? It is simply embarrassing and even hazardous to derive inference
from any set of these results.

An Illustration

A similar exercise is conducted here by using monthly stock price indices
for 14 countries over the period January 2000 to December 2015 (obtained
from *International Financial Statistics*). Out of all possible combinations,
41 cases were chosen with a wide range of correlations to find out if correlation and cointegration go together. Testing for cointegration is based
on the following statistics: the DW statistic of the cointegrating regression
(CRDW), the ADF of the residuals of the cointegrating regression, the t
statistic of the coefficient on the error correction term, $t(\phi)$, and the F and
W statistics of the bounds test. Out of the 41 cases, only nine show cointegration as judged by at least one test statistic, as shown in Table 9.1 (the full
set of results is presented in the appendix to this chapter).

The first question that arises is what we are supposed to believe. The
markets of India and Canada are integrated (because their stock prices
are cointegrated) as judged by the t statistic but not according to the other
tests. On the other hand, the markets of France and Japan are integrated

Table 9.1   Cointegration according to at least one test

1	2	Corr.	CRDW	ADF	$t(\phi)$	F	W
Canada	India	0.91	0.14	−2.27	−2.25*	2.81	5.62
Canada	Malaysia	0.87	0.11	−2.39	−2.48*	3.07	6.15
Canada	Mauritius	0.88	0.13	−2.87	−2.23*	2.62	5.25
Canada	UK	0.86	0.07	−2.52	−2.42*	2.95	5.91
Denmark	New Zealand	0.92	0.12	−3.86*	−2.56*	3.43	6.87
Denmark	US	0.92	0.14	−3.83*	−3.14*	5.58	11.16
France	Japan	0.87	0.10	−3.78*	−2.39*	3.44	6.89
Germany	UK	0.93	0.02	−2.63	−3.37*	6.69*	13.99*
UK	US	0.90	0.02	−2.47	−2.51*	3.90	7.80

Note: * Significant at the 5% level.

as judged by the ADF and t test but not by the other three. Naturally, explaining the results in economic terms is almost impossible. Why would the Canadian market be integrated with the markets of India, Malaysia and Mauritius but (strangely) not with the US market? Why is it that the French market is not integrated with the German market but it is integrated with the Japanese market? Why is it that the Indian market is not integrated with the markets of Malaysia and Mauritius and that the market of Malaysia is not integrated with the Japanese market? It is any-body's guess.

Granger and Newbold (1974) suggested that a spurious regression is characterized by a high R^2 and a low DW statistic. Phillips (1986) argues that low values of DW and moderate values of R^2 indicate spurious regression, which means that a high value of R^2 should not, on the basis of traditional tests, be regarded as evidence for a significant relation. Banerjee et al. (1993) argue that a spurious regression is present when $R^2 > DW$. If this is true then the regressions listed in the Appendix Table 9A.1 are spurious because, with a few exceptions, $R^2 > DW$. So, are stock price indices cointegrated, correlated or spuriously correlated?

Introducing Johansen

If the Johansen test is used, then the sky is the limit, as anything can be proved. For this purpose we choose stock price indices that are cointe-grated according to at least one of the tests already used and some that are not. In all cases it can be shown that the two price series are cointegrated or not cointegrated. The procedure gives several possibilities for model specification by taking combinations of no trend, restricted trend and unrestricted trend as well as no intercept, restricted intercept and no inter-cept. Once a combination of the intercept and trend has been selected, the model can be modified further by changing the lag length. So we start with a basic specification (with respect to the intercept and trend) and a lag of one, then we change the lag progressively to report the results of the alter-native specification. Two test statistics are used: the maximum eigenvalue (EV) and the trace statistics.

The results, which are very interesting, are reported in Table 9.2. No case of cointegration is obtained by using the basic specification, but by manipulating the lag length, cointegration is found to be present in all cases. This is why the Johansen test is a life-saver for those subject to confirmation bias. Some would say that the optimal lag length has to be determined by using one of the information criteria. This is easy because it is always possible to find a criterion that supports the selection of the lag. Otherwise, another procedure can be used to select the lag length such

Table 9.2   Results of the Johansen test

1	2	3	EV		Trace	
			Basic	Alternative	Basic	Alternative
Canada	India		13.21	19.90	16.99	25.57
Canada	Mauritius		11.62	21.47	14.62	26.20
Denmark	US		11.12	22.43	14.09	28.39
Germany	UK		13.73	21.33	19.43	28.12
Australia	Canada		11.60	21.20	15.05	27.44
Australia	New Zealand		6.85	19.98	6.95	20.05
India	Malaysia		8.63	18.6	12.34	25.01
India	New Zealand		12.32	19.36	12.79	20.16
France	India		9.03	18.54	11.17	25.84
France	Malaysia		7.59	19.09	9.89	27.97
Japan	Mauritius		14.42	23.6	15.77	24.96
China	Japan	Malaysia	18.68	27.84	35.44	49.04
Egypt	India	Mauritius	14.30	26.69	19.20	37.59
France	Mauritius	New Zealand	24.79	39.76	30.82	47.78
Canada	India	Egypt	13.38	27.75	21.46	42.61
Australia	New Zealand	UK	11.04	29.18	17.84	43.21
Australia	Egypt	Mauritius	21.28	24.57	37.93	40.13

Notes: The 5% critical values are as follows: eigenvalue EV = 18.33 and 24.35 for two and three countries, respectively; Trace = 23.83 and 39.33 for two and three countries, respectively.

as the general-to-specific methodology or the lag needed to obtain white noise residuals. In any case, no one mentions how the lag length is selected in published papers – the results are reported for a lag length that gives "good" results.

The picture becomes more interesting when the test is conducted on three or more markets. For example, it can be seen that the Australian, Egyptian and Mauritian stock prices form a cointegrating vector, and the same is true of Canada, India and Egypt. What does a cointegrating vector mean here? And what is the connection between these markets? Of course we can always claim that these markets do not form a cointegrating vector by choosing the results derived from the basic specification. Conversely, we can choose the alternative specification to claim that the markets of Australia, New Zealand and the UK form a cointegrating vector, because this is more plausible. We can get the results we wish.

Cointegration and Correlation

Next we consider the relation between cointegration and correlation.
In Figure 9.1, we observe scatter diagrams of three cointegration test

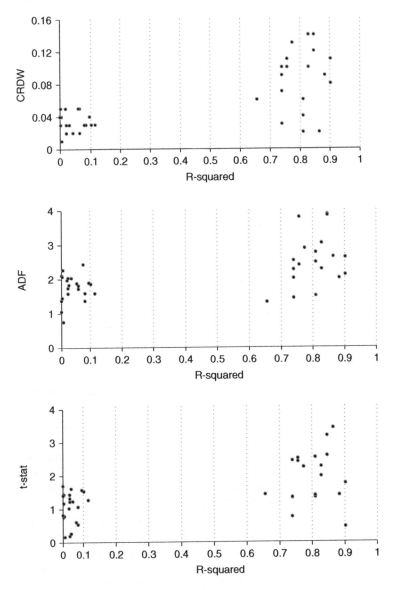

Figure 9.1   Cointegration statistics against R-squared

statistics (CRDW, ADF and the t statistic) and the coefficient of determination (the square of the correlation coefficient). Irrespective of the cointegration test statistic, we observe two clusters of points in the scatter diagrams: a cluster in the high correlation range and another cluster in the low correlation range. We can see that high values of the cointegration test statistics are associated with high correlations, and vice versa. High correlation, it seems, is at least a necessary condition for cointegration – that is, cointegration is correlated with correlation. It is for this reason that cointegration cannot and should not be used as a test for spurious correlation.

Stock Prices and Returns

We can use the same set of data on stock price indices to examine two propositions that were presented in Chapter 8 about correlation between stock prices and returns. The two propositions are (1) correlation of price is time dependent but correlation of returns is not, and (2) it is easier to forecast returns than prices. For this purpose, four pairs of stock prices indices are used: Australia–Canada, India–Malaysia, New Zealand–UK, and Mauritius–US. For each pair (say A and B) rolling regressions are run as follows. For a sample of n observations on P_A and P_B, the regression takes the form:

$$P_{A,t} = \alpha + \beta P_{B,t} + \varepsilon_t \qquad (9.1)$$

The regression is estimated over the sub-sample $t = 1,2,\ldots,k$, where $k < n$. Then it is estimated successively over the sub-samples $t = 2,3,\ldots,k,k+1$, $t = 3,4,\ldots,k+1,k+2$, and so on. The slope coefficient β is related to the correlation coefficient (r) between the two prices because:

$$\beta = \frac{r(\sigma_A \sigma_B)}{\sigma_A^2} \qquad (9.2)$$

where σ_A is the standard deviation of P_A, σ_B is the standard deviation of P_B and σ^2_A is the variance of P_A. The process is repeated for the returns measured as the percentage changes in prices.

The results are reported in Table 9.3 for the four price pairs, including the mean value of the slope coefficient, its standard deviation and the coefficient of variation, which is a measure of time dependence. We can see that the coefficient of variation of the slope coefficient is slightly higher for prices than for returns, but the results also show that return correlations are far away from being time-invariant. In one case, Mauritius–US, correlation of returns is more time dependent than correlation of prices.

As far as forecasting is concerned, one-step ahead forecasts are generated

Table 9.3   Rolling regression slope coefficients

1	2	Correlation	Mean	SD	CV (%)
Prices					
Australia	Canada	0.91	0.97	0.19	19.96
India	Malaysia	0.95	1.14	0.35	30.94
New Zealand	UK	0.77	1.10	0.53	48.01
Mauritius	US	0.67	0.72	0.43	59.65
Returns					
Australia	Canada	0.68	0.71	0.12	16.64
India	Malaysia	0.51	0.99	0.27	26.79
New Zealand	UK	0.39	0.33	0.15	45.05
Mauritius	US	0.36	0.49	0.31	62.77

from recursive regressions to calculate, as a measure of forecasting accuracy, the range of the ratio of the forecasting error to its standard deviation. The actual and forecast values for prices and returns are shown in Figures 9.2 and 9.3, respectively. Table 9.4 displays the minimum and maximum values of the ratio of the error to its standard deviation, showing no evidence that it is easier to forecast returns than prices.

Causality Testing

The last exercise that is conducted on the data sample of stock price indices is causality. Table 9.5 reports the results of testing for causality from one market to another, and vice versa, when the prices are cointegrated, including the F statistic for the null of no causality and the associated p-value. The results are all over the place, as this is what we find: (1) Canadian prices cause Indian prices, but not vice versa; (2) Danish prices cause Canadian prices, and vice versa; and (3) Canadian prices cause Mauritian prices, but not vice versa. No causality is found in any other case, not even between the UK and Germany or between the UK and US. What is the connection between Canada and Mauritius to find causality in this case? And what about the proposition that if two variables are cointegrated then causality should exist in at least one direction? Testing causality by using an error correction model when the prices are cointegrated produces no qualitative difference. In Table 9.6, which reports causality in the absence of cointegration, we find causality between New Zealand and Australia (which makes sense), India and Malaysia (which is reasonable) and Malaysia and France (which is unreasonable).

We must remember that causality in economics is not causality but

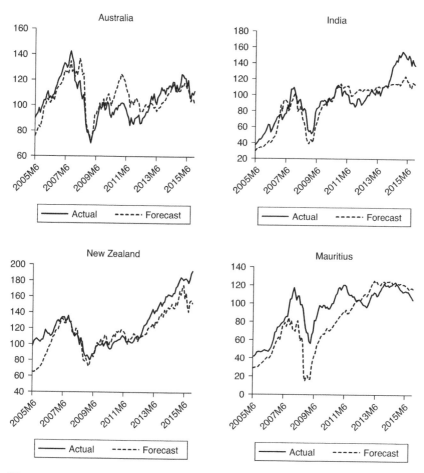

Figure 9.2 Actual and forecast prices

rather temporal ordering. But the mere fact that something happens before something else does not mean that the first something causes the second something. The use of monthly data may be inappropriate but so is the use of daily data because the effect is supposed to happen very quickly.

9.3 PAIRS TRADING

One of the applications of cointegration in finance is an investment strategy known as "pairs trading". The underlying idea is that the spread between (or ratio of) two cointegrated stock prices may widen temporarily,

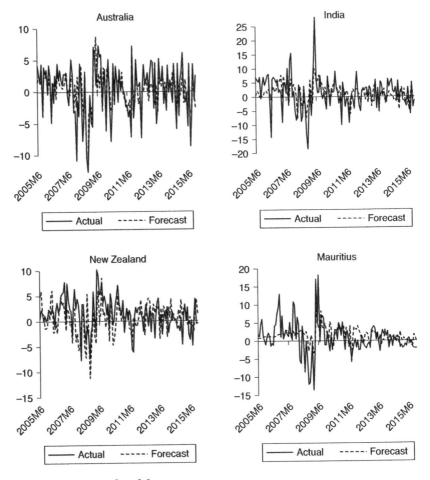

Figure 9.3   Actual and forecast returns

which provides the opportunity to go short on one of the stocks and long
on the other, then exiting the two positions when the spread is back where
it should be – in other words, when the spread has gone through mean
reversion. Hence what matters is cointegration, not correlation, because
cointegration implies mean reversion.

Schmidt (2008) uses the Johansen test to identify stock pairs for this
strategy as applied to some stocks listed on the Australian Stock Exchange.
Based on the results, it is stated that "two cointegrated stocks can be combined in a certain linear combination so that the dynamics of the resulting
portfolio are governed by a stationary process". Without experimenting

Table 9.4   One-step rolling forecasts of prices and returns

1	2	Standard Deviation of Forecasting Error	Ratio to Standard Deviation	
			Min.	Max.
Prices				
Australia	Canada	9.07	−2.02	2.06
India	Malaysia	18.29	−1.15	2.89
New Zealand	UK	15.48	−0.68	3.99
Mauritius	US	60.44	−0.21	6.35
Returns				
Australia	Canada	2.79	−3.04	2.39
India	Malaysia	4.72	−3.41	4.04
New Zealand	UK	2.80	−2.22	2.14
Mauritius	US	3.95	−2.64	3.76

Table 9.5   Causality testing of cointegrated series

Countries	F	p-value
India→Canada	0.173	0.91
Canada→India	9.47*	0.00
Denmark→Canada	2.91*	0.04
Canada→Denmark	14.14*	0.00
Mauritius→Canada	2.04	0.11
Canada→Mauritius	10.51*	0.00
UK→Canada	1.64	0.50
Canada→UK	1.09	0.35
New Zealand→Denmark	2.04	0.11
Denmark→New Zealand	1.32	0.27
US→Denmark	1.59	0.19
Denmark→US	0.59	0.63
Japan→France	0.85	0.47
France→Japan	0.67	0.57
UK→Germany	1.49	0.217
Germany→UK	2.07	0.11
US→UK	1.99	0.12
UK→US	23.18*	0.00
India→Canada	0.15	0.92
Canada→India	9.58*	0.00
Denmark→Canada	2.87*	0.04
Canada→Denmark	12.51*	0.00

Note: * Significant at the 5% level.

Table 9.6   Causality testing of non-cointegrated series

Direction of Causality	F	p-value
Canada→Australia	0.69	0.56
Australia→Canada	0.41	0.74
New Zealand→Australia	0.94	0.42
Australia→New Zealand	22.24*	0.00
Malaysia→India	0.45	0.65
India→Malaysia	3.31*	0.02
New Zealand→India	1.45	0.23
India→New Zealand	0.46	0.71
India→France	1.67	0.17
India→France	2.46	0.06
Malaysia→France	3.76*	0.01
France→Malaysia	3.58*	0.02
Mauritius→Japan	0.56	0.64
Japan→Mauritius	2.04	0.11

Note: * Significant at the 5% level.

with a trading rule and based on plots of the residual series (showing a high rate of "zero crossings" and large deviations around the mean), she concludes that "this strategy would likely be profitable". I would imagine that it is typical to find that those suggesting these investment strategies are not willing to bet their own money on the predictions of cointegration-based tests. I would certainly not advise anyone to invest superannuation money by using a trading strategy based on the Johansen test.

Cointegration or Correlation

This description of pairs trading brings back the issue of distinction between correlation and cointegration, because other descriptions of carry trade are based on correlation and because high correlation (in prices) produces mean reversion. For example, Folger (2014) describes pairs trading without reference to cointegration as follows:

> Pairs trading is a market neutral trading strategy that matches a long position with a short position in a pair of highly correlated instruments such as two stocks, exchange-traded funds, currencies, commodities or options. Pairs traders wait for weakness in the correlation and then go long on the under-performer while simultaneously going short on the over-performer, closing the positions as the relationship returns to its statistical norms. . . . Central to their research was the development of quantitative methods for identifying pairs of securities whose prices exhibited similar historical price movements, or that

were highly correlated. . . . Central to pairs trading is the idea that if the two stocks (or other instruments) are correlated enough, any changes in correlation may be followed by a reversion to the pair's mean trend, creating a profit opportunity.

Folger traces the origin of pairs trading to a group of computer scientists, mathematicians and physicists assembled by Morgan Stanley in the early to mid-1980s to study arbitrage opportunities in the stock markets, employing advanced statistical modelling and developing an automated trading program to exploit market discrepancies. Computer scientists, mathematicians and physicists do not talk about cointegration but rather correlation, particularly in the early 1980s when the concept of cointegration had not been developed yet. This is yet another attempt to give credibility to cointegration as distinct from correlation by cointegration enthusiasts. Folger explains the importance of correlation for pairs trading as follows:

If the two instruments were not correlated to begin with, any divergence and subsequent convergence in price might, in general, be less meaningful. As an example, let's consider a main road along a river. In general, the road follows the river very closely. Occasionally, the road must diverge away from the river due to terrain or development (comparable to the "spread" in price). Each time this happens, however, the road eventually reverts to its spot parallel to the river. In this example, the road and the river have a correlated relationship. If we compare the river to another nearby dirt road, however, with no definable correlation to the river (i.e., their movements are completely random), it would be futile to predict how the two would behave relative to one another. The positive correlation between the main road and the river, however, is what makes it reasonable to anticipate that the main road and the river will eventually reunite.

Likewise, van Dam (2012) describes pairs trading without mentioning cointegration but he talks about a pair of stocks from the same sector, which are expected to be correlated. But then he tells a story of a German billionaire who had a go at pairs trading with Volkswagen's two share classes and ended up jumping in front of a train. As a result, van Dam warns that "if pairs trading can drive a billionaire to suicide, that tells you that you should stay away as well". He makes the following recommendation: "Keep your life simple – don't do pairs trading". Cointegration enthusiasts do not agree with the warning or recommendation, because for them cointegration reveals something similar to the laws of nature. Like van Dam, Elliott et al. (2005) do not mention cointegration but rather talk about "two similar stocks which trade at some spread". Gatev et al. (2006) refer to "pairs with minimum distance between normalized historical prices".

Table 9.7   Mean reversion in stock price indices

1	2	Corr.	SD	Min.	Max.	Range
Denmark	New Zealand	0.916	0.179	−0.289	0.496	0.785
Denmark	US	0.918	0.162	−0.413	0.388	0.801
France	India	−0.017	0.317	−0.506	0.615	1.116
India	Mauritius	0.953	0.148	−0.362	0.349	0.712

Correlation and Mean Reversion

It can be demonstrated that high correlation implies mean reversion, irrespective of whether or not the two series are cointegrated. For this purpose, we use four pairs that encompass high correlation and cointegration, high correlation and no cointegration and low correlation: Denmark–New Zealand, Denmark–US, France–India and India–Mauritius. In this exercise we examine mean reversion in the residuals of the cointegrating regression using the range of values assumed by the residuals as a measure of the strength of mean reversion. In Table 9.7 we can see that the most highly correlated pair (India–Mauritius) produces the lowest standard deviation and the narrowest range of values although the two stock price indices are not cointegrated. Conversely, the pair with the weakest correlation (France and India) produces the weakest mean reversion, as shown in Figure 9.4.

9.4   PURCHASING POWER PARITY

In international finance, one of the most popular applications of cointegration is the testing of international parity conditions, starting with purchasing power parity (PPP), which was initiated by Taylor (1988) and Enders (1988). The production of papers testing PPP by cointegration is yet to come to an end, but we are not better off with respect to our understanding of PPP. This hypothesis may work well over very long periods of time, but it is definitely valid under hyperinflation. The use of cointegration analysis to test PPP, particularly with the Johansen test, gives a false indication that PPP works under normal conditions and short periods of time. For any observer, exchange rates are too volatile to be explained by the smooth price movements over time.

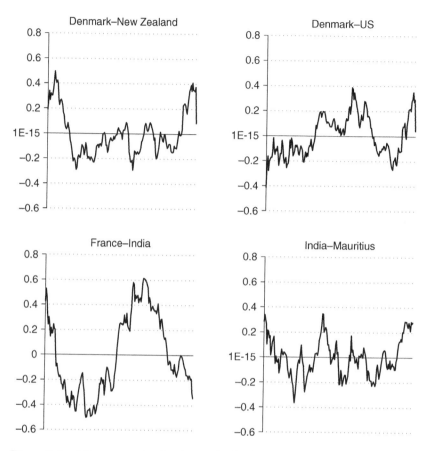

Figure 9.4   Mean reversion in the residuals of stock price indices

An Illustration

In this section we illustrate how misleading cointegration analysis can be by testing PPP. For this purpose, we employ six cointegration test statistics: CRDW, ADF, the t statistic of the coefficient on the error correction, $t(\phi)$, the two statistics used in conjunction with the bounds test (F and W) and Johansen's maximum eigenvalue test. PPP is tested using two specifications: the restricted specification in which the exchange rate is a function of the price ratio, and the unrestricted specification in which the exchange rate is a function of the price indices of the two countries. The two specifications are written in logarithmic form respectively as:

Table 9.8   Cointegration tests of PPP

1	2	Form	CRDW	ADF	$t(\phi)$	F	W	EV
Japan	US	R	0.12	−2.48	−1.75	2.43	4.87	62.62*
Japan	US	U	0.18	−3.95*	−2.24*	2.36	7.08	79.92*
UK	US	R	0.20	−3.93*	−3.03*	5.24	10.49	19.47*
UK	US	U	0.21	−3.86*	−3.82*	6.26*	18.80*	64.06*
Canada	US	R	0.08	−1.81	−1.59	1.13	2.26	3.55
Canada	US	U	0.10	−1.96	−1.95	2.58	7.76	54.73*
Switzerland	US	R	0.19	−2.95	−2.43*	3.07	6.14	49.43*
Switzerland	US	U	0.70	−3.08	−2.57*	2.29	6.87	16.35*
Sweden	US	R	0.12	−3.10	−2.67*	4.23	8.47	17.99*
Sweden	US	U	0.14	−3.02	−2.47*	2.81	8.49	16.57*
UK	Japan	R	0.11	−2.63	−2.23*	4.34	8.68	21.84*
UK	Japan	U	0.16	−3.25	−2.86*	5.69*	17.08*	31.22*
Canada	Japan	R	0.10	−2.02	−1.68	2.67	5.35	51.52*
Canada	Japan	U	0.24	−4.18*	−3.07*	6.83*	20.52*	71.04*
Switzerland	Japan	R	0.15	−2.41	−2.43*	4.14	8.27	9.45
Switzerland	Japan	U	0.24	−4.32*	−2.86*	3.56	10.68	56.31*
Sweden	Japan	R	0.02	−2.08	−2.78*	3.91	7.83	13.31
Sweden	Japan	U	0.20	−3.97*	−3.03*	4.13	12.39	77.64*

Note: * Significant at the 5% level.

$$s_t = \alpha_0 + \alpha_1(p_{a,t} - p_{b,t}) + \varepsilon_t \qquad\qquad (9.3)$$

and

$$s_t = \beta_0 + \beta_1 p_{a,t} - \beta_2 p_{b,t} + \zeta_t \qquad\qquad (9.4)$$

where s is the (log of) exchange rate (measured as the price in terms of currency a as the price of one unit of currency b), p_a is the (log of) price level in the country a. and p_b is the (log of) price level in country b. The US and Japan represent country b while country a is represented by the UK, Canada, Switzerland and Sweden. The data series (obtained from *International Financial Statistics*) are quarterly covering the period 2000:1 to 2015:3.

The results are reported in Table 9.8, showing (as expected) a mixed bag. One test (CRDW) tells us that PPP does not hold in any case. The ADF test indicates that PPP holds in five out of the nine cases, but the t statistic shows that PPP holds in more cases. The bounds test results show that PPP holds only for UK–US, UK–Japan and Canada–Japan. And the Johansen test results show that PPP holds in all cases except two, but it is always possible to turn this result of no cointegration into the affirmative by manipulating model specification. So, confirmation bias would dictate the reporting of the Johansen results and hide the others. Those arguing against PPP would tend to report the CRDW, F and W. In some cases, a test would tell us that PPP holds in one form but not the other. For example, PPP holds for Japan–US in the unrestricted form but not in the restricted form, which may sound plausible because the imposition of the proportionality and symmetry restrictions may render the model misspecified.

Is it wise to use results like these for policy making and business decisions? Policy making in this case involves the determination of exchange rate misalignment. The claim made by politicians and some anti-Chinese, right-wing economists that the Chinese currency is undervalued and calls for a trade war with China are based, *inter alia*, on PPP (for example, Moosa, 2011c, 2011d; Moosa and Ma, 2015). Business decisions may take the form of using PPP as a currency trading rule or for measuring economic exposure to foreign exchange risk. The answer to the question if it is wise to use results like these for policy or business decisions is in the negative, unless one wishes to start a trade war with China.

9.5   COVERED INTEREST PARITY

I am puzzled by attempts to use cointegration to test CIP because this condition must hold by definition, as an arbitrage or a hedging condition (Moosa, 2004). Strangely, cointegration tests may tell us that CIP does not work although it represents a formula that is used by bankers to calculate the forward rates they quote to their customers. CIP is not a theory but a deterministic equation, which means that it is an untestable hypothesis. In fact testing CIP is indicative of the fact that academic economists are out of touch with reality.

It has been demonstrated repeatedly that deviations from CIP are observed whenever published data are used for empirical testing even if allowance is made for bid-offer spreads in interest and exchange rates (Moosa, 2016b). The malpractice of testing CIP is a direct result of the "retire-to-your-study" approach, as Bergmann (1999) puts it. Motivated by the arsenal of tools provided by econometricians, economists retire to their studies and "test, test, test" without bothering to ask bankers how they quote forward rates to customers.

One way to test CIP is to find out if the actual and forward exchange rates are cointegrated. However, CIP must hold as a truism because a bank will never quote a forward rate that is different from the rate that is compatible with CIP, the so-called interest parity forward rate. This is because the interest parity rate is the only rate that precludes the possibility of profitable risk-free arbitrage (hence CIP is a no-arbitrage condition) and it is the only rate that enables the quoting bank to hedge its exposure perfectly (hence CIP is a hedging condition). The interest parity forward rate is calculated as:

$$F_t = S_t \left[\frac{1 + i_a}{1 + i_b} \right] \tag{9.5}$$

where F is the forward rate, S is the spot rate (both defined as the price of one unit of currency b), i_a is the interest rate on currency a and i_b is the interest rate on currency b. Although CIP must hold by definition and design, cointegration tests may reveal that it does not hold. Consider the cointegrating regression:

$$F_t = \alpha + \beta S_t + \varepsilon_t \tag{9.6}$$

Cointegration between F_t and S_t requires that $\varepsilon_t \sim I(0)$. Since we know that $\alpha = 0$ and $\beta = (1 + i_a)/(1 + i_b)$, F and S are related by a deterministic equation, in which case they are cointegrated by definition.

Irrespective of the results of cointegration testing, CIP must always hold in the sense that a bank can only quote the forward rate implied by equation (9.5). There cannot be any deviations from this condition because deviation implies the availability of riskless arbitrage profit. Cointegration results have no meaning whatsoever in the case of CIP, and the hundreds of tests that have been done to find out whether or not CIP holds are a total waste of time. Sometimes CIP is tested not by cointegration but by specifying the model in terms of stationary variables, the forward spread and interest rate differential. It still does not make sense because the formula used by bankers to calculate the forward rate is compatible with the equality of the spread and differential.

An Illustration

The results presented here are based on quarterly data on the exchange rates and three-month interest rates of the US, Canada, Japan, Sweden, Switzerland and the UK. The CIP equation is estimated for 14 currency combinations, including the exchange rates against the dollar and cross exchange rates. The ADF of the cointegrating regressions corresponding to the 14 combinations are displayed in Figure 9.5 (the horizontal line represents the critical value of the ADF statistic). Only in four cases are the forward and spot rates found to be cointegrated. This is a mechanical relation that should hold irrespective of the currency combinations

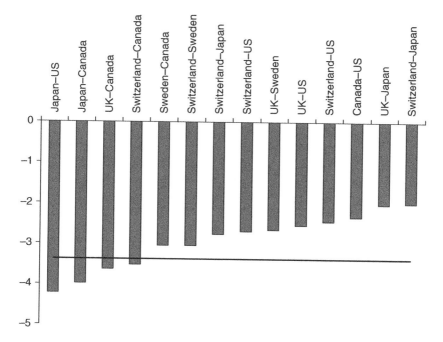

Figure 9.5   ADF statistics for the CIP equation

as F is derived by adjusting S by a factor that reflects the interest rate differentials.

Economists frequently test the so-called unbiased efficiency hypothesis (UEH), which postulates a lagged (as opposed to contemporaneous) relation between the spot and forward rates. Unlike CIP, which is a definitional relation, the unbiased efficiency hypothesis is theoretically implausible, simply because the spot and forward rates are determined jointly and contemporaneously according to CIP. Those economists who find no support for the unbiased efficiency hypothesis call it a puzzle, when in fact there is no puzzle whatsoever. It is either that the test is valid but the theory is not, or that the theory is valid but the test is not. The truth in this case is that neither the theory, nor the test are valid. We will come back to this point in Chapter 11 that deals with econometric forecasting.

9.6 COINTEGRATION OF MACROECONOMIC VARIABLES

Cointegration tests invariably produce results that do not make sense – for example, showing two variables that are not related as cointegrated, most likely because they are highly correlated, and showing two variables that are related either theoretically or by definition to be not cointegrated. To demonstrate how misleading the results of cointegration testing are, three cointegration tests are conducted on pairs chosen from a total of 30 macroeconomic variables using quarterly data on the US over the period 1980:1 to 2015:3 (obtained from *International Financial Statistics*). The full set of results are presented in Appendix Table 9A.2.

To start with, there is contradiction between the results based on the t statistic of the coefficient on the error correction term and those based on the two statistics associated with the bounds test. Typically, the t test rejects the null of no cointegration more often than the bounds test. But what is surprising is that in so many cases the t statistic is positive or significantly positive, implying the absence of mean reversion, yet the bounds test rejects the null of no cointegration. Such cases include cointegration between the monetary base and a range of interest rates, as well as stock prices, wages, industrial production, employment and unemployment. The same can be said about the relation between the broader monetary aggregates (M1 and M2) and other macroeconomic variables.

How is it possible that the residual of the cointegrating regression shows the opposite of mean reversion, yet the variables are cointegrated according to the bounds test? Figure 9.6 shows the residuals of the following cointegrating regressions: (1) monetary base on 10-year bond yield; (2) monetary base on unemployment; (3) M1 on stock prices; and (4) M1 on industrial production. They are certainly nonstationary, in which case they should not be cointegrated as indicated by the bounds test.

Results Making No Sense

The results show cases of cointegration and no cointegration that do not make sense. In some cases the variables should be cointegrated as implied by theory or because they are related somehow. For example, the nominal and real effective exchange rates are cointegrated according to the t test, which makes sense because the two variables are related by a definitional relation: one is a weighted average of exchange rate relatives, while the other is a weighted average of the exchange rate relatives adjusted for inflation. What does not make sense is that the bounds

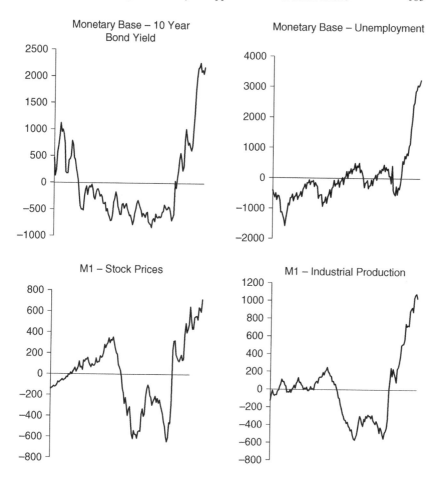

Figure 9.6 Non-mean reverting residuals of cointegrating regressions

test tells us that the two rates are not cointegrated. Other examples of when a finding of cointegration makes a lot of sense in terms of theory and intuition include NEER-exports, NEER-export prices, M1-stock prices, stock prices-consumption, PPI-wages and imports-consumption. In most of these, however, cointegration is rejected by one of the tests. In other cases, common sense and theory tell us that the two variables should be cointegrated, but the tests indicate the opposite. These include the monetary base and both M1 and M2, which should be related by the money multiplier model. M1 and M2 are not cointegrated although M1 is an integral part of M2. Other cases include bond yield–stock prices, stock prices–PPI, stock prices–CPI, PPI–CPI, PPI–export prices, industrial production–employment, industrial production–exports, industrial production–gross fixed capital formation, and import prices–current account.

Last, but not least, we examine the cointegration of interest rates, which should be cointegrated as implied by the theory of the term structure of interest rates or because all interest rates are so related that the spread (the difference between two rates) tends to be constant or at least stationary. In Figure 9.7 we observe how some of the rates are related. All interest rates must be connected to the discount rate, which is obvious from the graphs. The 3-year and 10-year government bond yields must be closely related because they are connected by the term structure. Yet, the bounds test produces results saying that these four pairs of interest rates are not cointegrated. How do we explain the finding that the discount rate is cointegrated with the 3-year bond yield but not with the 10-year bond yield? I suppose that we cannot.

9.7 CONCLUSION

It seems that the cointegration revolution was not a revolution at all. Cointegration is yet another econometric "trick" that does not help our understanding of how the economy and financial system work. On the contrary, cointegration analysis may produce results that are highly misleading (for example, CIP does not hold, hence free money is available for no risk). One can only wonder why this gimmick is considered as important for our lives as the discovery of Penicillin (at least in the eyes of the Nobel Prize committee).

The problems associated with cointegration analysis are plentiful. To start with, the results obtained by using different tests typically vary considerably and they are not robust with respect to model specification (for example, linear versus log linear, restricted versus unrestricted, changing the lag structure, changing the direction of normalization, and the addition or deletion of a time trend). Hence, the technique offers the opportunity for anyone to prove whatever they like. This can be very dangerous if the results are used for policy formulation or for financial decision making. The claim to fame of cointegration analysis that it makes it possible to distinguish spurious relations from genuine ones is false. We can only do this by using common sense, theory and/or intuition. Furthermore, some of the pillars of cointegration analysis are not supported by the results presented in this study: cointegration does not necessarily imply and is implied by a valid error correction representation; and it does not necessarily imply that causality must be present in at least

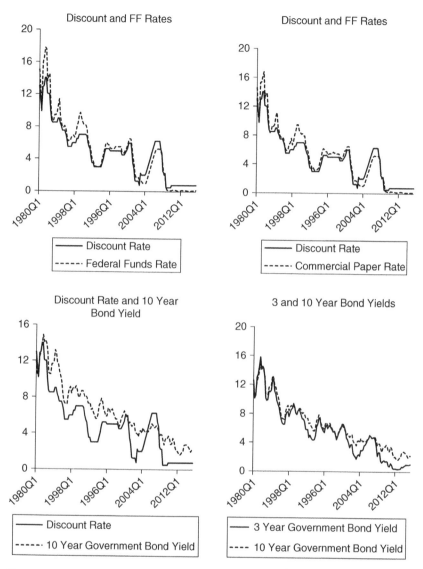

Figure 9.7   Non-cointegrated interest rates

one direction. In some cases simple correlation analysis does a better job than cointegration testing.

Cointegration analysis, like many of the techniques of econometrics, is not worthy of the brain power spent on its development. While it has provided the means for finance and economics academics to publish papers and for students in the two disciplines to obtain their PhDs, the technique has not provided any useful insights. On the contrary, it typically provides faulty, inconsistent and robustness-lacking results that may be hazardous to use. I would certainly advocate the use of a warning phrase such as "handle with care" to describe results based on cointegration testing.

APPENDIX

Table 9A.1 A full set of cointegration results (stock price indices)

1	2	Corr.	CRDW	ADF	$t(\phi)$	F	W
Australia	Canada	0.91	0.10	-3.02	-1.97	2.19	4.39
Australia	New Zealand	0.86	0.09	-2.01	-1.34	1.41	2.82
Canada	India	0.91	0.14	-2.27	-2.25*	2.81	5.62
Canada	Malaysia	0.87	0.11	-2.39	-2.48*	3.07	6.15
Canada	Mauritius	0.88	0.13	-2.87	-2.23*	2.62	5.25
Canada	New Zealand	0.86	0.10	-2.26	-1.36	1.32	2.65
Canada	UK	0.86	0.07	-2.52	-2.42*	2.95	5.91
Canada	US	0.81	0.06	-1.32	-1.44	2.14	4.28
China	France	0.25	0.05	-1.81	-1.62	3.27	6.54
China	Japan	0.24	0.05	-1.88	-1.45	4.35	8.71
Denmark	Egypt	0.15	0.02	-2.04	-0.19	0.02	0.04
Denmark	France	0.25	0.02	-1.72	-0.32	0.06	0.11
Denmark	New Zealand	0.92	0.12	-3.86*	-2.56*	3.43	6.87
Denmark	US	0.92	0.14	-3.83*	-3.14*	5.58	11.16
Egypt	France	0.20	0.02	-2.03	-1.45	1.26	2.53
Egypt	Germany	0.15	0.03	-1.58	-1.32	113	2.28
Egypt	India	0.29	0.03	-1.37	-1.09	2.21	4.41
Egypt	Japan	0.32	0.03	-1.85	-1.54	1.53	3.07
Egypt	Malaysia	0.15	0.03	-1.74	-1.22	1.18	2.37
Egypt	Mauritius	0.34	0.03	-1.58	-1.29	2.24	4.48
Egypt	New Zealand	0.29	0.03	-1.59	-0.58	0.56	1.12
Egypt	UK	0.18	0.03	-1.83	-1.23	0.83	1.66
Egypt	US	0.05	0.03	-1.45	-1.17	1.09	2.17
France	India	-0.02	0.04	-2.11	-1.40	1.22	2.45

Table 9A.1 (continued)

1	2	Corr.	CRDW	ADF	$t(\phi)$	F	W
France	Japan	0.87	0.10	-3.78*	-2.39*	3.44	6.89
France	Malaysia	-0.05	0.05	-2.08	-0.76	1.03	2.05
France	Mauritius	-0.14	0.05	-1.97	-1.02	2.13	4.28
France	New Zealand	0.07	0.04	-2.27	-0.79	0.42	0.85
France	US	0.28	0.03	-2.43	-0.65	0.23	0.46
Germany	UK	0.93	0.02	-2.63	-3.37*	6.69*	13.99*
India	Japan	0.08	0.01	-0.75	-0.16	0.23	0.47
India	Malaysia	0.95	0.08	-2.61	-1.76	1.78	3.56
India	Mauritius	0.95	0.11	-2.11	-0.50	0.13	0.26
India	New Zealand	0.90	0.04	-1.50	-1.36	0.94	1.88
Japan	Malaysia	0.01	0.04	-1.05	-0.82	1.75	3.50
Japan	Mauritius	-0.01	0.04	-1.37	-1.70	1.76	3.51
Japan	New Zealand	0.31	0.04	-1.89	-1.58	2.26	4.53
Malaysia	Mauritius	0.94	0.09	-2.01	-1.42	1.02	2.04
Malaysia	New Zealand	0.86	0.03	-1.43	-0.79	0.52	1.03
New Zealand	US	0.90	0.06	-2.75	-1.41	2.09	4.15
UK	US	0.90	0.02	-2.47	-2.51*	3.90	7.80

Note: * Significant at the 5% level.

Table 9A.2   A full set of cointegration results (US macroeconomic data)

1	2	$t(\phi)$	F	W
NEER	REER	−2.51*	4.30	8.61
NEER	Monetary Base	−2.58*	3.23	6.46
NEER	M1	−2.59*	3.43	6.87
NEER	M2	−1.99	2.55	5.10
NEER	Discount Rate	−1.55	2.52	5.03
NEER	Federal Funds Rate	−0.98	2.73	5.46
NEER	3-month CP Rate	−0.84	2.83	5.66
NEER	10-year Bond Yield	−0.89	2.58	5.17
NEER	Stock Prices	−2.09*	2.64	5.29
NEER	CPI	−1.95	3.98	7.96
NEER	Wages Rate	−1.36	2.52	5.05
NEER	Industrial Production	−1.29	2.56	5.13
NEER	Employment	−1.19	2.54	5.08
NEER	Unemployment	−2.32*	3.59	7.18
NEER	Exports	−2.48*	3.22	0.05
NEER	Imports	−1.60	2.07	0.02
NEER	Export Prices	−3.74*	7.80	15.60*
NEER	Import Prices	−3.04*	4.83	9.64
NEER	Current Account	−0.20	4.05	8.10
REER	Monetary Base	−1.01	1.19	2.39
REER	M1	−1.24	1.02	2.04
REER	M2	−1.44	1.12	2.24
REER	3-month CP Rate	−2.54*	4.63	9.26
REER	3-month TB Rate	−2.50*	4.87	9.79
REER	10-year Bond Yield	−2.71*	4.18	8.36
REER	Stock Prices	−1.46	1.42	2.84
REER	CPI	−1.68	1.36	2.72
REER	Industrial Production	−1.56	1.16	2.32
REER	Employment	−1.85	1.77	3.53
REER	Unemployment	−1.45	1.18	2.36
REER	Gross saving	−1.22	1.02	2.05
Monetary Base	M1	−0.98	3.82	7.65
Monetary Base	M2	−0.53	2.15	4.31
Monetary Base	Discount Rate	1.82	8.65*	17.30*
Monetary Base	Federal Funds Rate	1.90	8.48*	16.97*
Monetary Base	3-month CP Rate	1.99	8.57*	17.14*
Monetary Base	3-month TB Rate	1.80	8.62*	17.25*
Monetary Base	3-year Bond Yield	1.74	8.72*	17.45*
Monetary Base	10-year Bond Yield	2.21	8.39*	16.78*
Monetary Base	Stock Prices	2.37	9.58*	19.17*
Monetary Base	PPI	−1.55	16.03*	32.07*
Monetary Base	Wages Rate	1.03	9.30*	18.60*
Monetary Base	Industrial Production	2.88	9.38*	18.77*
Monetary Base	Employment	2.47	8.36*	16.72*
Monetary Base	Unemployment	2.26	9.92*	19.85*
Monetary Base	Exports	−0.75	13.04*	0.00

Table 9A.2 (continued)

1	2	$t(\phi)$	F	W
Monetary Base	Imports	0.43	11.75*	0.00
Monetary Base	Export Prices	−0.89	12.08*	24.17*
Monetary Base	Import Prices	−1.55	16.72*	33.44*
M1	M2	0.57	0.28	0.56
M1	Discount Rate	1.83	11.84*	23.68*
M1	Federal Funds Rate	1.67	9.65*	19.27*
M1	3-month CP Rate	1.59	9.91*	19.82*
M1	3-month TB Rate	1.34	9.84*	19.68*
M1	3-year Bond Yield	1.25	9.69*	19.39*
M1	10-year Bond Yield	2.18	9.49*	18.98*
M1	Stock Prices	3.64	12.9*	25.58*
M1	CPI	1.61	8.73*	17.46*
M1	Wage Rate	1.73	9.42*	18.85*
M1	Industrial Production	4.58	14.59*	29.19*
M1	Employment	3.62	10.59*	21.18*
M1	Exports	−0.58	10.93*	0.00
M1	Imports	0.91	10.71	0.00
Discount Rate	Federal Funds Rate	−2.75*	4.44	8.89
Discount Rate	3-month CP Rate	−3.23*	5.67	11.34
Discount Rate	3-month TB Rate	−3.50*	6.32*	12.65*
Discount Rate	3-year Bond Yield	−3.38*	6.29*	12.58*
Discount Rate	10-year Bond Yield	−2.80*	4.70	9.41
Discount Rate	Stock Prices	−2.54*	3.34	6.68
Discount Rate	CPI	−3.31*	6.13*	12.27*
Discount Rate	Industrial Production	−1.57	1.82	3.64
Federal Funds Rate	3-month CP Rate	−7.23*	26.18*	52.36*
Federal Funds Rate	3-month TB Rate	−6.34*	20.37*	40.74*
Federal Funds Rate	3-year Bond Yield	−4.67*	11.16*	22.33*
Federal Funds Rate	10-year Bond Yield	−3.64*	7.11*	14.23*
Federal Funds Rate	Stock Prices	−2.51*	3.72	7.45
3-month CP Rate	3-month TB Rate	−6.55*	21.61*	43.22*
3-month CP Rate	3-year Bond Yield	−4.63*	10.98*	21.96*
3-month CP Rate	10-year Bond Yield	−3.63*	7.08*	14.17*
3-month CP Rate	Stock Prices	−2.54*	3.73	7.46
3-month TB Rate	3-year Bond Yield	−4.56*	10.89*	21.78*
3-month TB Rate	10-year Bond Yield	−3.47*	6.71*	13.42*
3-month TB Rate	Stock Prices	−2.52*	3.78	7.57
3-year Bond Yield	10-year Bond Yield	−2.59*	3.66	7.33
3-year Bond Yield	Stock Prices	−1.76	1.62	3.25
3-year Bond Yield	PPI	−2.37*	2.86	5.72
10-year Bond Yield	Stock Prices	−1.51	1.81	3.62
Stock Prices	PPI	−0.50	0.52	1.03
Stock Prices	CPI	−1.71	2.40	4.81
Stock Prices	Wage rate	−1.43	1.75	3.51
Stock Prices	Industrial production	−0.98	0.75	1.50
Stock Prices	Employment	−0.29	0.19	0.37

Table 9A.2   (continued)

1	2	$t(\phi)$	F	W
Stock Prices	Unemployment	0.37	1.68	3.37
Stock Prices	Exports	−1.25	1.22	0.02
Stock Prices	Imports	−0.27	0.14	0.02
Stock Prices	Export prices	−0.90	1.81	3.6
Stock Prices	Import prices	−0.03	0.41	0.81
Stock Prices	Consumption	−3.44*	6.78*	13.57*
Stock Prices	Government Expenditure	−0.65	0.63	1.26
Stock Prices	Gross Capital Formation	−1.77	1.67	3.35
PPI	CPI	−1.95	3.58	7.16
PPI	Wage rate	−2.19*	2.49	4.99
PPI	Industrial production	−1.23	0.92	1.84
PPI	Employment	−1.36	0.57	1.14
PPI	Exports	−2.85*	4.16	0.002
PPI	Imports	−2.80*	3.92	0.008
PPI	Export prices	−1.73	2.37	4.74
PPI	Import prices	−2.03*	2.76	5.52
PPI	Consumption	0.58	5.30	10.61
PPI	Government Expenditure	−1.57	1.24	2.47
PPI	Gross Capital Formation	−1.44	1.07	2.14
PPI	Gross saving	−0.67	0.22	0.45
CPI	Wage rate	−2.29*	3.91	7.82
CPI	Industrial production	−2.05*	2.27	4.54
CPI	Imports	−2.34*	3.58	0.002
CPI	Export prices	−0.67	0.26	0.54
CPI	Consumption	−2.64*	9.73*	19.47*
CPI	Government Expenditure	−2.03*	2.82	5.64
CPI	Gross Capital Formation	−2.14*	2.69	5.39
Industrial production	Employment	−1.46	1.09	2.18
Industrial production	unemployment	−0.20	0.02	0.05
Industrial production	Exports	−0.42	0.11	0.002
Industrial production	Imports	0.09	0.19	0.001
Industrial production	Consumption	−2.26*	7.21*	14.44*
Industrial production	Government Expenditure	0.28	0.08	0.16
Industrial production	Gross Capital Formation	−1.28	1.12	2.25
Industrial production	Gross saving	−2.31*	2.70	5.40
Imports	Consumption	−3.12*	8.30*	0.00
Imports	Gross Capital Formation	−2.41*	2.92	0.00
Export Prices	Current Account	−2.44*	2.11	4.22
Import Prices	Current Account	−1.69	2.17	3.54

Note: * Significant at the 5% level.

10. Sensitivity and insensitivity of empirical results

10.1 INTRODUCTION

In Chapter 7 we saw that the empirical results derived from a cross-sectional model of the capital structure are highly sensitive to model specification with respect to the explanatory variables included in the model and the definitions and measurement of these variables. In this chapter we investigate the sensitivity of results derived from time series models with respect to model specification, estimation method, and variable definition and measurement. The problem with sensitivity is that it allows the researcher to obtain desirable results, thus data mining becomes tantalizing. We will also investigate insensitivity of the results with respect to model specification and estimation method, which occurs when the effects of specification and estimation are dominated by the effect of another factor. This observation is nowhere else more apparent than in the models used to estimate the hedge ratio and measure hedging effectiveness where the only thing that matters is correlation. In this case, sophisticated econometric models and methods do not have any value added over and above what can be obtained from the simple concept of correlation.

Sensitivity of the empirical results obtained from time series models to various factors is the rule rather than the exception. Take, for example, vector autoregressive (VAR) models where every variable is regressed on the contemporaneous and lagged values of every other variable, typically without any consideration of theory on the grounds that theory does not tell us much about the structure of the economy or the flawed practice of "let the data do the talking". The results of any VAR model are highly sensitive to the lag length in the autoregressive structure as well as the definitions of variables and sample period. VAR models may be specified in levels or first differences. The results obtained from a symmetric model are different from those obtained from an asymmetric model. In studies of the environmental Kuznets curve, the results depend on whether the model is represented by a polynomial of degree two or three and whether it is specified in levels or log levels. Typically, logarithmic specifications (implying nonlinearity) are used in a haphazard manner without any theoretical or empirical justification. Then let us not forget the arsenal of ARCH/ GARCH models.

Examples of sensitivity to variable measurement are plentiful. In the news model, where what matters are the unanticipated components of the explanatory variables, the results are sensitive to how the anticipated components are derived. In studies of cyclical co-variation, such as the cyclical behaviour of wages and prices, the results are highly sensitive to how the cyclical components are extracted. When the underlying model involves expected values, the results are highly sensitive to the underlying expectation formation mechanism (static, adaptive, regressive, mixed, contrarian, rational, and so on).

Any set of results can be obtained by changing the estimation method. Try, for example, the following menu: ordinary least squares, nonlinear least squares, restricted least squares, fully modified least squares, two-stage least squares, dynamic ordinary least squares, generalized method of moments, dynamic generalized least squares, full-information maximum likelihood, limited information maximum likelihood, instrumental variables, logit and probit models, ordered choice models, quantile regression, generalized linear models, step-wise least squares, unobserved component models, time-varying parametric estimation, and censored regression. Later on in this chapter we will come across estimation methods such as maximum likelihood with an autoregressive process in the residuals, the Cochrane–Orcutt method with an autoregressive process in the residuals, the Gauss–Newton method with an autoregressive process in the residuals, and maximum likelihood with a moving average process in the residuals. And there is more where these come from.

In this chapter the sensitivity of the results of time series models is demonstrated by using Wagner's law, Okun's law and the J-curve effect. Researchers always find it embarrassing to report the results of studies of laws and empirical regularities (if at all) for a large number of countries. Those who dare to report the full set of results for, say, 30 countries are typically incapable of explaining cross-country differences – for example, why Wager's law works in Austria and Somalia but not in Switzerland, which has a similar pattern to that of Nepal. Insensitivity of the results is demonstrated by using models of cross-currency hedge ratios.

10.2   WAGNER'S LAW

Wagner's law, which is named after the German economist Adolph Wagner, states that economic growth leads to increasing share of public expenditure in GDP. Cross-country differences in Wagner's law are apparent in the empirical literature. Ram (1987) uses data on income and government expenditure for 115 countries, covering the period 1950–1980. He observes a "tremendous diversity in the position for various countries", indicating that while there is support for the hypothesis in some time-series data sets, such support is lacking in most cross-section estimates. Much of the support for the hypothesis (sorry, the law) reported in many earlier studies is probably due to either use of limited samples or inadequate data comparability across the observations studied.

Model Specification

Wagner's law is expressed in various shapes and forms. Henrekson (1992) points out that testing Wagner's law should focus on the time series behaviour of public expenditure in a country for as long a time period as possible rather than on a cross-section of countries at different income levels, which sounds plausible. Following Henrekson, the results of the empirical work reported here is based on the time series specifications:

$$g_t = \alpha + \beta y_t + \varepsilon_t \tag{10.1}$$
$$g_t = \alpha + \beta(y_t - n_t) + \varepsilon_t \tag{10.2}$$
$$g_t - n_t = \alpha + \beta(y_t - n_t) + \varepsilon_t \tag{10.3}$$
$$g_t - y_t = \alpha_i + \beta(y_t - n_t) + \varepsilon_t \tag{10.4}$$
$$g_t - y_t = \alpha + \beta y_t + \varepsilon_t \tag{10.5}$$

where g is the log of government expenditure, y is the log of GDP, n is the log of population, which means that $(y_t - n_t)$ is the log of real GDP per capita and that $(g_t - y_t)$ is the log of the share of government expenditure in GDP. Further variations can be tried by specifying the model without logs, by using GNP instead of GDP, by using various definitions of government expenditure and by using the nominal rather than real values of the variables. This is not to forget that testing these equations implies that all other variables that affect the dependent variables are held constant.

An Illustration

In this exercise, 15 equations representing Wagner's law are estimated, encompassing five different specifications, two estimation methods (the Phillips–Hansen fully modified OLS and the ARDL approach to cointegration) and three different measures of government expenditure and GDP (current US dollars, current local currency and constant US dollars). The estimates are based on an annual sample of Australian data covering the period 1960–2014 (obtained from the World Bank database). The

Table 10.1   Estimated equations of Wagner's law

Estimated Equation	Phillips–Hansen FMOLS (t)	t (Coefficient on EC term)	F (Bounds)	W (Bounds)
(10.1):A	50.57*	−1.99	4.33	8.67
(10.1):B	78.63*	−0.81	3.57	7.14
(10.1):C	37.72*	−2.61*	10.48*	20.96*
(10.2):A	5.12*	−2.89*	7.62*	15.24*
(10.2):B	6.07*	−0.36	4.73	9.47
(10.2):C	12.31*	−2.70*	10.08*	20.02*
(10.3):A	42.93*	−1.98	4.21	8.41
(10.3):B	76.99*	−0.69	3.48	6.97
(10.3):C	21.62*	−1.94	5.36	10.72
(10.4):A	4.25*	−1.97	4.20	8.41
(10.4):B	8.01*	−1.34	3.41	6.82
(10.4):C	3.52*	−2.19*	7.38*	14.62*
(10.5):A	36.64*	−1.11	1.98	3.96
(10.5):B	52.46*	−0.70	2.31	4.62
(10.5):C	27.19*	−1.78	5.61	11.22

Notes: (10.1) to (10.5) refer to equation numbers as they appear in the text. A, B and C refer to how the variables g and y are measured: current US dollar, current local currency and constant US dollars. * Significant at the 5% level.

results reported in Table 10.1 for equations (10.1) to (10.5) where A, B and C refer to the measurement of variables respectively in terms of current US dollars, current local currency and constant US dollars.

Four test statistics are reported: the t statistic on the slope coefficient in the Phillips–Hansen fully modified OLS, the t statistic of the coefficient on the error correction term, and the F and W statistics associated with the bounds test of cointegration. The Phillips–Hansen test produces supportive evidence in all cases as the t statistic of the slope coefficient is significantly positive. Note, however, that these variables are strongly trended, implying the possibility of spurious regression. The bounds test shows cointegration in four out of the 15 cases. The t statistic of the coefficient on the error correction term shows significant mean reversion of the residuals in three out of 15 cases. Therefore if I want to produce evidence in favour of Wagner's law, I would report equations (10.1):C, (10.2):A, (10.2):C and (10.4):C. On the other hand, if I want to produce evidence against Wagner's law, I would report equations (10.1):A. (10.2):B, (10.4):A and (10.5):C. This is quite a contribution to human knowledge!

10.3   OKUN'S LAW

Empirical studies of the relation between unemployment and output growth have produced a range of values for the coefficient on output growth, or what has come to be known as Okun's coefficient. The range of estimates is wide because of a number of factors that have given rise to different interpretations of the coefficient. These factors include: (1) using dynamic versus static specifications, which brings about the question whether the relation is contemporaneous or lagged; (2) allowing, or otherwise, for the effect of other variables such as capacity utilization, hours per worker and labour force participation; (3) the method used to extract the cyclical components of unemployment and output; (4) distinguishing between demand and supply shocks; (5) the econometric method used to estimate the model; (6) distinguishing between long-run and short-run effects; and (7) the sample period. Point (1) boils down to whether the relation should be tested on the basis of a static regression, allowing for the contemporaneous effect only, or by using a dynamic model that also allows for the lagged effect. Point (2) pertains to whether the relation should be tested in a bivariate or a multivariate framework.

In general, more recent studies have produced results suggesting that output growth exerts greater impact on unemployment than what is implied by the original results produced by Okun (1962). The main reason for this conclusion seems to be the use of dynamic specifications which allow the estimation of the long-run effect. For example, while Okun (1962) produced a value of −0.32 using a static regression, Gordon (1984) and Evans (1989) used an autoregressive distributed lag (ARDL) model to estimate the lagged effect and produced values of the coefficient exceeding 0.4 in absolute value. On the other hand, allowing for other factors seems to reduce the value of the coefficient. For example, by incorporating other factors in his model, Prachowny (1993) has shown that the coefficient is much smaller than what was obtained by Gordon (1984), Evans (1989) and Okun (1962). The reason for this finding is a combination of incorporating other variables and not allowing for the lagged effects. Weber (1995) reported 18 estimates of Okun's coefficient using static OLS regression, cointegrating regression, ARDL model with lags two and four, and Blanchard's (1989) method of innovations in VAR. The three sample periods are 1948:1–1988:4, 1948:1–1973:3 and 1973:4–1988:4. Moosa (1997) produced varying results for the G7 countries.

Model Specification

The relation between cyclical unemployment and cyclical output, u^c and y^c, may be written in a stochastic form as:

$$u_t^c = \phi y_t^c + \varepsilon_t \tag{10.6}$$

This equation can be modified by introducing a lagged dependent variable, which gives:

$$u_t^c = \alpha + \beta u_{t-1}^c + \phi y_t^c + \varepsilon_t \tag{10.7}$$

A model that encompasses more dynamics is represented by the ARDL equation:

$$u_t^c = \sum_{i=1}^{m} \delta_i u_{t-i}^c + \sum_{i=0}^{m} \alpha_i y_{t-i}^c + \upsilon_t \tag{10.8}$$

By using equation (10.8), Okun's coefficient may be represented by the impact coefficient (that is, the coefficient on y^c_t) or as the long-run coefficient:

$$\varphi = \frac{\sum_{i=0}^{m} \alpha_i}{1 - \sum_{i=0}^{m} \delta_i} \tag{10.9}$$

The question that arises here is whether Okun's coefficient is α_0 or φ in equations (10.8) and (10.9). The reason for defining Okun's coefficient as the long-run effect is that the relation between unemployment and output is not necessarily contemporaneous, in which case Okun's coefficient is taken to be φ. Weber (1995) considers Okun's coefficient to be the long-run coefficient but he calculates it by excluding the impact coefficient, α_0. This is bound to produce a smaller value of Okun's coefficient than otherwise.

Instead of using the cyclical components, percentage changes can be used. In this case the simple model is specified as:

$$\Delta u_t = \phi \Delta y_t + \varepsilon_t \tag{10.10}$$

Alternatively, a lagged dependent variable may be introduced such that the model becomes the following:

$$\Delta u_t = \alpha + \beta \Delta u_{t-1} + \phi \Delta y_t + \varepsilon_t \tag{10.11}$$

Table 10.2   Estimates of Okun's coefficient (Australian data)

Model	GDP	GNI	Industrial Production
Cyclical components – Static (10.6)	−0.27 (−6.14)	−0.03 (−1.93)	−0.37 (−0.20)
Cyclical components – Limited Dynamics (10.7)	−0.15 (−3.15)	−0.12 (−2.79)	−0.78 (−0.50)
ARDL – impact coefficient (10.8)	−0.16 (−2.16)	−0.13 (−1.90)	−0.72 (−1.25)
ARDL – long-run coefficient (10.8)+(10.9)	−0.17 (−1.46)	−0.08 (−0.69)	−0.31 (−0.94)
Percentage changes (10.10)	−0.13 (−2.07)	−0.12 (−1.97)	−0.07 (−1.55)
Percentage changes (10.11)	−0.16 (−2.58)	−0.13 (−2.29)	−0.11 (−2.35)

Note: * t-statistics are placed in parentheses.

It is noteworthy that even without an explicit lagged dependent variable, an implicit one is included in equation (10.10) as we are going to see in Chapter 11. The empirical illustration presented here covers equations (10.6) to (10.11).

The Results

Here we conduct an exercise to demonstrate the sensitivity of the estimates of Okun's coefficient to model specification and the definition of output. For this purpose quarterly Australian data (obtained from *International Financial Statistics*) are used covering the period 1990:1 to 2015:3. Three measures of output are used: GDP, GNI and industrial production. The results are presented in Table 10.2, showing clearly that the estimated value of Okun's coefficient is sensitive to the choice of the output variable and model specification.

Other Sources of Sensitivity

In this exercise the cyclical components are extracted by using the Hodrick–Prescott (HP) filter, which is not the only possible way of doing so – for example, they can be extracted as deviations from a time polynomial or by using Harvey's (1989) structural time series model (as in Moosa, 1997). The choice of the detrending method introduces yet another source of sensitivity. Furthermore, other model specifications can be used. For example, it can be hypothesized that the output–unemployment relation is asymmetric, in the sense that the response of unemployment to output growth is different when the economy is expanding from that when the economy is contracting. This is different from the conventional specification, which encompasses symmetry in the sense that expansions and contractions in output have the same absolute effect on unemployment.

With respect to asymmetry, Neftci (1984) demonstrated that the US unemployment rate has gone through much sharper increases during downswings than declines during upswings. Using alternative estimation methods, Brunner (1997) found similar asymmetric features in US output data. Likewise, Rothman (1991) provides some evidence indicating that unemployment responds asymmetrically to positive and negative growth shocks. Palley (1993) attributes increasing cyclical asymmetry to changes in the pattern of employment growth, which has become more cyclically sensitive to changes in female labour supply behaviour; the latter is now less affected by downturns. Using an asymmetric model brings about yet another source of sensitivity. It must be mentioned here that there are different ways of representing asymmetry – for example by splitting changes in output into positive and negative changes or by creating a variable denoting the sign of the error correction term in an error correction specification.

10.4 THE J-CURVE EFFECT

The J-curve effect is a description of the time path taken by the trade balance (or the current account) following the devaluation or depreciation of the domestic currency. The underlying theory is that the trade balance deteriorates immediately after devaluation, then it starts to improve, which is why a plot of the trade balance shows a J-shaped time path. The available evidence on this phenomenon is indeed a mixed bag.

In a study of Canadian data over the period 1981:1–2005:12, Georgopoulos (2008) concludes that "the J-curve does not exist". He is critical of the underlying literature because it overlooks two crucial points: the degree to which exchange rate movements are passed through into local currency prices and the degree to which trade volumes respond to the exchange rate. These are two of the factors that impede not only the emergence of a J-curve effect but any effect of the exchange rate on the trade balance. Some studies found evidence for N-curve, M-curve, I-curve, V-curve, L-curve, S-curve, inverse J-curve and delayed J-curve. This is awesome – there is still space for a PhD on the J-curve effect.

The literature is surveyed by Bahmani-Oskooee and Ratha (2004) who conclude that "while there are reasons to believe that the J-curve phenomenon characterizes the short-run dynamics, there are also reasons why it may not" and that "the empirical evidence has been rather mixed, or inconclusive". It turns out that the J-curve effect may be no more than an aberration. Some of the conclusions reached by the studies surveyed by Bahmani-Oskooee and Ratha are the following: (1) there may or may not be a J-curve; (2) evidence for the inverse J-curve; (3) no evidence for the J-curve or delayed J-curve; (4) no support for the J-curve; (5) the evidence supports the J-curve in some cases; (6) the results support a new definition of the J-curve in 11 out of 18 cases; (7) evidence for the delayed J-curve; (8) evidence for the J-curve, N-curve, M-curve and I-curve; (9) evidence for the S-curve; (10) no specific short-run pattern supporting the J-curve phenomenon; (11) evidence for the J-curve in two out of five cases; and (12) significant differences in the duration and extent of the J-curve effect across countries.

In another survey of the literature on the J-curve and S-curve conducted by Bahmani-Oskooee and Hegerty (2010), the results are all over the place: the J-curve is present; the J-curve is not present; it is present for some countries but not for others; there is J-curve for Japan only; there is a J-curve for all except Japan; 41 out of 60 cases have S-curve; and so on and so forth. Bahmani-Oskooee and Alse (1994) found a mixed bag of results when they tested the J-curve effect for 19 developed and 22 less developed countries. They found evidence for the J-curve effect in Costa Rica, Ireland, the Netherlands and Turkey, but not for other countries. It is not clear what special characteristics these countries have to exhibit a J-curve effect, while other countries do not. It is not that easy to envisage that Ireland and the Netherlands have something in common with Turkey and Costa Rica.

In yet another study, Bahmani-Oskooee et al. (2015) summarize the results of a number of studies of the J-curve effect conducted over the period from 1985 to 2014. They find a mixed bag of results, a sample of which is reported in Table 10.3. Given that no conclusion can be derived from a large number of studies over a long period of time, it is not worthwhile repeating this useless exercise here.

10.5   INSENSITIVITY OF RESULTS: THE HEDGE RATIO

In this section, it is demonstrated that hedging effectiveness does not depend on model specification or the estimation method. This issue arose out of the "cointegration revolution" as a view emerged that

Table 10.3   The findings of some J-curve studies

Study	Findings
1	No support for the J-curve effect in the short run but some support in the long run
2	No support in the short run or long run
3	J-curve is supported
4	J-curve is supported on short-run deterioration combined with long-run improvement
5	Support for the J-curve phenomenon
6	Minor long-run effect
7	The J-curve phenomenon does not exist
8	No J-curve effect is established by majority of short-run dynamics
9	Cointegration between trade balance and exchange rate but no evidence for the J-curve
10	No evidence for the J-curve effect
11	Long-run relationship among trade balance, exchange rate and the two incomes
12	Long-run effect but no J-curve effect
13	Following depreciation, trade balance could move in either direction in the short run
14	In the long run currency appreciation has no effect on the trade balance
15	Following an interest rate shock, exchange rate falls and trade balance worsens
16	Evidence for the J-curve effect is found for 58 industries out of 148 industries

hedging effectiveness depends on cointegration rather than correlation. For example, Alexander (1999) explains how cointegration can be used for the purpose of hedging, arguing that "hedging methodologies based on cointegrated financial assets may be more effective in the long term" and that "investment management strategies that are based only on volatility and correlation of returns cannot guarantee long term performance". She suggests that "since high correlation alone is not sufficient to ensure the long term performance of hedges, there is a need to augment standard risk-return modelling methodologies to take account of common long-term trends in prices", which is "exactly what cointegration provides".

Likewise, it has been suggested by Lien (1996) that if the price of the unhedged position and that of the hedging instrument are cointegrated, the position will be under-hedged if the hedge ratio is estimated from a first difference model. This follows from Granger's representation theorem, which implies that if the prices are cointegrated the first difference model will be misspecified because it ignores cointegration. Lien (1996) shows analytically that the hedger makes a mistake if the hedging decision is based on the hedge ratio derived from a first-difference model that does not contain an error correction term. This view is supported by Ghosh (1993) who finds the hedge ratios obtained from the first difference model to be underestimated because the model is misspecified.

This issue is not only about cointegration and error correction but about model specification in general. For example, it is argued that the hedge ratio should be estimated from conditional rather than unconditional moments, which has been dealt with by Kroner and Sultan (1993) as well as Brooks and Chong (2001). A large number of studies use GARCH models to estimate the hedge ratio (for example, Scarpa and Manera, 2006). Other models used in the literature for the same purpose include BEKK, EWMA, VAR, VECM and EGARCH. With respect to estimation methods, Coffey et al. (2000) use the Cochrane–Orcutt method (generalized least squares), whereas Scholes and Williams (1977) use instrumental variables.

An Alternative View

It has been demonstrated that the econometric modelling of the hedge ratio has no value added whatsoever to the improvement of hedging effectiveness and that using the so-called naïve model (a hedge ratio of one) produces similar results to those obtained from elaborate model specifications and "sophisticated" estimation methods (Moosa, 2003, 2011a). Maharaj et al. (2008) utilize wavelet analysis to estimate the hedge ratios for spot positions on the WTI crude oil, soybeans and the S&P500 index. A two-stage regime switching threshold model is used to estimate asymmetric hedge ratios corresponding to positive and negative returns on futures contracts. Other simple and sophisticated techniques are also used as a benchmark for the purpose of comparison, including the naïve model and the asymmetric error correction GJR-GARCH model. On the basis of the variance ratio test and variance reduction, it is revealed that econometric sophistication does not boost hedging effectiveness.

The Effectiveness of Cross-Currency Hedging

Cross-currency hedging is implemented by taking a position on a currency whose exchange rate against the base currency is correlated with the exchange rate between the base currency and the exposure currency. Let x, y and z be the base currency, currency of exposure and the third currency, respectively. In the case of cross-currency hedging, the price of the unhedged position is $S(x/y)$ while the price of the hedging instrument is $S(x/z)$. Let s_1 and s_2 be the logarithms of the two exchange rates, respectively in which case the rate of return on the unhedged position is Δs_1, while the rate of return on the hedging instrument is Δs_2. To hedge a position on currency y, an opposite position must be taken on currency z, in which case the rate of return on the hedged position is $\Delta s_1 - h\Delta s_2$ where h is the hedge ratio.

The effectiveness of hedging exposure to foreign exchange risk can be measured by the variance of the rate of return on the unhedged position relative to the variance of the rate of return on the hedged position. Thus we test the equality of the variances of the rates on return on the unhedged position and hedged positions where the null hypothesis is $\sigma^2(\Delta s_1) = \sigma^2(\Delta s_1 - h\Delta s_2)$. If the null is rejected in favour of the alternative that $\sigma^2(\Delta s_1) > \sigma^2(\Delta s_1 - h\Delta s_2)$, this means that the hedge is effective. The null hypothesis is rejected if:

$$VR = \frac{\sigma^2(\Delta s_1)}{\sigma^2(\Delta s_1 - h\Delta s_2)} > F(n-1, n-1) \tag{10.12}$$

where VR is the variance ratio and n is the sample size. This test can be complemented by calculating variance reduction:

$$VD = 1 - \frac{1}{VR} \tag{10.13}$$

which should take values such that $0 < VD < 1$ if the hedge is effective.

The Models

The basic first difference model is specified as:

$$\Delta s_{1,t} = \alpha + h\Delta s_{2,t} + \varepsilon_t \tag{10.14}$$

To examine the effect of the estimation method, equation (10.14) is estimated by using OLS, maximum likelihood with an AR(2) process in the residuals, the Cochrane–Orcutt method with an AR(2) process in the residuals, the Gauss–Newton method with an AR(2) process in the residuals, and maximum likelihood with an MA(2) process in the residuals.

The corresponding restricted and unrestricted error correction models are specified as:

$$\Delta s_{1,t} = \alpha + h\Delta s_{2,t} + \phi\varepsilon_{t-1} + \zeta_t \tag{10.15}$$

And:

$$\Delta s_{1,t} = \alpha + h\Delta s_{2,t} + \sum_{i=1}^{n}\beta_i \Delta s_{1,t-i} + \sum_{i=1}^{n}\gamma_i \Delta s_{2,t-i} + \phi\varepsilon_{t-1} + \zeta_t \qquad (10.16)$$

Following Broll et al. (2001) a nonlinear model is used to estimate the hedge ratio, which can be written in first differences as:

$$\Delta s_{1,t} = \alpha + h\Delta s_{2,t} + \gamma\Delta s_{2,t}^2 + \varepsilon_t \qquad (10.17)$$

A restricted nonlinear error correction model is used for the same purpose. This model is specified as:

$$\Delta s_{1,t} = \alpha + h\Delta s_{2,t} + \sum_{i=1}^{3}\phi_i\varepsilon_{t-1}^i + \zeta_t \qquad (10.18)$$

which includes a polynomial of order 3 in the error correction term. Hendry and Ericsson (1991) suggest that a polynomial of degree three in the error correction term is sufficient to capture the adjustment process. The last model specification used in this exercise to estimate the hedge ratio is an autoregressive distributed lag (ARDL) model of the form:

$$\Delta s_{1,t} = h\Delta s_{2,t} + \sum_{i=1}^{m}\alpha_i\Delta s_{1,t-i} + \sum_{i=1}^{n}\beta\Delta s_{2,t-i} + \zeta_t \qquad (10.19)$$

A summary of the model specifications and estimation methods used to estimate the cross-currency hedge ratio is presented in Table 10.4.

Table 10.4 Model specifications and estimation methods of the hedge ratio

	Specification	Estimation Method
1	First difference	OLS
2	First difference	Maximum likelihood with an AR(2) process in the residuals
3	First difference	The Cochrane–Orcutt method with an AR(2) process in the residuals
4	First difference	The Gauss–Newton method with an AR(2) process in the residuals
5	First difference	Maximum likelihood with an MA(2) process in the residuals
6	Restricted EC model	OLS
7	Unrestricted EC model	OLS
8	Quadratic first difference	OLS
9	Restricted nonlinear EC model	OLS
10	Autoregressive distributed lag model in first differences	OLS

Table 10.5   Cross-currency hedge ratios and variance reduction

Model/Method	JPY/USD-JPY/GBP		CHF/USD-CHF/SEK		GBP/USD-GBP/CAD	
	h	*VD*	*h*	*VD*	*h*	*VD*
1	0.602	0.422	0.661	0.242	0.821	0.664
2	0.616	0.422	0.667	0.242	0.806	0.664
3	0.623	0.423	0.682	0.242	0.502	0.664
4	0.623	0.423	0.682	0.242	0.802	0.664
5	0.618	0.423	0.682	0.242	0.797	0.664
6	0.600	0.422	0.652	0.242	0.801	0.664
7	0.623	0.423	0.675	0.242	0.793	0.664
8	0.653	0.421	0.645	0.241	0.814	0.664
9	0.602	0.422	0.661	0.242	0.809	0.664
10	0.626	0.423	0.677	0.242	0.804	0.664
h = correlation	0.650	0.422	0.491	0.224	0.815	0.664

Results

In this exercise quarterly data (obtained from *International Financial Statistics*) are used covering the period 1973:1–2014:3. Three pairs of exchange rates are used: JPY/USD-JPY/GBP, CHF/USD-CHF/SEK and GBP/USD-GBP/CAD. The hedge ratios estimated by using various model specifications and estimation methods are hardly different from each other as shown in Table 10.5. Likewise, hedging effectiveness as measured by variance reduction barely differs. Hedging effectiveness depends on correlation, not on model specification or estimation method. If we choose not to estimate the hedge ratio and put it as equal to the correlation coefficient, the results hardly change. Why then do we bother about estimating the hedge ratio by using this method or that specification when hedging effectiveness is the same by choosing a hedge ratio that is equal to the correlation coefficient?

Another issue that is worthy of investigation here is whether a consideration of correlation in levels rather than in returns matters for hedging effectiveness. If the objective of the hedger is to stabilize price rather than return, then what matters should be correlation in levels rather than in returns. Consider the JPY/USD-JPY/GBP case, where the hedge ratio from the first difference model is 0.602, while the hedge ratio from the model in levels is 0.408. The calculations show that if the hedge ratio derived from the first difference model is used to stabilize price, *VD* turns out to be 0.691. On the hand, if the hedge ratio derived from the model in levels is used to stabilize price, the hedge becomes much more effective as *VD* turns out to be 0.871. Therefore, it is worthwhile to take into account price correlation (which we are not supposed to talk about because there is no such thing as price correlation!).

10.6 CONCLUDING REMARKS

Like the results based on cross-sectional data, results based on time series data are sensitive with respect to model specification, estimation method and variable definition and measurement. The problem with sensitivity is that it allows the researcher to obtain desirable results, thus the temptation to indulge in data mining. On the other hand, the results may be insensitive to these variations but this is not good either because it means that there is no point in developing supposedly more sophisticated estimation and testing methods. In this chapter, these propositions were examined empirically by estimating relations and testing hypotheses pertaining to Wagner's law, Okun's law and the J-curve effect in the case of sensitivity and by evaluating the results obtained from models of the hedge ratio in the case of insensitivity.

The issue of sensitivity of the empirical results is largely ignored in the literature. Hardly anyone casts doubt on the usefulness of results that are all over the place. However, some of those who believe in the work of Leamer (1983) consider these issues explicitly, although this kind of work is largely ignored. For example, Young and Kroeger (2015) acknowledge the seriousness of the problem of "model uncertainty" in social science and raise the question as to "how robust empirical results are to sensible changes in model specification". They contend that while theory provides empirically testable ideas, it does not give concrete direction on how the testing should be done and that theory rarely says which explanatory variables should be in the model, how to define the variables, what the functional form should be, and how to specify the standard errors. As a result, the argument goes, theory can be tested in many different ways, and modest differences in methods may have large influence on the results.

To remedy this problem, they suggest an approach whereby they determine the modelling distribution of estimates across all combinations of possible explanatory variables and model specifications, as well as variable definitions. By following this procedure, they argue, researchers can present their "core, preferred estimate in the context of a distribution of plausible estimates". They also propose a "model influence analysis", showing how each model ingredient affects the coefficient of interest. The problem is that the choice of the core preferred model is subjective, propelled mainly by a preconceived belief and confirmation bias. This suggestion does not solve the problem of the sensitivity of empirical results to model specification, estimation method and variable definition. Sticking with econometrics is a lost cause.

11. The forecasting fiasco

11.1 INTRODUCTION

We have seen that econometrics has two main functions: hypothesis testing and forecasting, with some econometricians claiming that forecasting is the main function (for example, Brown, 2010). Econometrics is elevated to the status of natural science by claiming that econometric models estimated on the basis of historical data can be used to generate forecasts of the dependent variable. However, forecasting with econometric models is a travesty that can lead to disastrous results if decision makers place too much faith on the reliability of the forecasts. It is true that all decision making situations involve forecasting of some sort, but it is untrue that econometric forecasting produces more accurate forecasts than those generated by practitioners using judgment and special information.

In reality successful forecasters do not use econometrics. George Soros made a killing in 1992 by taking short positions against the pound and Italian lira, based on his forecast that the two currencies would come under pressure within the European Monetary System. He made a killing again during the Asian financial crisis of the late 1990s when he took a massive short position on the Thai baht. Warren Buffett has made his massive wealth by betting on the appreciation of undervalued assets, where values were calculated from the analysis of financial statements. Michael Burry, who is a physician, not an econometrician, correctly predicted that the real estate bubble would burst as early as 2007, reaching this conclusion by conducting research on the values of residential real estate and mortgage-backed securities. He took a short position on the market by persuading Goldman Sachs to sell him credit default swaps against the subprime deals he saw as vulnerable. He was right and he did it without econometrics. On the other hand, those who put their faith in econometric forecasting caused a big hedge fund (Long-Term Capital Management) to collapse with massive losses (and this is not the only story).

The fact of the matter is that econometric forecasting is not really forecasting. In-sample forecasting is simply a curve-fitting exercise. Out-of-sample *ex post* forecasting cannot be used for decision making although it is good for writing academic papers. Forecasts are generated out of samples by using the actual realized values of the explanatory variables, yet these forecasts turn out to be dreadful. *Ex ante* forecasting, which is useful for decision making, must involve the forecasting of the explanatory variables to be able to forecast the dependent variable, which augments the forecasting error. This is why simple trend extrapolation produces less bad forecasts than those produced by "structural" econometric models.

In this chapter several forecasting-related issues are considered. First we deal with the so-called Meese–Rogoff puzzle that no model can outperform the random walk in out-of-sample forecasting and argue that the alleged puzzle is not really a puzzle. Then we consider the con job of forecasting with dynamic models in an attempt to outperform the random walk. This is followed by a critical evaluation of the (mal)practice of using spot and futures prices as forecasters and the random walk as a benchmark for evaluating forecasting accuracy. Linking forecasting accuracy to cointegration is also dealt with, although this is no more than an attempt to glorify cointegration as argued in previous chapters. An illustration is presented to demonstrate the con job of forecasting with dynamic models and the malpractice of forecasting with forward and futures prices.

11.2   THE MEESE–ROGOFF PUZZLE

In what has become a highly cited and supposedly a "seminal" paper, Meese and Rogoff (1983a) demonstrated that none of the macroeconomic and time series models they used to forecast exchange rates produced a lower mean square error (and similar metrics) than the random walk. They interpreted this finding to imply that no exchange rate model can outperform the random walk in out-of-sample forecasting. This sounds like a puzzle, because it makes no sense for companies to pay for forecasts generated internally and externally while the random walk provides superior forecasts for free. However, Meese and Rogoff failed to point out that their conclusion is conditional upon the use of quantitative measures of forecasting accuracy that depend entirely on the magnitude of the forecasting error (Moosa and Burns, 2012, 2014b, 2014c, 2015).

Subsequent Research

The proposition that no model can outperform the random walk in out-of-sample forecasting has been accepted at face value by the profession, giving rise to a lingering and an unnecessary controversy. The proposition should take the form of the conditional statement that no model can outperform the random walk in terms of measures of forecasting accuracy that depend on the magnitude of the forecasting error only. This is because it has been demonstrated that the random walk can be outperformed in terms of the ability of the model to predict the direction of change and the profitability of forecasting-based trading operations.

The Meese–Rogoff results stimulated significant research in the area, and numerous attempts have been made to overturn the results using a variety of data, sample periods, methodologies and model specifications. Most of these attempts have been "unsuccessful" in the sense that they could not produce lower forecasting errors than the random walk. Some economists, however, have claimed victory over the random walk (by producing numerically smaller forecasting errors), thus overturning the Meese–Rogoff results, but they failed to conduct formal testing and opted instead to derive inference from the numerical values of measures of forecasting accuracy. Otherwise, they (the "victors") used dodgy procedures that boil down to beating the random walk with a random walk augmented with explanatory variables – that is, dynamic models. Although a minority of economists attempted and succeeded in resolving the puzzle by using alternative measures of forecasting accuracy, they undermined the significance of their work by not claiming that their results overturned the Meese–Rogoff conclusion. This is a manifestation of confirmation bias at its best and the reason why a trivial issue has become the subject of a one-sided debate, as economists repeatedly confirm the myth of the unbeatable random walk.

The Meese–Rogoff puzzle has become a sacred cow, and the paper in which the puzzle was exposed became a "seminal" paper. In reality, the seminal paper is not seminal and the myth is not a myth. The Meese–Rogoff paper was celebrated on its 25th anniversary by a series of papers commemorating the occasion, when it was revealed that the paper had been rejected by the *American Economic Review* because the editor felt that the results would offend and embarrass any potential referee! The implication was that the results were damaging to the profession who could not come up with a model that is better than the naïve random walk. If anything, the paper is flawed, which makes it bewildering why some brilliant economists feel ashamed for not being able to beat the random walk (in the Meese–Rogoff sense) when this is a natural outcome as has been demonstrated.

Explaining the Puzzle

Believing that there is a puzzle, economists have put forward several explanations to demystify the puzzle. Meese and Rogoff themselves explained the puzzle in terms of some econometric problems, including simultaneous equations bias, sampling errors, stochastic movements in the true underlying parameters, model misspecification, failure to account for non-linearities, and the proxies for inflationary expectations. Many economists support the model inadequacy proposition that exchange rate models do not provide a valid representation of exchange rate behaviour in practice (for example, Cheung and Chinn, 1998). Many more explanations have been suggested to resolve the puzzle by economists who do not realize that the best explanation is most likely the simplest one.

The main reason underpinning, and the root cause of, the Meese–Rogoff puzzle has been overlooked in the literature. Assessing forecasting accuracy exclusively by the magnitude of the forecasting error (which is what Meese and Rogoff did) may explain why the random walk cannot be outperformed. In fact, we should expect nothing other than the failure of exchange rate models to produce smaller forecasting errors than the random walk (Moosa, 2013). Actually, this observation is equally valid for other financial prices and for macroeconomic variables, as demonstrated by Moosa and Burns (2014b, 2014c, 2015) and by Moosa and Vaz (2015). When forecasting accuracy is assessed by a broader range of metrics, the Meese and Rogoff results can be overturned with considerable ease. Moosa and Burns (2015) reconsider the Meese–Rogoff puzzle by utilizing a wider range of forecasting accuracy measures that do not rely exclusively on the magnitude of the forecasting error. The main proposition that they put forward is that exchange rate models can outperform the random walk in out-of-sample forecasting when forecasting accuracy is assessed by measures that take into account more than just the magnitude of the forecasting error. They also demonstrate that other explanations, such as those suggested by Meese and Rogoff themselves, cannot explain the puzzle.

The Meese–Rogoff Analysis

In the original study that triggered the controversy, Meese and Rogoff (1983a) set out to assess the predictive power of models explaining the nominal exchange rate in terms of contemporaneous macroeconomic variables, as well as some time series models and the forward rate. Specifically they used three monetary models of exchange rate determination: the flexible-price monetary model, the sticky-price monetary model and the Hooper–Morton model. They estimated the models by using monthly data over the period 1973 to 1981 for three bilateral exchange rates (the US dollar against the German mark, Japanese yen and British pound) and various econometric techniques, including ordinary least squares (OLS), generalized least squares (GLS), and Fair's (1970) instrumental variables (IV) technique. GLS and IV were used to "correct" for serial correlation and account for simultaneous bias, respectively. Out-of-sample forecasts were generated for the period from 1976 to 1981.

Meese and Rogoff compared the forecasts generated by the models with those generated by the random walk (with and without drift). By comparing the numerical values of the forecasting errors, they concluded that the random walk could not be outperformed in exchange rate forecasting. This was the case despite the fact that the forecasts were generated by using the actual out-of-sample values of the explanatory variables (rather than forecasting them) to provide the model with the maximum forecasting ability (which is a common practice in *ex post* forecasting). They did not conduct formal testing to determine the statistical significance of the difference between the forecasting errors of a model and the random walk. In their follow-up study, Meese and Rogoff (1983b) undermined the strength of their original conclusion by stating that the random walk performs "as well as" the structural models, which means that the mighty random walk cannot be outperformed.

The Glory of the Meese–Rogoff Finding

The Meese–Rogoff finding has been discussed widely by the profession since 1983, but the tyranny of the status quo invariably led to the conclusion that the Meese–Rogoff finding is yet to be overturned "comprehensively", that it constitutes a puzzle, and that it represents a serious weakness in the field of international monetary economics. For example, Abhyankar et al. (2005) describe the Meese–Rogoff findings as a "major puzzle in international finance". Evans and Lyons (2005) comment that the Meese–Rogoff finding "has proven robust over the decades" despite it being "the most researched puzzle in international macroeconomics". Fair (2008) describes exchange rate models as "not the pride of open economy macroeconomics" and contends that the "general view still seems pessimistic".

The belief that the Meese–Rogoff work has put international monetary economics to shame is common, even amongst high-calibre economists. Engel et al. (2007) summarize the current state of affairs by stating that the "explanatory power of these [exchange rate] models is essentially zero". Frankel and Rose (1995) argue that the puzzle has a "pessimistic effect" on the field of exchange rate modelling in particular and international finance in general. Bacchetta and van Wincoop (2006) describe the "puzzle" as most likely the major weakness of international macroeconomics. Neely and Sarno (2002) consider the Meese and Rogoff conclusion to be a "devastating critique" of the monetary approach to exchange rate determination and to have "marked a watershed in exchange rate economics". Flood and Rose (2008) emphasize the point that the Meese–Rogoff results are "devastating for the field of international finance", going as far as claiming that "the area [international finance] fell into disrepute" and that "the area is not even represented on many first-rate academic faculties"!! This is dramatization at its best and an illustration of how a trivial issue is blown out of proportions.

There is an apparent bewilderment as to why exchange rate models cannot outperform the random walk, leading to gross overstatements about the miserable state of international finance and international monetary economics, which allegedly have fallen into disrepute. Even economists who actually overturned the Meese–Rogoff results by using alternative measures of forecasting accuracy portrayed their results so modestly as to perpetuate the myth of the puzzle and the historical significance of the Meese–Rogoff work. It is no exaggeration to say that those economists who have ridden the bandwagon make the Meese and Rogoff work look as if it were in the same league as the work of Grigori Perelman, the Russian mathematician who in the early 21st century solved the Poincaré conjecture which had been one of the most important and difficult open problems in topology since 1904. If this is what leading, high-calibre economists and econometricians say, what hope have we got that an early career researcher or a PhD student would sometime challenge the establishment?

Flaws in the Meese–Rogoff Work

It is surprising that the Meese–Rogoff puzzle has been taken as seriously as it has been despite the flaws in the Meese–Rogoff work, which no econometrician has complained about although these flaws are econometric in nature. The first of these flaws is failure to test for the statistical significance of the difference between two root mean square errors (RMSEs). While most subsequent studies made the same mistake, some of them correctly used the Diebold–Mariano (1995) test without emphasizing the point that Meese and Rogoff failed to do that, hence their (Meese and Rogoff's) results could not be taken seriously. Yes, the Diebold–Mariano test was not available in the early 1980s but the Ashley et al. (1980) test was available. Even if no test is available, deriving inference from the numerical values of statistics estimated with standard errors is not exactly right, particularly in a paper that has received so much attention. What has happened to the motto "test, test, test"? This, however, does not mean that testing would have shown that exchange rate models can outperform the random walk in terms of the magnitude of the forecasting error.

The most serious flaw, however, is that failure to outperform the random walk in terms of the magnitude of the forecasting error is a natural outcome, not a puzzle. We should expect nothing but failure, particularly over short forecasting horizons and when high-frequency data are used. Kilian and Taylor (2003) raise the question as to why it is so difficult to beat the random walk in the title of their paper, but they do not suggest that the Meese–Rogoff results are not surprising and that opposite results would have been so. By using simulated data to account for a wide range of exchange rate volatility, Moosa (2013) demonstrates that as volatility rises, the forecasting error of any model rises more rapidly than that of the random walk. Likewise, Moosa and Vaz (2015) demonstrate, by using two stock price models, that as price volatility rises, the RMSE of the random walk rises but the RMSE of the model rises more rapidly. It follows that the Meese–Rogoff finding is a natural outcome, not a puzzle and that nothing is remarkable about their results.

Meese and Rogoff used three, magnitude-only, measures of forecasting accuracy: mean error, mean absolute error and mean square error (hence the root mean square error). However, forecasting accuracy should be assessed by reference to the purpose for which forecasts are generated and used. In the real world, exchange rate forecasts are used as an input in the financial decision making process. Accordingly, the ultimate test of forecasting power should be the profitability of forecasting-based trading, which is more related to the ability of the model to predict the direction of change (Moosa, 2014). The critical question is whether or not the Meese and Rogoff results are robust when forecasting accuracy is assessed by measures that do not rely exclusively on the magnitude of the forecasting error. Moosa and Burns (2014b, 2014c, 2015) demonstrate that the Meese–Rogoff results are not robust in this sense.

Although the forecasts generated by the random walk look great, the random walk is a dumb forecasting model. Intuitively we should expect any model to outperform a dumb model like the random walk because the random walk without drift tells us that the best forecast is that of a no-change while the random walk with drift implies that the exchange rate always rises or falls. The random walk (in a stochastic form) conveys a plausible idea that the exchange rate is as likely to rise as to fall, but using it (in a deterministic form) as a benchmark to measure forecasting accuracy is inappropriate. This is why the random walk is justifiably dubbed "naïve". If we look at a time plot of the actual exchange rate and the random walk forecast we will see two graphs that move together but one of them turns before the other. This should be a good property for a forecaster except that in this case the forecast follows the actual, which means that the actual value forecasts the forecast value. This sounds rather dumb, which means that any model should be better than the random walk.

Likewise, the forward rate (more precisely, the lagged forward rate), which Meese and Rogoff used as forecaster, is a bad forecaster – it is exactly as bad as the lagged spot rate implied by the random walk. The forward rate is not a good forecaster of the future spot rate because the two rates are determined simultaneously and related via covered interest parity. Since the two rates are related contemporaneously, the lagged rate (the forecaster) turns after the actual rate (the "forecastee"). Using the lagged forward rate as a forecaster and the random walk as a benchmark is inappropriate (to say the least) because the lagged spot and forward rates are almost perfectly correlated. We will come back to this point later on.

Resolving the Puzzle

Studies that have been conducted to resolve the Meese–Rogoff puzzle may be classified under one of three categories. The first category includes those that followed the Meese–Rogoff methodology, making the same mistakes, obtaining similar results and preserving the myth of the puzzle, with all the praise that goes with it. Under the second category we find studies claiming victory over the random walk by using econometric modifications such as the introduction of dynamics and nonlinearities and by using time-varying parametric (TVP) estimation. Most of the economists claiming victory did so by using dynamic modelling, which effectively boils down to beating the random walk with a random walk. Most studies, however, preserved the myth of the puzzle by overlooking the fact that beating the random walk does not necessarily mean producing lower forecasting errors, which meant that attention was diverted away from the root cause of the puzzle (improper measures of forecasting accuracy) to the econometric problems highlighted by Meese and Rogoff.

No wonder then that the Meese–Rogoff puzzle has survived the test of time. Economists working in this field (and economists in general) demonstrate an incredible lack of resolve in challenging established ideas, albeit faulty. This is confirmation bias at its best: if you challenge an established idea, your paper will be rejected. Since it has become more important to publish papers than to reveal the truth, it is tantalizing to report results that confirm the Meese–Rogoff results. The field is in a bad shape, not because exchange rate models cannot outperform the random walk in terms of the RMSE, but because of the lack of will to challenge well-established but faulty ideas such as the Meese–Rogoff puzzle. Economic and financial models in general are not that great in terms of explanatory and predictive power but they are not as bad as not being able to outperform the random walk in out-of-sample forecasting.

11.3 FORECASTING WITH DYNAMIC MODELS: A CON JOB?

Some economists have attempted to boost the forecasting power of exchange rate models by introducing dynamics, including the use of error correction mechanisms. For example, Taylor (1995) suggests that "researchers have found that one key to improving forecast performance based on economic fundamentals lies in the introduction of equation dynamics". He points out that:

> [T]his has been done in various ways: by using dynamic forecasting equations for the forcing variables in the forward-looking, rational expectations version of the flexible-price monetary model, by incorporating dynamic partial adjustment terms into the estimating equation, by using time-varying parameter estimation techniques, and – most recently – by using dynamic error correction forms.

However, the use of dynamics, including error correction models, implicitly and effectively introduces a lagged dependent variable, which makes the underlying model some sort of an "augmented" random walk. The random walk component, which is represented by the lagged dependent variable, typically dominates the effect of the explanatory variables suggested by theory to be important determinants of the exchange rate. It may be disingenuous, therefore, to claim that a model outperforms the random walk just because it has been augmented by a random walk component. Moosa and Burns (2014a) demonstrate that dynamic specifications outperform the corresponding static models but improvement in the forecasting power may not be sufficient for the dynamic models to do a better job than the random walk. They explain these results by suggesting that any dynamic specification or transformation of the static model leads to the introduction of a lagged dependent variable, which in effect is a random walk component. The analysis leads to the conclusion that it is implausible to aim at beating the random walk by augmenting a static model with a random walk component.

The very act of adding a lagged dependent variable to a model is tantamount to converting the model into random walk, an "augmented" random walk. Adding a lagged dependent variable to enhance predictive accuracy is equivalent to saying that introducing a random walk component is desirable to boost the forecasting power of the model. It is a con job.

Econometrics as a con art

Model Specification

Consider the flexible-price monetary model, which is specified as:

$$s_t = a_0 + a_1(m_t - m_t^*) + a_2(y_t - y_t^*) + a_3(i_t - i_t^*) + \varepsilon_t \qquad (11.1)$$

where s is the log of the exchange rate (measured as the domestic currency price of one unit of the foreign currency), m is the log of the money supply, y is the log of industrial production, i is the short-term interest rate. The simplest way to introduce dynamics into equation (11.1) is to add a lagged dependent variable, which gives:

$$s_t = a_0 + a_1(m_t - m_t^*) + a_2(y_t - y_t^*) + a_3(i_t - i_t^*) + a_4 s_{t-1} + \varepsilon_t \qquad (11.2)$$

More elaborate dynamic specifications are represented by a general error correction model, an error correction model without explicit lagged dependent variables, a first difference model with lagged dependent variables, and a first difference model without lagged dependent variables. The general error correction model is specified as:

$$\Delta s_t = \alpha_0 + \sum_{j=1}^{\ell} \alpha_j \Delta s_{t-j} + \sum_{j=0}^{\ell} \beta_j \Delta(m_{t-j} - m_{t-j}^*) + \sum_{j=0}^{\ell} \gamma_j \Delta(y_{t-j} - y_{t-j}^*) +$$
$$\sum_{j=0}^{\ell} \delta_j \Delta(i_{t-j} - i_{t-j}^*) + \phi \varepsilon_{t-1} + \zeta_t \qquad (11.3)$$

By moving from general to specific we can obtain more parsimonious specifications by imposing the appropriate coefficient restrictions on equation (11.3). First, by imposing the restriction $\alpha_j = 0$ for $j = 1,\ldots,\ell$, we obtain an error correction model without explicit lagged dependent variables. This model can be written as:

$$\Delta s_t = \alpha_0 + \sum_{j=0}^{\ell} \beta_j \Delta(m_{t-j} - m_{t-j}^*) + \sum_{j=0}^{\ell} \gamma_j \Delta(y_{t-j} - y_{t-j}^*) +$$
$$\sum_{j=0}^{\ell} \delta_j \Delta(i_{t-j} - i_{t-j}^*) + \phi \varepsilon_{t-1} + \zeta_t \qquad (11.4)$$

We can also specify first difference models with and without lagged dependent variables by imposing the restriction $\phi = 0$ on equations (11.3) and (11.4), respectively. These models are written as follows:

$$\Delta s_t = \alpha_0 + \sum_{j=1}^{\ell} \alpha_j \Delta s_{t-j} + \sum_{j=0}^{\ell} \beta_j \Delta(m_{t-j} - m_{t-j}^*) + \sum_{j=0}^{\ell} \gamma_j \Delta(y_{t-j} - y_{t-j}^*)$$
$$+ \sum_{j=0}^{\ell} \delta_j \Delta(i_{t-j} - i_{t-j}^*) + \zeta_t \qquad (11.5)$$

$$\Delta s_t = \alpha_0 + \sum_{j=0}^{\ell} \Delta \beta_j (m_{t-j} - m_{t-j}^*) + \sum_{j=0}^{\ell} \gamma_j \Delta (y_{t-j} - y_{t-j}^*)$$
$$+ \sum_{j=0}^{\ell} \delta_j \Delta (i_{t-j} - i_{t-j}^*) + \zeta_t \tag{11.6}$$

The introduction of dynamics to the static models, which boosts forecasting accuracy, results from the fact that this process boils down to the introduction of a random walk component. Schinasi and Swamy (1989) make this point quite explicit with respect to exchange rate models, suggesting that "the random walk model and the structural models with lagged dependent variables are nested". This is why they uncover the "striking observation" that "adding a lagged dependent variable makes a substantial difference in the forecasting ability of all three structural models". Schinasi and Swamy (1989) view a structural model with a lagged dependent variable as a model in which the lagged variable (representing a random walk process) and the explanatory variables "are allowed to explain the spot exchange rate". However, experience shows that the random walk component invariably prevails (Kling, 2010, 2011), in which case a random walk with explanatory variables rarely performs better (in terms of the RMSE) than a pure random walk.

Dynamics Implies Random Walk

It can be demonstrated that no matter what shape or form is taken by dynamics, all dynamic specifications boil down to the introduction of a lagged dependent variable. Hence, forecasting accuracy does not change much as a result of changing the dynamic form of the model. Start, for example, with the error correction specification represented by equation (11.3). The equation can be simplified by replacing the three explanatory variables with a vector, x_t, and imposing the restriction $\ell = 1$. Since $\Delta s_t = s_t - s_{t-1}$ and $\Delta x_t = x_t - x_{t-1}$ equation (11.3) becomes:

$$s_t - s_{t-1} = \alpha_0 + \alpha_1(s_{t-1} - s_{t-2}) + \beta_0(x_t - x_{t-1}) + \beta_1(x_t - x_{t-2}) +$$
$$\phi(s_{t-1} - a_0 - a_1 x_{t-1}) + \zeta_t \tag{11.7}$$

which can be simplified to:

$$s_t = (\alpha_0 - \phi a_0) + (1 + \alpha_1 + \phi)s_{t-1} - \alpha_1 s_{t-2} + \beta_0 x_t + (-\beta_0 + \beta_1 - \phi a_1)x_{t-1}$$
$$-\beta_1 x_{t-2} + \zeta_t \tag{11.8}$$

The process $s_t = (\alpha_0 - \phi a_0) + (1 + \alpha_1 + \phi)s_{t-1}$ represents random walk without drift if $(\alpha_0 - \phi a_0) = 0$ and $(1 + \alpha_1 + \phi) = 1$. Because the exchange rate is an integrated process, the value of the coefficient on the lagged dependent variable is typically close to one (insignificantly different from one). Hence, an error correction model that is written in first difference form can be re-written as a model (in levels) with a lagged dependent variable. This is effectively introducing a random walk component.

The same result can be obtained by manipulating equation (11.4) (with the same restrictions). In this case we have:

$$s_t - s_{t-1} = \alpha_0 + \beta_0(x_t - x_{t-1}) + \beta_1(x_{t-1} - x_{t-2}) + \phi(s_{t-1} - a_0 - a_1 x_{t-1}) + \zeta_t \tag{11.9}$$

which can be rearranged as follows:

$$s_t = (\alpha_0 - \phi a_0) + (1 + \phi)s_{t-1} + \beta_0 x_t + (\beta_1 - \phi a_1)x_{t-1} + \beta_1 x_{t-2} + \zeta_t \tag{11.10}$$

where the random walk process is $s_t = (\alpha_0 - \phi a_0) + (1 + \phi)s_{t-1} + \zeta_t$. Hence even the first difference model without an explicit lagged dependent variable can be shown to have a random walk component.

Likewise, equation (11.6) can be re-written as:

$$\Delta s_t = \alpha_0 + \beta_0 \Delta x_t + \beta_1 \Delta x_{t-1} + \zeta_t \tag{11.11}$$

which gives:

$$s_t = \alpha_0 + s_{t-1} + \beta_0 x_t + (\beta_1 - \beta_0)x_{t-1} + \zeta_t \tag{11.12}$$

where the process $s_t = \alpha_0 + s_{t-1} + \zeta_t$ is random walk without drift if $\alpha_0 = 0$. In this case the lagged dependent variable has a coefficient of one by construction.

It can be shown that the use of the partial adjustment mechanism of Nerlove (1958b) produces a model with a lagged dependent variable. Here we distinguish between the actual, s_t, and equilibrium, $\bar{s}_t$, exchange rates. Assume that:

$$\bar{s}_t = \alpha + \beta x_t + \varepsilon_t \tag{11.13}$$

The partial adjustment mechanism is written as:

$$s_t - s_{t-1} = k(\bar{s}_t - s_{t-1}) + u_t \tag{11.14}$$

where k is the adjustment coefficient. By substituting equation (11.13) into equation (11.14), we obtain:

$$s_t - s_{t-1} = k(\alpha + \beta x_t + \varepsilon_t - s_{t-1}) + u_t \tag{11.15}$$

or

$$s_t = k\alpha + k\beta x_t + (1 - k)s_{t-1} + (u_t - k\varepsilon_t) \tag{11.16}$$

which obviously involves a lagged dependent variable, hence a random walk component.

Likewise, it can be demonstrated that a model with an autoregressive distributed lag structure in the explanatory variables can be manipulated to produce a model with a lagged dependent variable, which is the essence of the Koyck transformation (Koyck, 1954). Let us start with the ARDL model:

$$s_t = \alpha + \sum_{j=0}^{\ell} \beta_j x_{t-j} + \varepsilon_t \tag{11.17}$$

Assume that the distributed lag is geometrically declining such that $\beta_j = k^j \beta_0$ where k falls between zero and one. Equation (11.17) can be re-written as:

$$s_t = \alpha + \sum_{j=0}^{\ell} k^j \beta_0 x_{t-j} + \varepsilon_t \tag{11.18}$$

By applying the lag operator to (11.18) we obtain:

$$s_{t-1} = \alpha + \sum_{j=0}^{\ell} k^j \beta_0 x_{t-j-1} + \varepsilon_{t-1} \tag{11.19}$$

Multiplying (11.19) by k and subtracting from (11.18), we have:

$$s_t - ks_{t-1} = \alpha(1 - k) + \beta_0 x_t + (\varepsilon_t - k\varepsilon_{t-1}) \tag{11.20}$$

or

$$s_t = \alpha(1 - k) + \beta_0 x_t + ks_{t-1} + (\varepsilon_t - k\varepsilon_{t-1}) \tag{11.21}$$

which again contains a lagged dependent variable. Kling (2010) argues that the assumption of geometrically declining lags saved Nerlove from having to estimate a regression including many lagged explanatory variables, which "was no small consideration in the 1950s, when econometricians were solving for regression coefficients by hand".

It seems, therefore, that no matter how dynamics is introduced, we end up with an equation that contains a lagged dependent variable, which effectively represents a random walk component. This is why a model with any dynamic specification produces forecasts that are not different from the forecasts produced by a simple random walk (at least in terms of the RMSE). This point is illustrated with an example in Section 11.6.

11.4 FORECASTING WITH FORWARD AND FUTURES PRICES

Following Meese and Rogoff (1983a), it has become customary in any exchange rate forecasting exercise to use the random walk (the lagged spot rate) as a benchmark for measuring forecasting accuracy. In terms of the level (not the log) of the exchange rate, the general random walk (with drift) model is specified as:

$$S_t = \alpha_0 + \alpha_1 S_{t-1} + \varepsilon_t \tag{11.22}$$

If the coefficient restriction $(\alpha_0, \alpha_1) = (0,1)$ is imposed, which is empirically plausible, the forecaster becomes the lagged spot rate – that is, $\hat{S}_t = S_{t-1}$.

The use of the forward rate as a forecaster is based on the unbiased efficiency hypothesis (UEH), which postulates that the forward rate is an unbiased and efficient predictor of the future spot rate (the spot rate observed on the maturity date of the forward contract). The UEH is written as:

$$S_t = \beta_0 + \beta_1 F_{t-1} + \varepsilon_t \tag{11.23}$$

Again, if the coefficient restriction $(\beta_0, \beta_1) = (0,1)$ is imposed, which is empirically plausible, the forecaster becomes the lagged forward rate – that is, $\hat{S}_t = F_{t-1}$.

The Failure of UEH in the FX Market

Explanations for the failure of unbiased efficiency in the foreign exchange market include covered interest parity, the peso problem, central bank intervention, transaction costs, political risk, foreign exchange risk, purchasing power risk, interest rate risk, differences in real interest and exchange rates, and the effect of news (see Moosa, 2000, for details). Out of these explanations, the least emphasized but most plausible explanation is that of covered interest parity (CIP) because the CIP condition implies that the spot and forward rates are related contemporaneously, which makes the lagged relation representing the UEH (11.23) misspecified.

In practice, banks quote forward rates for various maturities, not on the basis of expectations or forecasting of the future level of the spot rate but rather by adjusting the spot rate for a factor that reflects the interest rate differential. The resulting quote is the only value of the forward exchange rate that eliminates no-risk arbitrage opportunities and allows banks to hedge the underlying short forward position (Moosa, 2004). Given this simple and realistic explanation, it is not clear why the forward-spot relation "remains a theoretical and empirical puzzle" (Aggarwal and Zong, 2008) and why "an important puzzle in international finance is the failure of the forward exchange rate to be a rational forecast of the future spot rate" (Aggarwal et al., 2009). This is just another neoclassical puzzle that is not a puzzle (like the Meese–Rogoff puzzle). The forward exchange rate is not an expectation variable but rather the result of a "simple arithmetic operation" (Lavoie, 2000).

Commodity Futures

In the international finance literature it is no longer universally accepted that the forward exchange rate is an accurate, unbiased and efficient forecaster of the spot exchange rate. However, the proposition that futures prices of crude oil can be used to forecast spot prices seems to be accepted without much scrutiny. This proposition can be challenged both theoretically and empirically, suggesting instead that futures prices have nothing to do with forecasting. Since spot and futures prices are related contemporaneously, futures prices are as good or as bad forecasters as spot prices, in which case it is not sound to use the futures price as a forecaster and the spot price as a benchmark. Moosa (2016c) produces results showing that spot and futures prices are not as good forecasters as they are portrayed to be. While futures prices produce small forecasting errors, because they are related contemporaneously to spot prices, they fail to capture turning points and exhibit signs of biasedness and inefficiency. Adjusting the random walk and the unbiased efficiency equations, by including a time-varying risk premium or drift factor, does not make the models better in terms of predicting turning points.

Numerous attempts have been made to examine the forecasting power of futures prices on the same basis of unbiased efficiency. These studies are motivated by the view that one of the functions of commodity futures markets is the provision of unbiased forecasting of the spot price. The empirical evidence on the predictive power of futures prices is mixed. Some of those finding evidence for unbiased efficiency, hence the legitimacy of using futures prices as forecasters, base their conclusion on a finding of cointegration between spot and futures prices, which is not a necessary and sufficient condition for unbiased efficiency – that is, cointegration between spot and lagged futures prices does not preclude the possibility of the forecaster over- or under-predicting actual values consistently, which is a sign of biasedness. When weak evidence for cointegration is found, the failure of unbiased efficiency is explained in terms of irrationality of expectations and/or the presence of time-varying risk premia. Unlike the international finance literature, the literature on the use of futures prices as forecasters does not seem to acknowledge the proposition that futures prices are linked to spot prices by the cost of carry relation or a modified version thereof. What is overlooked is that spot and futures prices are determined contemporaneously and that futures prices have nothing to do with forecasting because they are not determined on the basis of expectations.

The empirical evidence on unbiased efficiency is mixed at best. Serletis and Banack (1990) find evidence that is "consistent with efficiency", showing that the current spot price dominates the current futures price in explaining movements in the future spot price. The problem is that they define efficiency to be implied by cointegration between spot and lagged futures prices, when cointegration is not a necessary and sufficient condition for unbiased efficiency. Serletis (1991), on the other hand, finds evidence suggesting the presence of a time-varying risk premium. Bopp and Lady (1991) compare the use of futures and lagged spot prices as explanatory variables in a forecasting model, concluding that either the spot or the futures price can be the superior forecasting variable, depending upon market conditions, and that the information content of the two price series is essentially the same. Samii (1992) demonstrates that futures prices are unbiased predictors of spot prices whereas Quan (1992) finds that spot and futures prices quoted less than or equal to three months ahead are cointegrated, but no cointegration is found if futures prices are quoted more than three months ahead. Moosa and Al-Loughani (1994) report results indicating that futures prices are neither unbiased nor efficient forecasters of spot prices, whereas Gulen (1998) finds that futures prices are efficient predictors of spot prices. Ma (1989) and Kumar (1992) find that futures prices outperform the no-change model (random walk) in out-of-sample forecasting, which is almost impossible.

Even in more recent literature, it is suggested that futures oil prices are used as a proxy for the market's expectation of the spot price. For example, Alquist and Arbatli (2010) suggest that "it is common for policy-makers and market analysts to use the price of crude oil futures contracts to interpret developments in the global crude oil market". However, they cast a shadow of doubt on the adequacy of forecasting by futures prices, suggesting that "such forecasts are volatile". The fact of the matter in this case is that the forecasts can only be as volatile as the series being forecast because the forecasts follow the actual values. They cannot be (by definition and design) "highly volatile relative to the no-change forecasts". It is rather strange for them to suggest that the available evidence is broadly supportive of the proposition (which they call assumption) that futures prices can be used as a measure of the expected spot price.

It seems that most of those claiming that futures prices are better forecasters than spot prices (the no-change model) base their conclusions on the numerical values of measures of forecasting accuracy that depend on the magnitude of the forecasting error. For example, Chernenko et al. (2004) provide evidence indicating that "futures-based forecasts have a marginally lower mean-squared prediction error than the no-change forecast". They seem to overlook the fact that "marginally" means nothing as these metrics are estimated with standard errors, which means that what matters is statistical significance, not the numerical value, of the difference. It is more likely that the marginal difference is statistically insignificant, which means that futures-based forecasting is no better than the no-change forecast.

While Chinn et al. (2005) conclude that "futures-based forecasts are unbiased predictors of the spot price of oil" and that "they perform better than the random-walk forecasts", Chinn and Coibion (2009) find that "futures prices do not systematically outperform the random-walk forecasts". Wu and McCallum (2005) also find that "futures prices tend to be less accurate than the no-change forecast". Likewise, Alquist and Kilian (2010) conclude that the no-change forecast outperforms futures prices. The evidence is by no means favourable to unbiased efficiency, as suggested by Alquist and Arbatli (2010). The fact of the matter is that futures prices are not meant to be forecasters, but only Knetsch (2007) concludes that futures prices should not be used as a predictor of spot prices. As an alternative he suggests the use of the cost of carry equation and forecasting the marginal convenience yield from an autoregressive process.

The belief that forward and futures prices can be used to forecast spot prices is driven by number crunching rather than by thinking logically about the issue. By putting time series on spot and lagged forward prices in a computer, a researcher would find "good" results in terms of the root mean square error or similar metrics. The researcher would obey the econometric results because they are "nice", without thinking about the rationale for why forward and futures prices seem to forecast spot prices and why the root mean square error tends to be small. However, a graph of the actual and forecast prices would show clearly that forward and futures prices are dumb forecasters as they fail to pick the turning points consistently. Naturally, no author would report a graph like this because it is embarrassing, to say the least.

11.5   FORECASTING AND COINTEGRATION

In section 11.6 it will be demonstrated that error correction models do not forecast better than the corresponding first difference models. This issue has been investigated in the literature because one of the reasons that has been put forward to explain the Meese–Rogoff puzzle is failure to take into account cointegration.

Studies of the effect of cointegration on forecasting accuracy involve a comparison of the forecasting power of an ECM with a straight first difference model (or VAR in levels and first differences). The general finding of this strand of literature is that taking account of cointegration does not pay off in the sense that it does not boost forecasting accuracy. More specifically, it has been found that a cointegration-based error correction model does not forecast better than the corresponding first difference model. This finding has been explained in terms of many factors such as measurement errors in the long-run relation, measures of forecasting accuracy, structural breaks, the length of forecasting horizon, and inadequacy of the basic ECM. Moosa and Vaz (2016b) take this matter further by comparing the forecasting power of dynamic models that exhibit no cointegration with models that exhibit cointegration with and without the error correction term, arguing against the prevailing explanation of measurement errors and suggesting a new explanation for what seems to be a puzzle.

The Rationale

It follows from Granger's Representation Theorem that if variables are cointegrated, a first difference model will be misspecified and may not forecast well, regardless of the relevance of the included variables. To illustrate this proposition we start with the long-run relation:

$$y_t = a + bx_t + \varepsilon_t \qquad (11.24)$$

According to Granger's Representation Theorem, cointegration implies and is implied by the presence of a valid ECM, which means that if $x_t \sim I(1)$, $y_t \sim I(1)$ and $\varepsilon_t \sim I(0)$, then the corresponding ECM is specified as:

$$\Delta y_t = \alpha + \sum_{i=1}^{k} \beta_i \Delta y_{t-i} + \sum_{i=0}^{k} \gamma_i \Delta x_{t-i} + \phi \varepsilon_{t-1} + \zeta_t \qquad (11.25)$$

such that $\phi < 0$. In other words, for equation (11.25) to be a valid ECM, ϕ must be negative and statistically significant. This is how cointegration implies the presence of a valid EC model. Conversely, error correction implies cointegration, in which case we start with the ECM:

$$\Delta y_t = \alpha + \sum_{i=1}^{k} \beta_i \Delta y_{t-i} + \sum_{i=0}^{k} \gamma_i \Delta x_{t-i} + \phi(y_{t-1} - x_{t-1}) + \zeta_t \quad (11.26)$$

If ϕ is significantly negative, then $\varepsilon_t \sim I(0)$. The difference between the EC models represented by (11.25) and (11.26) is that in equation (11.26) the restriction $(a,b) = (0,1)$ is imposed on the error correction term – this restriction may be implied by theory.

The underlying proposition is that if x and y are cointegrated, then the error correction model (11.25) will produce more accurate forecasts than a first difference model that excludes the error correction term – that is, a model of the form:

$$\Delta y_t = \alpha + \sum_{i=1}^{k} \beta_i \Delta y_{t-i} + \sum_{i=0}^{k} \gamma_i \Delta x_{t-i} + \zeta_t \quad (11.27)$$

In reality, however, equation (11.25) does not forecast better than equation (11.27).

Explanations

Christofferson and Diebold (1998) provide an explanation as to why the exclusion of the error correction term leads to deterioration in forecasting accuracy. Recall that the value of the error correction term at any point in time is a measure of the deviation of the actual value of the dependent variable from the long-run relation as represented by equation (11.24). The coefficient on the error correction term, ϕ, is a measure of the rate at which deviation from long-run equilibrium is eliminated. They suggest that information about whether the cointegrating relation is in equilibrium or not (and if not, how far it is from equilibrium) helps to predict how the dependent variable moves in the near future since deviation from equilibrium tends to be eliminated. Therefore, the value of the EC term at any point in time is valuable for near-horizon forecasting as it contains information that can boost forecasting accuracy. However, they argue that since the long-run forecast of the EC term is always zero, it is doubtful that it can provide any information to improve long-run forecasting.

While Christofferson and Diebold (1998) provide an explanation as to why cointegration matters, they also identify the condition under which it does not matter. And while it is intuitively plausible to suggest that the exclusion of the error correction term is detrimental to forecasting power if cointegration is present, the common finding is that vector error correction (VEC) models do not predict better than vector autoregression (VAR) models (for example, Clements and Hendry, 1996; Hoffman and Rasche, 1996; Lin and Tsay, 1996).

One explanation that has been suggested in the literature for this empiri-cal observation (which sounds like a puzzle) is that the ECM represented by equation (11.25), unlike equation (11.26), does not incorporate the coefficient restrictions suggested by economic theory, which means that the ECM represented by equation (11.26) should produce better forecasts than the ECM (11.25). In other words, it is suggested that equation (11.25) may not forecast well because of errors in the estimation of the coefficients of the long-run relation. For example, if the estimates of the coefficients a and b are $\hat{a}$ and $\hat{b}$, respectively, then forecasts are generated from the ECM:

$$\Delta y_t = \alpha + \sum_{i=1}^{k}\beta_i\Delta y_{t-i} + \sum_{i=0}^{k}\gamma_i\Delta x_{t-i} + \phi(y_{t-1} - \hat{a} - \hat{b}x_{t-1}) + \zeta_t \quad (11.28)$$

If $\hat{a} = a + \eta$ and $\hat{b} = b + \omega$ where η and ω are estimation errors then fore-casts are generated from the ECM:

$$\Delta y_t = \alpha + \sum_{i=1}^{k}\beta_i\Delta y_{t-i} + \sum_{i=0}^{k}\gamma_i\Delta x_{t-i} + \phi[y_{t-1} - (a + \eta) - (b + \omega)x_{t-1}] + \zeta_t \quad (11.29)$$

when the true EC model is:

$$\Delta y_t = \alpha + \sum_{i=1}^{k}\beta_i\Delta y_{t-i} + \sum_{i=0}^{k}\gamma_i\Delta x_{t-i} + \phi[y_{t-1} - a - bx_{t-1}] + \zeta_t \quad (11.30)$$

This explanation is put forward by a number of economists. For example, Swanson (2002) provides a theoretical basis for why imposing the long-run relations suggested by economic theory on cointegrating vectors could improve the forecasting performance of ECMs. Hoffman and Rasche (1996) impose the restrictions suggested by economic theory and find some advantage in incorporating cointegration, particularly as compared to VAR models. Bachmeier and Swanson (2005) allow for estimated and theoretically specified cointegrating relations and find that forecasting gains are obtained by allowing monetary aggregates to enter into predic-tion models via the restrictions among money, prices and output as rep-resented by the quantity theory. They even argue that the random walk routinely forecasts better than correctly specified alternative models due to parameter estimation errors – this is the wrong explanation for the Meese–Rogoff puzzle.

Another explanation for the observed inferiority of cointegration-based ECMs is presented by Clements and Hendry (1999) who show that equi-librium mean shifts could induce major forecast failure, which means that imposing cointegration improves forecasting accuracy only if there is no shift in equilibrium means. If a structural break occurs and the equilibrium mean shifts, the ECM interprets this shift as disequilibrium. Since the

ECM is designed to remove any disequilibrium by adjusting in the oppo-site direction, the ECM forecasts a change downwards when the under-lying variable is going up. Clements and Hendry (1996) show that VAR models forecast better than cointegration-based ECMs when the means of the cointegrating relations are non-constant. In another paper, Hendry and Clements (2001) suggest that cointegration makes the resulting models sensitive to shifts in equilibrium means.

Some explanations have been put forward for the failure of ECMs to outperform the random walk in terms of measures of forecasting accuracy and the way in which forecasts are generated. Anderson et al. (2002) dem-onstrate that when the generalized forecast error second moment is used as a measure of forecasting accuracy, ECMs deliver better forecasts than the random walk (particularly at short-term horizons), which is not the case when the RMSE is used. On the other hand, Assenmacher-Wesche and Pesaran (2008) and Pesaran et al. (2009) show that pooled forecasts gener-ated from ECMs beat the random walk. Banerjee et al. (2013) suggest that a more robust ECM specification can perform better than a straight ECM. For this purpose they advocate the use of the factor-augmented error correction model (FECM) proposed by Banerjee and Marcellino (2009). They examine the forecasting performance of the FECM by means of an analytical example, Monte Carlo simulations and several empirical appli-cations and find that, relative to the FAVAR, FECM generally produces a higher forecasting precision and in general "marks a very useful step forward for forecasting with large datasets". Once more, it is suggested that a new model can do what its predecessors could not although any dynamic model is no different from the random walk.

The finding that cointegration-based ECMs do not perform well has been attributed to several factors. However, the most widely accepted view is that ECMs are inferior to VARs because of measurement errors in the estimated EC term, which explains why the imposition of the restrictions suggested by theory leads to more accurate forecasts. This argument can be questioned on the grounds that the underlying theory may not be sound. For example, the monetary model of exchange rates is derived by imposing the proportionality and symmetry restrictions on purchasing power parity – these should be testable hypotheses rather than theory-implied restric-tions (for example, Moosa, 1994).

In fact the imposition of these restrictions may be a reason for the poor forecasting power of the monetary model. Baum et al. (2001) examine nonlinear adjustment in purchasing power parity and consider as a contri-bution to the literature the estimation of deviations from equilibrium using cointegration analysis rather than imposing the strict PPP cointegrating vector to calculate the real exchange rate. They suggest that "strong PPP" (that is, unrestricted PPP) might not hold because of differential composition of price indices across countries, differential productivity shocks, and measurement errors in prices as a result of aggregation and index construction. Likewise, Neely and Sarno (2002) and Tawadros (2001) argue that the imposition of the proportionality and symmetry restrictions may be a source of misspecification that can be detrimental to forecasting accuracy. It is strange that econometrics is supposed to be about "test, test, test" but what we hear now is that we can do away with testing.

Moosa and Vaz (2016b) put forward another explanation for why cointegration-based ECMs do not perform better than the corresponding first difference models. They believe that there is no value added in the EC term over and above what is offered by the distributed lag structure of the dependent and explanatory variables. The assumption made in the literature is that the forecasting power of ECMs lies in the error correction mechanism because deviations from the long-run relation determine in which direction the dependent variable should move and by how much. While this proposition is intuitively plausible, it can be demonstrated that an ECM and the corresponding first difference model have similar dynamic structures, meaning that which model outperforms the other is an empirical issue. This is a simple but more logical explanation for the underlying issue.

11.6   AN ILLUSTRATION

Assuming a sample of n observations ($t = 1,2,\ldots n$), out-of-sample forecasts are generated recursively by estimating the model over the estimation period $t = 1,2,\ldots m$, then generating a forecast for the period in time $m+1$. For the flexible-price monetary model represented by equation (11.1) the equation used to calculate the forecasts is:

$$\hat{s}_{m+1} = \hat{a}_0 + \hat{a}_1(m_{m+1} - m^*_{m+1}) + \hat{a}_2(y_{m+1} - y^*_{m+1}) + \hat{a}_3(i_{m+1} - i^*_{m+1}) \quad (11.31)$$

where $\hat{a}_i$ is the estimated value of a_i. The process is then repeated by estimating the model over the period $t = 1,2,\ldots m+1$ to generate a forecast for point in time $m + 2$, $\hat{S}_{m+1}$ and so on until we get to $\hat{S}_n$ where n is the total sample size.

In this exercise a sample of quarterly data is used spanning the period 1980:1 to 2015:3 on the exchange rate between the yen and US dollar (measured as the price of one US dollar) and the corresponding explanatory variables. The data series were obtained from *International Financial Statistics*. Recursive out-of-sample, one-period ahead forecasts are generated for the period 1998:1 to 2015:3. The models used to generate the forecasts are the static flexible price monetary model (equation 11.1), the same model with a lagged dependent variable (equation 11.2), the general error correction model (equation 11.3), the error correction model without lagged dependent variables (equation 11.4), the first difference model with lagged dependent variables (equation 11.5) and the first difference model without lagged dependent variables. We call these specifications Model A to Model F, respectively. Also used are the lagged spot rate (random walk without drift) and the lagged forward rate.

The Results

The root mean square errors of the eight models/forecasters are displayed in Figure 11.1. We can see that once dynamics is introduced, the RMSE drops sharply, but there is hardly any difference among the six dynamic specifications. They are just as good as the random walk and the forward rate. In Figure 11.2, we can see that the forecasts generated from the six dynamic models follow a similar pattern to what is generated from the random walk or the forward rate.

These results lead to two conclusions, the first of which is that dynamic models are as good as, or in some cases better than, the random walk. This should be no surprise, given that the introduction of any form of dynamics invariably leads to the introduction of a lagged dependent variable, which

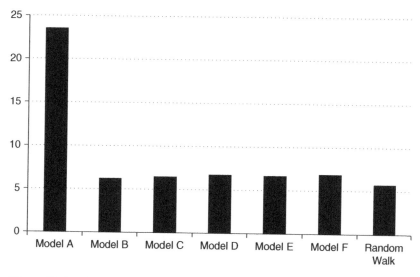

Figure 11.1   Root mean square errors of the models

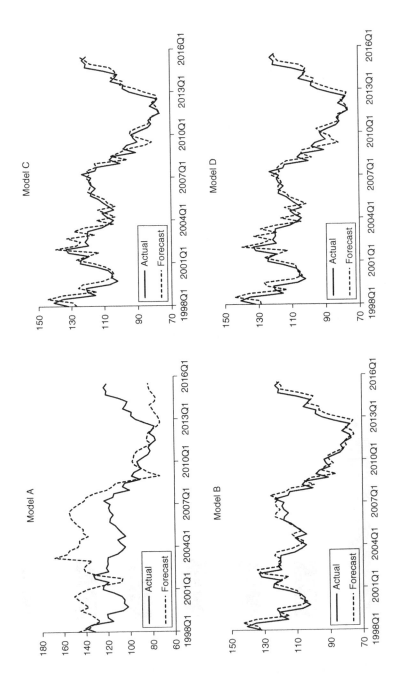

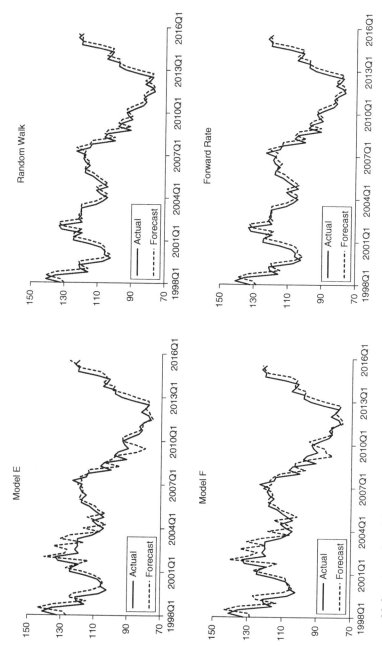

Figure 11.2   Actual and forecast JPY/USD

231

represents a random walk component. It follows that claiming victory over the random walk by using a dynamic model is a con job. The second is that it does not make sense to use the forward rate as a forecaster and the spot rate as a benchmark, which is typical in any forecasting exercise.

In view of these results, one must raise the following question: what has happened to the claim that error correction models are superior to first difference models because the former incorporate short-term and long-term information? There seems to be no difference, at least as far as out-of-sample forecasting is concerned. Once more this is evidence indicating that the case for cointegration is overstated and that it does not matter whether the coefficient on the error correction term is significant or not.

11.7   CONCLUDING REMARKS

Forecasting by using econometric methods is indeed a fiasco. This does not mean that we do not need forecasting, because the output of a forecasting exercise is used as an input in the decision making process. We generate forecasts, perhaps unconsciously, in our daily life and act upon these forecasts, but we do not need econometric models to do that. No one would deny the fact that econometric forecasting has an appalling track record and many would agree that good judgment is perhaps the best way to generate forecasts. Those who do not subscribe to this view still suggest that judgment has value added in economic forecasting (for example, Turner, 1990; Wallis and Whitley, 1991). Others would argue that good forecasters tend to use some informal judgments to form their forecasts without following blindly what formal models tell about the future. In this case the information produced by formal models is combined with their own experience and analytical skills to do their job.

I experienced the value of judgment in exchange rate forecasting in the 1980s when I was in investment banking. The firm I worked for had subscriptions to the reports produced by two forecasters, one was based in Geneva and another in Philadelphia. The forecaster based in Geneva used judgmental forecasting, producing a weekly report containing a narrative of what may and may not happen in the foreign exchange market in the coming weeks and months. The forecaster based in Philadelphia used a state-of-the-art simultaneous equation model to produce forecasts for specific US dollar exchange rates against several currencies on a monthly basis over the following 12, 24 or 36 months.

As an economist I read these reports and tried to reach a consensus view, which I would convey to senior management and the dealing room. With the passage of time, I found the descriptive report produced by the forecaster based in Geneva to be more useful than the point forecasts of the forecaster based in Philadelphia, which were all over the place. At one time I travelled to Philadelphia to spend time with the forecasting firm and observe how they generated their forecasts. Typically, the forecasts produced by the model looked very odd and inconsistent with the sentiment prevailing in the market. What happened next was that the fresh forecasts coming out of a computer would be changed haphazardly to look more reasonable. I wondered what was the point of using the computer to produce forecasts in the first place.

The theory of economic forecasting is based on two assumptions: (1) the model is a good representation of the economy, and (2) the structure of the economy is relatively stable (see, for example, Klein, 1971). However, these two assumptions are not valid – more like wishful thinking – because econometric models are invariably misspecified and all economies have been subject to fundamental unanticipated structural changes. This is what led to the demise of large-scale econometric models in the 1970s. For example, Barrell (2001) discusses six examples of endemic structural change since the 1990s while Clements and Hendry (2001) seek to ascertain the historical prevalence of failure in output forecasts for the UK and any association of such poor forecasts with major economic events. The forecasting theory of Clements and Hendry (1999) is based on two watered-down assumptions: (1) models are simplified representations which are incorrect in many ways; and (2) economies evolve and shift suddenly.

Furthermore, Clements and Hendry (1998, 1999) identify nine sources of forecasting error: (1) shifts in the coefficients of deterministic terms; (2) shifts in the coefficients of stochastic terms; (3) misspecification of deterministic terms; (4) misspecification of stochastic terms; (5) mis-estimation of the coefficients of deterministic terms; (6) mis-estimation of the coefficients of stochastic terms; (7) mis-measurement of the data; (8) changes in the variances of the errors; and (9) errors cumulating over the forecasting horizon. This is a formidable list that makes inaccurate forecasts all but inevitable. How can we even hope to obtain reasonably accurate economic forecasts? If, as Brown (2010) claims, forecasting is "perhaps the main reason for econometrics", then econometricians have done a terribly bad job.

12. Concluding thoughts

12.1 RECAPITULATION

In the previous 11 chapters, arguments were presented as to why econometrics is useful, successful, useless, misleading, dangerous, irrelevant, fragile and a con art. The enthusiasts tend to portray econometrics as essential for the progress of economics and that it is not possible to turn the clock back and revert to economic analysis à la J.M. Keynes, Joan Robinson, Karl Marx, J.K. Galbraith and Hayman Minsky. This sounds like the situation in banking as the so-called "financial innovation" has taken us from one financial disaster to another – yet we cannot turn the clock back. We have to live with shadow banking, derivatives that no one knows how they work, the culture of greed, and rampant corruption. In econometrics we cannot turn the clock back as we should carry on with "econometric innovation" to produce more and more ARCH/GARCH models.

According to the enthusiasts, econometrics is indispensible. Jevons (1871) said the following more than a century ago:

> The deductive science of Economy must be verified and rendered useful by the purely inductive science of Statistics. Theory must be invested with the reality and life of fact. But the difficulties of this union are immensely great.

Yes, indeed, the difficulties of the union between economics and statistics are immensely great – actually, so great that they make econometrics useless and a junk science. It is the obsession of making economics look and sound like science that drives the inevitability of using econometrics. When scientists talk about the Laplace transform, which has significant applications in electrical engineering, econometricians rise to the challenge by coming up with the Bewley transformation that is used to estimate a long-run coefficient, which means absolutely nothing. Nuclear physicists talk about half-life, a term that is commonly used in nuclear physics to describe how quickly unstable atoms undergo, or how long stable atoms survive, radioactive decay. Econometricians talk about half-life with respect to purchasing power parity, a proposition that is theoretically implausible and empirically unsupportable, concluding that a long half-life of a shock to the real exchange rate represents a puzzle, when in fact there is no puzzle whatsoever.

Econometricians believe that they perform the vital task of verifying or refuting a theory by using data and statistical tools, but whether or not this is possible is another question. Magnus (1999) deals with this issue with reference to Keuzenkamp and Magnus (1995) by writing the following:

> At the end of our paper we invited the readers to name a published paper that contains a test which, in their opinion, significantly changed the way economists think about some economic proposition. Such a paper, if it existed, would be an example of a successful theory test. The most convincing contribution, we promised, would be awarded with a one week visit to CentER for Economic Research, all expenses paid. What happened? One (Dutch) colleague called me up and asked whether he could participate without having to accept the prize. I replied that he could, but he did not participate. Nobody else responded. Such is the state of current econometrics.

Magnus (1999) attributes this state of affairs to the fact that individuals, households and firms behave so irrationally that it is hard to think of an economic law with any claim to universality. The fact of the matter is that there is no such thing as a law in economics. Why then do econometricians claim that econometrics has been a success? Even Magnus, who sounds as if he has mixed feelings about econometrics, mentions the s-word (success) by writing:

> Econometric theory has achieved much, but there is unmistakably a certain amount of gloom among the profession. This gloom, I believe, is the result of the fact that we [econometricians?] are not really doing our job. That is, we are not providing the applied economist with the tools that he needs. It is not that we are not providing tools. We are working hard and produce more and more sophisticated tools all the time. They are just not the tools that are required.

There seems to be some contradiction in this statement. Econometric theory could not have achieved much by providing tools that are not required. Providing "more and more sophisticated tools" is the problem because it has led the profession to believe blindly in the results of empirical work and forget about common sense, theory and intuition. We must believe that margarine causes divorce because time series on the consumption of margarine and divorce are cointegrated, in which case correlation between the two series cannot be spurious. For some, common sense and intuition are things of the past – for example, Stigler (1939) wrote the following a long time ago:

> The inconclusiveness of the present statistical demand curves should not be taken as an excuse for lapsing back into the use of "common sense" and "intuition".

The use of quotation marks with common sense and intuition implies that these are not to be taken seriously and that we should only believe a theory if it is verified by econometric testing. The problem is that econometric testing can be used to verify or refute any theory, as we have seen throughout this book.

Yet Magnus (1999) refers to the "wonderful success" of econometric theory and the "terrific speed" and "depth" with which econometric theory has developed. So, let us once more go through the indicators of the alleged success. Econometrics, it is claimed, has been a success because the applications of econometric methods can be found in almost every field of economics; because econometric models have been used extensively by government agencies, international organizations and commercial enterprises; because macroeconometric models have been constructed for almost every country in the world; and because, both in theory and practice, econometrics has already gone well beyond what its founders envisaged. Yet another indicator of the success of econometrics is that there is now scarcely a field of applied economics into which mathematical and statistical theory has not penetrated, including economic history. Econometrics, according to Pagan (1987), is an "outstanding success" because the work of econometric theorists has become "part of the process of economic investigation and the training of economists". Last, but not least, econometrics has been a success because of the excess demand for well-trained econometricians. In Chapter 1 it was demonstrated that these claims represent nothing more than empty rhetoric.

From another perspective, doing sophisticated econometric work has nothing to do with the quest for the truth, but rather more with publishing, which often involves confirmation bias. The use of econometrics and quantitative methods in general has become a minimum requirement to have a paper accepted in a highly rated academic journal. The alleged success of econometrics has led to brain drain inflicted on society by the movement of physicists, mathematicians and engineers to economics and finance, particularly looking for lucrative jobs in the financial sector. At the same time, some good economists have left the field or retired early because they could not cope with the success of econometrics. Econometrics is no longer about measurement in economics as it has become too abstract. Success of econometrics must be measured in one sense only – in terms of enhancing our understanding of the economy and financial markets. In this sense, econometrics has been a total failure.

Econometrics as a junk science has produced some "precise numerical facts" such as the following. One econometric study tells us that a 1 per cent increase in the number of people carrying concealed guns "causes" a 3.3 per cent decline in the murder rate. Naturally we are not told how this happens, but what is important is that this result is music to the ears of the gun lobby. Another study tells us that every time a prisoner is executed, eight future murders are deterred. Other studies tell us that 10–20 per cent of the decline in crime in the 1990s was caused by an increase in abortions in the 1970s, that the murder rate would have increased by 250 per cent since 1974 if it were not for the building of new prisons, and that the welfare reform of the 1990s would force 1,100,000 children into poverty. There is also a study telling us that firing a regulator leads to the creation of a precise number of new jobs and another telling us that slavery is a good business. Econometrics has been used to advocate extreme inequality, to argue for the immoral trickle-down effect and financial deregulation, and to put a case against minimum wage legislation. Econometric evidence has been used to support the proposition that cutting taxes on the rich is good for the economy at large, thus benefiting the 1 per cent at the expense of the 99 per cent.

In reality econometric modelling cannot produce an accurate representation of the working of the economy. The knowledge acquired from econometric work is neither impartial nor systematic and the results of econometric studies could lead to complacency. A bank manager may be advised that the internal model says that there is nothing to worry about since the capital held by the bank is adequate to protect it from insolvency with a confidence level of 99.99 per cent. Econometric models, or quantitative models in general, may also tell us that an event is supposed to happen only once every billion years – this is at least what the management of Long-Term Capital Management believed just before the collapse of 1998 and what the management of AIG believed before the collapse of 2008. Econometrics is not harmless, not just innocent tools that help academics publish papers whose results are of interest only to the authors who do that to get promoted or keep their jobs.

12.2 THE TYRANNY OF THE STATUS QUO

Academia is highly self-censored in the sense that you would not dare criticize the establishment or challenge the status quo. The situation represents the dictatorship of the prevailing orthodoxy, which says that good economics must involve sophisticated econometrics. This is why we should abandon common sense and intuition and go by what the results of econometric studies tell us. However, in most situations common sense is adequate to tell us right from wrong. For example, it is easy to produce empirical evidence telling us that fiscal stimulus does not work, a conclusion that appeals to those who are opposed to the fiscal intervention of the government in the economy. However, common sense and descriptive economic analysis tell us that fiscal expansion does work if it is used properly. Using public funds to finance infrastructure projects depending primarily on local labour and resources is bound to create new jobs. Using fiscal expansion to import tanks and killing machines will not create jobs except for those few who practise war profiteering. No empirical evidence is required in this case.

No empirical evidence is required to tell us that cutting taxes for the rich does not boost growth. This is because the funds arising from the redistribution of income from the public purse to the rich will find their way to tax havens rather than used to start new projects and employ the unemployed, and there is a limit to what a rich individual can consume. No empirical evidence is required to tell us that bailing out (or bailing in) failed financial institutions is economically implausible and morally reprehensible. And no empirical evidence is required to tell us that too much financial deregulation brings about financial instability. In the US, financial stability prevailed for some 50 years following the implementation of the Glass–Steagal Act in the 1930s, but problems started in the 1980s with the Reagan wave of deregulation, and the situation was aggravated by Bill Clinton's final abolition of the act in the late 1990s. In this case, we learn much more from history than from econometrics. And no evidence is needed to tell us that quantitative easing is a very bad idea.

Try to criticize econometrics and you will be in trouble because no major journal will publish a paper questioning the status quo. Even someone like J.M. Keynes was accused time and again that he did not know anything about anything because he rejected econometrics as a tool of economic analysis. Once I came across a few papers published in an obscure journal that were very critical of econometrics and quantitative models in general. The papers, appearing under the general title of "economists' hubris", address the issue of whether or not academic thought (predominantly based on quantitative analysis) is relevant to business or policy applications. In the first paper, which deals with mergers and acquisitions, Shojai (2009) finds little or no value in academic papers when it comes to the strategic issues that are essential to the management, concluding that "the academic literature adds very little to our knowledge of how each specific case is to be handled" and that "very few papers from the world of economics/finance that are actually able to suggest how business combinations can be integrated post-merger, which is what seems to be of greatest value to business managers". In another paper, Shojai and Feiger (2009) discuss asset pricing models and conclude that "the unwavering acceptance of these [asset pricing] models has resulted in research that merely cements their acceptance, discouraging an examination of how those pricing models could be adapted to suit the practical world". In yet another paper, Shojai and Feiger (2010) highlight the shortcomings of academic thought in developing models that can be used by financial institutions to put in place effective enterprise-wide risk management systems and policies. They find that pretty much all of the models fail when put under intense scientific scrutiny. In the fourth paper Shojai et al. (2010) find that while the theoretical aspects of the modern portfolio theory offer little insight into the operations of the asset management industry, very few, if any, portfolio managers look for the efficiency frontier in their asset allocation processes.

I was encouraged by reading these papers and decided to go for the same journal, thinking that getting critical papers in an obscure journal is better than not getting them published at all. I wrote and published (in the obscure journal) three papers under the theme "failure of financial econometrics" (Moosa, 2011a, 2011b, 2012) in which I reached the following conclusions: (1) the econometric modelling of the hedge ratio has no value added whatsoever to the improvement of hedging effectiveness and that using the so-called naïve model (a hedge ratio of one) produces similar results to those obtained from elaborate model specifications and "sophisticated" estimation methods; (2) the results obtained by using different cointegration tests vary considerably and they are not robust with respect to model specification; and (3) "stir-fry" regressions are used extensively in financial research to produce desirable results by reporting only one or a small number of regressions out of the tens or hundreds that are typically estimated.

Once I came across a paper that is highly critical of cointegration, which was also published in an obscure journal. In that paper Guisan (2001) demonstrated that "cointegration tests fail very often to recognize causal relations and, on the other hand, that approach does not always avoid the peril of accepting as causal relations those that really are spurious". As a result, I was encouraged to write a paper on cointegration and spurious correlation, which was rejected four times in as many weeks because it is critical of Nobel-Prize winning work. Eventually, I managed to get the paper published in a very well read and popular journal (Moosa, 2016a). While I have received positive responses from down-to-earth economists, I am yet to find an econometrician who would agree with the proposition I put forward in that paper, that cointegration cannot be used to detect spurious correlation. On another occasion, I was told by an anonymous reviewer that my claim that the case for cointegration was overstated was not valid and that I did not understand cointegration. This is the tyranny of the status quo – if you raise concerns about established ideas and procedures, no one wants to hear about it.

12.3   THE WAY FORWARD

Economics is an important discipline because economic mismanagement
and bad policy decisions can bring about catastrophic consequences.
Hyperinflation and depression can cause more misery than wars and
natural disasters. Economics must be done well, but econometrics is not
the way to do good economics. The way forward is to turn the clock back
and rely on clear thinking, and yes, intuition and common sense, rather
than the principle of "let the data do the talking". We should go back
to the days when everyone could read *Econometrica* and participate in
the debate. We should go back to the days when all seminar and conference participants could understand the presenter and participate in the
discussion in contrast to what we have today, when only one or two of
the participants can understand the presenter because they are 98-Octane
econometricians.

We should stop treating economics as a branch of applied mathematics
in the same sense that physics is. Economists must recognize and accept
the nature of economics as a social science and avoid formalism that
makes economic analysis more amenable to quantification. We should
stop building models based on the unrealistic assumption of a "representative agent", just because it makes it easier to formulate an optimization
problem leading to a testable model.

In this book it was suggested time and again that econometrics is used
to support ideology. Perhaps leaving ideology aside and starting from
the premise of the urge to reveal the truth will curb the tendency to use
econometric analysis that not many people can understand to prove a
point. Economists should be more open-minded in their discussion of
the research results from other economists, even if they are perceived as
ideological opponents. This also implies that editorial boards of some
influential journals need to be willing to consider papers that are less conventional, less mathematical, more applied, and critical of econometric
analysis. Economic research must involve more emphasis on explaining
social institutions such as financial institutions and to take into account
the knowledge provided by other disciplines and social sciences, including
history, philosophy, sociology, ethics and so on.

One of the adverse consequences of the rapid growth of econometrics is
that courses in economic history and the history of economic thought have
all but disappeared from the curriculum of any economics degree. This is
one aspect of going back to the good old days when economic statistics
was more important than econometrics. Chang and Aldred (2014) argue
that "what makes economics so unique is the fact that it is the only academic discipline in which a significant and increasing number of students

are in an open revolt against the content of their degree courses". The discontent, they argue, has been brewing since the outbreak of the 2008 financial crisis, when students found out that their professors have little to offer in terms of explanation of the biggest financial crisis in three generations, not to speak of some of them having been cheerleaders of reckless financial expansion. They also report that employers are not happy about the economics graduates. This is what they write:

> Employers complain that recent economics graduates, while being technically proficient, know very little about the real world. Lacking knowledge about the historical backgrounds, institutional details and political idioms of real-world economies, they end up being idiot savants – they can manipulate most complicated mathematical models but cannot translate their insights into business strategies and economic policies in the real world.

Because of the emphasis placed on econometric and quantitative analysis, modern economists cannot say anything useful about the real world, because they talk in a language that is incomprehensible to non-economists. Students and many employers feel that the typical economics graduate today receives training that is irrelevant to understanding real economies, incomprehensible to the target audiences for economic advice, and often just plain incorrect.

Chang and Aldred (2014) suggest a "back to the future" approach to deal with the situation. Students need to learn more about the real world. They need to know about the current state of the world economy, the history of capitalism (including the history of finance), and some details about specific contemporary economies – for example, the Chinese and German economies are so different from the UK economy. In other words we need to emphasize applied economics and economic history.

Economic pluralism would be desirable. Students should be introduced to different approaches to economics rather than insisting that only the current mainstream approach is the right way to do good economics because it is amenable to quantification. Even within the doctrine of free market economics, there are different approaches including the classical approach, the Austrian approach and the neoclassical approach, which is the current mainstream approach. Unlike neoclassical economists, Austrian economists cannot publish in top journals because they do not like quantitative formalism. Students should study other approaches, including Keynesian, Marxist, Schumpeterian, institutionalist, developmentalist and behaviouralist. In other words, let us bring back history of economic thought and comparative economic theory. Yes, the way forward is to turn the clock back.

12.4 ECONOMETRICS IS A CON ART

In Chapter 3 it was argued, against what some econometricians believe, that econometrics is not a science and that there are no laws in economics. For one thing, econometric models do not meet the desirable properties of scientific models such as theoretical plausibility, explanatory power, accuracy of the estimates of the model parameters, forecasting power and simplicity. Unlike the laws of physics, which can be represented by exact equations that hold universally, the so-called laws of economics are written as stochastic equations, sometimes estimated in a time-varying parametric framework and produce results that are not robust with respect to specification, estimation method and the data sample. This is not science, unless other words are used with "science" to describe econometrics as "junk science" or "science of hubris".

Magnus (1999), who seems to have mixed feelings about econometrics, brings our attention to an important point that rules econometrics as a science – this point pertains to the data. While physicists generate their own data and they are responsible for its soundness, econometricians rely on others to generate the data for them and they usually have no clue of how that data have been generated. This is what Magnus says:

> Why do we not assume responsibility for the data we use? If someone attacks us by pointing out a flaw in the data, we respond that this is not our fault, but the fault of whoever supplied the data. No other discipline would accept this lack of responsibility. Also, the data are not value-free, but often collected according to some economic theory. For example the filling in of missing observations is often done using the most relevant economic theory. Thus in testing an economic hypothesis one jointly tests the data and the theory.

Yet Magnus argues that "econometricians can continue to make important contributions and eventually, perhaps, become respectable scientists". What important contributions have econometricians made? Cointegration, causality and ARCH/GARCH models? The contribution of econometricians is that they have provided tools that allow anyone to prove anything, which can be rather "handy", particularly for those motivated by ideology. This is why econometrics is not a science – rather it is an art, a con art to be specific.

References

Abhyankar, A., Sarno, L. and Valente, G. (2005) Exchange Rates and Fundamentals: Evidence on the Economic Value of Predictability, *Journal of International Economics*, 66, 325–348.

Aggarwal, R. and Zong, S. (2008) Behavioral Biases in Forward Rates as Forecasts of Future Exchange Rates: Evidence of Systematic Pessimism and Under-Reaction, *Multinational Finance Journal*, 12, 241–277.

Aggarwal, R., Lucey, B.M. and Mohanty, S.K. (2009) The Forward Exchange Rate Bias Puzzle is Persistent: Evidence from Stochastic and Nonparametric Cointegration Tests, *Financial Review*, 44, 625–645.

Ahsan, M., Kwan, A.C.C. and Sahni, B.S. (1996) Cointegration and Wagner's Hypothesis: Time Series Evidence for Canada, *Applied Economics*, 28, 1055–1058.

Alexander, C. (1999) Optimal Hedging Using Cointegration, *Philosophical Transactions of the Royal Society*, Series A, 357, 2039–2085.

Allen, R.G.D. and Bowley, A.L. (1935) *Family Expenditure*, London: P.S. King.

Almon, S. (1965) The Distributed Lag between Capital Appropriations and Net Expenditures, *Econometrica*, 33, 178–196.

Al-Nakeeb, B. (2016) *Two Centuries of Parasitic Economics: The Struggle for Economic and Political Democracy on the Eve of the Financial Collapse of the West*, New York (Private Publication).

Alquist, R. and Arbatli, E. (2010) Crude Oil Futures: A Crystal Ball?, *Bank of Canada Review*, Spring, 3–11.

Alquist, R. and Kilian, L. (2010) What Do We Learn From the Price of Crude Oil Futures?, *Journal of Applied Econometrics*, 25, 539–573.

Amemiya, T. (1983) Nonlinear Regression Models, in Z. Griliches and M.D. Intriligator (eds) *Handbook of Econometrics*, Vol. 1, Amsterdam: North-Holland, 333–389.

Anderson, R.G., Hoffman, D.L. and Rasche, R.H. (2002) A Vector Autoregression Forecasting Model of the US Economy, *Journal of Macroeconomics*, 24, 569–598.

Anderson, T.W. and Rubin, H. (1949) Estimation of the Parameters of a Single Equation in a Complete System of Stochastic Equations, *Annals of Mathematical Statistics*, 20, 46–63.

Andreou, E., Ghyles, E. and Kourtellos, A. (2010) Regression Models with Mixed Sampling Frequencies, *Journal of Econometrics*, 158, 246–261.

Andrews, D.W.K. (1993) Tests for Parameter Instability and Structural Change with Unknown Change Point, *Econometrica*, 61, 821–856.

Angrist, J. and Pischke, J.S. (2010) The Credibility Revolution in Empirical Economics: How Better Research Design is Taking the Con out of Econometrics, NBER Working Paper, No. w15794.

Ansari, M.I., Gordon, D.V. and Akuamoah, C. (1997) Keynes versus Wagner: Public Expenditure and National Income for Three African Countries, *Applied Economics*, 29, 543–550.

Anthony, R.N. (1960) The Trouble with Profit Maximization, *Harvard Business Review*, 38, 126–134.

Antoine, B. and Lavergne, P. (2014) Conditional Moment Models under Semi-Strong Identification, *Journal of Econometrics*, 182, 59–69.

Ardeni, P.G. (1989) Does the Law of One Price Really Hold for Commodity Prices? *American Journal of Agricultural Economics*, 71, 661–669.

Ashley, R., Granger, C.W.J. and Schmalensee, R. (1980) Advertising and Aggregate Consumption: An Analysis of Causality, *Econometrica*, 48, 1149–1167.

Assenmacher-Wesche, K. and Pesaran, M.H. (2008) Forecasting the Swiss Economy Using VECX* Models and Observation Windows, *National Institute Economic Review*, 203, 91–108.

Avetisov, V.A., Bikulov, A.K, Vasilyev, O.A., Nechaev, S.K. and Chertovich, A.V. (2009) Some Physical Applications of Random Hierarchical Matrices, *Journal of Experimental and Theoretical Physics*, 109, 485–504.

Bacchetta, P. and van Wincoop, E. (2006) Can Information Heterogeneity Explain the Exchange Rate Determination Puzzle?, *American Economic Review*, 96, 552–576.

Bachelier, L.J. (1900) *Théorie de la Speculation*, Paris: Gauthier-Villars. Reprinted in Paul H. Cootner (ed.) *The Random Character of Stock Market Prices*, Cambridge: MIT Press (1964), 17–78.

Bachmeier, L. and Swanson, N.R. (2005) Predicting Inflation: Does The Quantity Theory Help? *Economic Inquiry*, 43, 570–585.

Bahmani-Oskooee, M. and Alse, J. (1994) Short-Run versus Long-Run Effects of Devaluation: Error Correction Modelling and Cointegration, *Eastern Economic Journal*, 20, 453–464.

Bahmani-Oskooee, M. and Hegerty, S.W. (2010) The J- and S-Curves: A Survey of the Recent Literature, *Journal of Economic Studies*, 37, 580–596.

Bahmani-Oskooee, M. and Ratha, A. (2004) The J-Curve: A Literature Review, *Applied Economics*, 36, 1377–1398.

Bahmani-Oskooee, M., Xu, J. and Saha, S. (2015) Commodity Trade between the US and Korea and the J-Curve Effect, *New Zealand Economic Papers* (published online 19 October).

Bai, J. and Perron, P. (1998) Estimating and Testing Linear Models with Multiple Structural Changes, *Econometrica*, 66, 47–78.

Baillie, R.T., Bollerslev, T. and Mikkelsen, H.O. (1996) Fractionally Integrated Generalized Autoregressive Conditional Heteroskedasticity, *Journal of Econometrics*, 74, 3–30.

Baltagi, B.H. (2002) *Econometrics* (3rd edition), New York: Springer.

Baltagi, B.H., Feng, Q. and Kao, C. (2016) Estimation of Heterogeneous Panels with Structural Breaks, *Journal of Econometrics*, 191, 176–195.

Banerjee, A. and Marcellino, M. (2009) Factor-Augmented Error Correction Models, in J. Castle and N. Shepard (eds) *The Methodology and Practice of Econometrics: A Festschrift for David Hendry*, Oxford: Oxford University Press, 227–254.

Banerjee, A., Marcellino, M. and Masten, I. (2013) Forecasting with Factor-Augmented Error Correction Models, *International Journal of Forecasting*, 30, 589–612.

Banerjee, A., Dolado, J.J., Galbraith, J.W. and Hendry, D.F. (1993) *Cointegration, Error Correction, and the Econometric Analysis of Nonstationary Data*, Oxford: Oxford University Press.

Banerjee, A., Dolado, J.J., Hendry, D.F. and Smith, G.W. (1986) Exploring Equilibrium Relationships in Econometrics Through Static Models: Some Monte Carlo Evidence, *Oxford Bulletin of Economics and Statistics*, 48, 253–277.

Barrell, R. (2001) Forecasting the World Economy, in D.F. Hendry and N.R. Ericsson (eds) *Understanding Economic Forecasts*, Cambridge (MA): MIT Press, 152–173.

Basmann, R.L. (1957) A Generalized Classical Method of Linear Estimation of Coefficients in a Structural Equation, *Econometrica*, 25, 77–83.

Baum, C.F., Barkoulas, J.T. and Caglayan, M. (2001) Nonlinear Adjustment to Purchasing Power Parity in the Post-Bretton Woods Era, *Journal of International Money and Finance*, 20, 379–399.

Baxter, J.L. and Moosa, I.A. (1996) The Consumption Function: A Basic Needs Hypothesis, *Journal of Economic Behavior and Organization*, 31, 85–100.

Beard, T.R., Ford, G.S., Kim, H. and Spiwak, L.J. (2011) Regulatory Expenditures, Economic Growth and Jobs: An Empirical Study, Phoenix Center Policy Bulletin No. 28. http://www.phoenix-center.org/PolicyBulletin/PCPB28Final.pdf (accessed 3 May 2016).

Bekker, P.A. and Crudu, F. (2015) Jackknife Instrumental Variable Estimation with Heteroscedasticity, *Journal of Econometrics*, 185, 332–342.

Benini, R. (1907) Sull'uso delle Formole Empiriche a Nell'economia Applicata, *Giornale Degli Economisti*, 2nd series, 35, 1053–1063.

Bentolila, S. and Saint-Paul, G. (2003) Explaining Movements in the Labor Share, *Contributions to Macroeconomics*, 3, 1–31.

Bera, A.K., Higgins, M.L. and Lee, S. (1992) Interaction Between Auto-Correlation and Conditional Heteroskedasticity: A Random-Coefficient Approach, *Journal of Business and Economic Statistics*, 10, 133–142.

Bergmann, B. (1999) Abolish the Nobel Prize for Economics, *Challenge*, 42, 52–67.

Bernanke, B. (1986) Alternative Explanations of the Money–Income Correlation, *Carnegie Rochester Conference Series on Public Policy*, 25, 49–101.

Bhabra, H.S., Liu, T. and Tirtiroglu, D. (2008) Capital Structure Choice in a Nascent Market: Evidence from Listed Firms in China, *Financial Management*, 37, 341–364.

Billio, M., Caporin, M. and Gobbo, M. (2006) Flexible Dynamic Conditional Correlation Multivariate GARCH Midels for Asset Allocation, *Applied Financial Economics Letters*, 2, 123–130.

Biswal, B., Dhawan, U. and Lee, H. (1999) Testing Wagner versus Keynes Using Disaggregated Public Expenditure Data for Canada, *Applied Economics*, 31, 1283–1291.

Bjerkholt, O. (1995) Ragnar Frisch, Editor of Econometrica, *Econometrica*, 63, 755–765.

Black, D. and Nagin, D. (1998) Do Right-to-Carry Laws Deter Violent Crime? *Journal of Legal Studies*, 27, 209–219.

Blanchard, O.J. (1989) A Traditional Interpretation of Macroeconomic Fluctuations, *American Economic Review*, 79, 1146–1164.

Blanchard, O.J. and Quah, D. (1989) The Dynamic Effects of Aggregate Demand and Supply Disturbances, *American Economic Review*, 79, 1146–1164.

Blanchard, O.J. and Summers, L.H. (1986) Hysteresis and the European Unemployment Problem, *NBER Macroeconomic Annual*, 1, 15–90.

Blinder, A.B. (1991) Why Are Prices Sticky? Preliminary Results from an Interview Study, *American Economic Review*, 81 (Papers and Proceedings), 89–96.

Blommestein, H.J. (2009) The Financial Crisis as a Symbol of the Failure of Academic Finance (A Methodological Digression), *Journal of Financial Transformation*, 27, 3–8.

Blumstein, A. and Wallman, J. (eds) (2000) *The Crime Drop in America*, New York: Cambridge University Press.

Bollerslev, T. (1986) Generalised Autoregressive Conditional Heteroskedasticity, *Journal of Econometrics*, 51, 307–327.

Bollerslev, T. (1987) A Conditionally Heteroskedastic Time Series Model for Speculative Prices and Rates of Return, *Review of Economics and Statistics*, 69, 542–547.

Bollerslev, T. (2008) Glossary to ARCH (GARCH), CREATES Research Papers, No. 2008–49.

Bollerslev, T. and Ghysels, E. (1996) Periodic Autoregressive Conditional Heteroskedastcity, *Journal of Business and Economic Statistics*, 14, 139–151.

Bollerslev, T. and Mikkelsen, H.O. (1996) Modeling and Pricing Long Memory in Stock Market Volatility, *Journal of Econometrics*, 73, 151–184.

Bollerslev, T., Engle, R.F. and Wooldridge, J.M. (1988) A Capital Asset Pricing Model with Time Varying Covariances, *Journal of Political Economy*, 96, 116–131.

Bonhomme, S. (2012) Functional Differencing, *Econometrica*, 80, 1337–1385.

Bonner, B. (2007) 25 Standard Deviations in a Blue Moon. www.money-week.com.

Booth, L., Aivazian, V., Demirguc-Kunt, A. and Maksimovic, V. (2001) Capital Structure in Developing Countries, *Journal of Finance*, 56, 87–130.

Bopp, A.E. and Lady, G.M. (1991) A Comparison of Petroleum Futures versus Spot Prices as Predictors of Prices in the Future, *Energy Economics*, 13, 274–282.

Bowers, W.J. and Pierce, G.L. (1975) The Illusion of Deterrence in Isaac Ehrlich's Research on Capital Punishment, *Yale Law Journal*, 85, 187–208.

Box, G.E.P. and Jenkins, G.M. (1970) *Time Series Analysis, Forecasting and Control*, San Francisco: Holden-Day.

Brandt, M.W. and Jones C.S. (2006) Volatility Forecasting with Range-Based EGARCH Models, *Journal of Business and Economic Statistics*, 24, 470–486.

Brenner, R.J., Harjes, R.H. and Kroner, K.F. (1996) Another Look at Models of the Short-Term Interest Rate, *Journal of Financial and Quantitative Analysis*, 31, 85–107.

Breusch, T.S. and Pagan, A.R. (1980) The Lagrange Multiplier Test and its Applications to Model Specification in Econometrics, *Review of Economic Studies*, 47, 239–253.

Brockes, E. (2009) He Told Us So, *The Guardian*, 24 January.

Broll, U., Chow, K.W. and Wong, K.P. (2001) Hedging and Nonlinear Risk Exposure, *Oxford Economic Papers*, 53, 281–296.

Brooks, C. and Chong, J. (2001) The Cross-Currency Hedging Performance of Implied versus Statistical Forecasting Models, *Journal of Futures Markets*, 21, 1043–1069.

Brooks, D. (2008) The Behavioral Revolution, *New York Times*, 28 October.

Brown, B.W. (2010) Econometrics. http://www.ruf.rice.edu/~bwbwn/econ400_files/ch1-ch5.pdf (accessed 19 August 2016).

Brown, T.M. (1952) Habit Persistence and Lags in Consumer Behaviour, *Econometrica*, 20, 355–371.

Brundy, J.M. and Jorgenson, D.N. (1971) Efficient Estimation of Simultaneous Equations by Instrumental Variables, *Review of Economics and Statistics*, 53, 207–224.

Brunner, A.D. (1997) On the Dynamic Properties of Asymmetric Models of Real GNP, *Review of Economics and Statistics*, 79, 321–326.

Buckley, J. and James, I. (1979) Linear Regression with Censored Data, *Biometrika*, 66, 429–436.

Burney, N.A. (2002) Wagner's Hypothesis: Evidence from Kuwait Using Cointegration Tests, *Applied Economics*, 34, 49–57.

Burns, A.F. and Mitchell, W.C. (1947) *Measuring Business Cycles*, New York: Columbia University Press.

Burns, P. (2005) Multivariate GARCH with Only Univariate Estimation. http://www.burns-stat.com (accessed 17 June 2016).

Burns, W.C. (1997) Spurious Correlations. https://hbr.org/2015/06/beware-spurious-correlations (accessed 12 April 2016).

Bushaw, D.W. and Clower, R.W. (1957) *Introduction to Mathematical Economics*, New York: Irwin.

Cagan, P. (1956) The Monetary Dynamics of Hyperinflation, in M. Friedman (ed.) *Studies in the Quantity Theory of Money*, Chicago: University of Chicago Press, 25–117.

Cai, J. (1994) A Markov Model of Switching-Regime ARCH, *Journal of Business and Economic Statistics*, 12, 309–316.

Cameron, A.C. and Trivedi, P.K. (1986) Econometric Models Based on Count Data: Comparisons and Applications of some Estimators and Tests, *Journal of Applied Econometrics*, 1, 29–53.

Caporin, M. and McAleer, M. (2006) Dynamic Asymmetric GARCH, *Journal of Financial Econometrics*, 4, 385–412.

Cappiello, L., Engle, R.F. and Sheppard, K. (2006) Asymmetric Dynamics in the Correlations of Global Equity and Bond Returns, *Journal of Financial Econometrics*, 4, 537–572.

Cassidy, J. (2010) After the Blowup: Laissez-Faire Economists Do Some Soul-Searching – and Finger-Pointing, *The New Yorker*, 11 January.

Castiglione, C. (2011) Verdoorn–Kaldor's Law: An Empirical Analysis with Time Series Data in the United States, *Advances in Management and Applied Economics*, 1, 135–151.

Castle, J.F., Doornik, J.A. and Hendry, D.F. (2012) Model Selection when There are Multiple Breaks, *Journal of Econometrics*, 169, 239–246.

Cavaliere, G., Nielsen, H.B. and Rahbek, A. (2015) Bootstrap Testing of Hypotheses on Co-Integration Relations in Vector Autoregressive Models, *Econometrica*, 83, 813–831.

Chait, B. (1949) *Sur l'conomtrie*, Brussels: J. Lebeque and Co.

Chambers, J.C. (2016) The Econometric Analysis of Mixed Frequency Data Sampling, *Journal of Econometrics*, 193, 390–404.

Champernowne, D.G. (1960) An Experimental Investigation of the Robustness of Certain Procedures for Estimating Means and Regressions Coefficients, *Journal of the Royal Statistical Society*, 123, 398–412.

Chan, E. (2006) Cointegration is Not the Same as Correlation, TradingMarkets.Com, 13 November. http://www.tradingmarkets.com/. site/stocks/commentary/quantitative_trading/Cointegration-is-not-the-same-as-correlation.cfm (accessed 1 June 2016).

Chang, H.J. and Aldred, J. (2014) After the Crash, We Need a Revolution in the Way We Teach Economics, *The Guardian*, 11 May.

Chen, J.J. (2004) Determinants of Capital Structure of Chinese-Listed Companies, *Journal of Business Research*, 57, 1341–1351.

Chen, S. and Zhou, X. (2011) Semiparametric Estimation of a Bivariate Tobit Model, *Journal of Econometrics*, 165, 266–274.

Chernenko, S., Schwarz, K. and Wright, J. (2004) The Information Content of Forward and Futures Prices: Market Expectations and the Price of Risk, Board of Governors of the Federal Reserve System, International Finance Discussion Paper No. 808.

Chernozhukov, V., Fernandez-Val, I. and Melly, B. (2013) Inference on Counterfactual Distributions, *Econometrica*, 81, 2205–2268.

Chesher, A. (2010) Instrumental Variable Models for Discrete Outcomes, *Econometrica*, 78, 575–601.

Cheung, Y. and Chinn, M. (1998) Integration, Cointegration, and the Forecast Consistency of Structural Exchange Rate Models, *Journal of International Money and Finance*, 17, 813–830.

Chinn, M. and Coibion, O. (2009) The Predictive Content of Commodity Futures, La Follette School of Public Affairs, University of Wisconsin (Madison), Working Paper No. 2009–2016.

Chinn, M., LeBlanc, M. and Coibion, O. (2005) The Predictive Content of Energy Futures: An Update on Petroleum, Natural Gas, Heating Oil and Gasoline, NBER Working Papers, No. 11033.

Cho, J.S. and White, H. (2007) Testing for Regime Switching, *Econometrica*, 75, 1671–1720.

Cho, J.S., Kim, T. and Shin, Y. (2015) Quantile Cointegration in the

Autoregressive Distributed-Lag Modeling Framework, *Journal of Econometrics*, 188, 281–300.

Chou, R.Y. (2005) Forecasting Financial Volatilities with Extreme Values: The Conditional Autoregressive Range (CARR) Model, *Journal of Money, Credit and Banking*, 37, 561–582.

Chow, G.C. (1960) Tests of Equality between Sets of Coefficients in two Linear Regressions, *Econometrica*, 28, 591–605.

Chow, Y., Cotsomitis, J.A. and Kwan, A.C.C. (2002) Multivariate Cointegration and Causality Tests of Wagner's Hypothesis: Evidence from the UK, *Applied Economics*, 34, 1671–1677.

Christiano, L.J., Eichenbaum, M. and Evans, C. (2005) Nominal Rigidities and the Dynamic Effects of a Shock to Monetary Policy, *Journal of Political Economy*, 113, 1–45.

Christodoulakis, G.A. and Satchell, S.E. (2002) Correlated ARCH (CorrARCH): Modelling Time-Varying Conditional Correlation Between Financial Asset Returns, *European Journal of Operational Research*, 139, 351–370.

Christoffersen, P.F. and Diebold, F.X. (1998) Cointegration and Long-Horizon Forecasting, *Journal of Business and Economic Statistics*, 16, 450–458.

Chung, E.Y. and Romano, J.P. (2016) Multivariate and Multiple Permutation Tests, *Journal of Econometrics*, 193, 76–91.

Clements, M.P. and Hendry, D.F. (1996) Intercept Corrections and Structural Change, *Journal of Applied Econometrics*, 11, 475–494.

Clements, M.P. and Hendry, D.F. (1998) *Forecasting Economic Time Series: The Marshall Lectures on Economic Forecasting*, Cambridge: Cambridge University Press.

Clements, M.P. and Hendry, D.F. (1999) *Forecasting Non-Stationary Economic Time Series*, Cambridge (MA): MIT Press.

Clements, M.P. and Hendry, D.F. (2001) An Historical Perspective on Forecast Errors, *National Institute Economic Review*, 177, 100–112.

Cochrane, P. and Orcutt, G.H. (1949) Application of Least Squares Regression to Relationships Containing Autocorrelated Error Terms, *Journal of the American Statistical Association*, 44, 32–61.

Coffey, B.K., Anderson, J.D. and Parcell, J.L. (2000) Optimal Hedging Ratios and Hedging Risk for Grain Co-Products, Paper presented at the annual meeting of the American Economic Association, January.

Colander, D., Föllmer, H., Haas, A., Goldberg, M., Juselius, K., Kirman, A. Lux, T. and Sloth, B. (2009) The Financial Crisis and the Systemic Failure of Academic Economics, Kiel Working Papers, No. 1489.

Confederation of British Industry (2013) Our Global Future: The Business

Vision for Reformed EU. http://news.cbi.org.uk/reports/our-global-future/our-global-future/ (accessed 28 May 2016).

Congdon, T. (2014) How Much Does the European Union Cost Britain? UKIP. http://www.timcongdon4ukip.com/docs/EU2014.pdf (accessed 7 January 2016).

Cooley, T.F. and LeRoy, S.F. (1981) Identification and Estimation of Money Demand, *American Economic Review*, 71, 825–844.

Cooley, T.F. and LeRoy, S.F. (1986) What will Take the Con Out of Econometrics? A Reply to McAleer, Pagan, and Volker, *American Economic Review*, 76, 504–507.

Cosslett, S.R. (1983) Distribution Free Maximum Likelihood Estimation of the Binary Choice Model, *Econometrica*, 51, 765–782.

Courakis, A.S., Moura-Roque, F. and Tridimas, G. (1993) Public Expenditure Growth in Greece and Portugal: Wagner's Law and Beyond, *Applied Economics*, 25, 125–134.

Cox, D.R. (1961) Tests of Separate Families of Hypotheses, *Proceedings of the Fourth Berkeley Symposium on Mathematical Statistics and Probability*, Vol. 1, Berkeley: University of California Press, 105–123.

Cox, D.R. (1962) Further Results of Tests of Separate Families of Hypotheses, *Journal of the Royal Statistical Society*, Series B, 24, 406–424.

Cox, D.R. (1972) Regression Models and Life Tables, *Journal of the Royal Statistical Society*, Series B, 34, 187–220.

Crawford, D. (2016) The Legacy of Joan Robinson, 4 May. http://angrybearblog.com/2016/05/the-legacy-of-joan-robinson.html (accessed 10 August 2016).

Crouhy, H. and Rockinger, M. (1997) Volatility Clustering, Asymmetry and Hysteresis in Stock Returns: International Evidence, *Financial Engineering and the Japanese Markets*, 4, 1–35.

Darolles, S., Fan, Y., Florens, J.P. and Renault, E. (2011) Nonparametric Instrumental Regression, *Econometrica*, 79, 1541–1565.

Davenant, C. (1698) *Discourses on the Public Revenues and on the Trade of England*, London: James Capton.

Davidson, J. (2004) Moment and Memory Properties of Linear Conditional Heteroskedasticity Models, and a New Model, *Journal of Business and Economic Statistics*, 22, 16–29.

Davis, H.T. (1941) *The Theory of Econometrics*, Bloomington (IN): The Principia Press.

Deaton, A. (1985) Panel Data from Time Series of Cross-Sections, *Journal of Econometrics*, 30, 109–126.

Debreu, G. (1991) The Mathematization of Economic Theory, *American Economic Review*, 81, 1–7.

Dehnad, K. (2009) Efficient Market Hypothesis: Another Victim of the Great Recession, *Journal of Financial Transformation*, 27, 35–36.

Den Hertog, R.G.J. (1994) Pricing of Permanent and Transitory Volatility for US Stock Returns: A Composite GARCH Model, *Economics Letters*, 44, 421–426.

Dharmapala, D. and McAleer, M. (1996) Econometric Methodology and the Philosophy of Science, *Journal of Statistical Planning and Inference*, 49, 9–37.

Dhrymes, P. (1971) A Simplified Estimator for Large-Scale Econometric Models, *Australian Journal of Statistics*, 13, 168–175.

Dickey, D.A. and Fuller, W. (1979) Distribution of the Estimators for Autoregressive Time Series with a Unit Root, *Journal of the American Statistical Association*, 74, 427–431.

Dickey, D.A. and Fuller, W. (1981) Likelihood Ratio Statistics for Autoregressive Time Series with a Unit Root, *Econometrica*, 49, 1057–1072.

Dickey, D.A., Jansen, D.W. and Thornton, D.L. (1991) A Primer on Cointegration with an Application to Money and Income, *Federal Reserve Bank of St. Louis Economic Review*, March/April, 58–78.

Diebold, F.X. and Mariano, R.S. (1995) Comparing Predictive Accuracy, *Journal of Business and Economic Statistics*, 13, 253–263.

Diebold, F.X. and Nerlove, M. (1989) The Dynamics of Exchange Rate Volatility: A Multivariate Latent Factor ARCH Model, *Journal of Applied Econometrics*, 4, 1–21.

Ding, Z., Granger, C.W.J. and Engle, R.F. (1993) A Long Memory Property of Stock Market Returns and a New Model, *Journal of Empirical Finance*, 1, 83–106.

Doan, T., Litterman, R. and Sims, C.A. (1984) Forecasting and Conditional Projections Using Realistic Prior Distributions, *Econometric Reviews*, 3, 1–100.

Doerig, H.U. (2003) Operational Risks in Financial Services: An Old Challenge in a New Environment, Credit Suisse Group, Working Paper.

Donaldson, R.G. and Kamstra, M. (1997), An Artificial Neural Network GARCH Model for International Stock Return Volatility, *Journal of Empirical Finance*, 4, 17–46.

Donohue, J.J. and Wolfers, J. (2005) Uses and Abuses of Empirical Evidence in the Death Penalty Debate, *Stanford Law Review*, 58, 791–845.

Dovonon, P. and Renault, E. (2013) Testing for Common Conditionally Heteroskedastic Factors, *Econometrica*, 81, 2561–2586.

Dowd, K. (2009) The Failure of Capital Adequacy Regulation, in P. Booth (ed.) *Verdict on the Crash Causes and Policy Implications*, London: Institute of Economic Affairs, 73–80.

Dowd, K. (2014) Math Gone Mad: Regulatory Risk Modeling by the Federal Reserve, The Cato Institute, *Policy Analysis*, Number 754.

Dowd, K., Cotter, J., Humphrey, C. and Woods, M. (2008) How Unlucky is 25-Sigma? *Journal of Portfolio Management*, Summer, 1–5.

Dowd, K., Hutchinson, M., Ashby, S. and Hinchcliffe, J.M. (2011) Capital Inadequacies: The Dismal Failure of the Basel Regime of Capital Regulation, *Policy Analysis*, No. 681.

Drost, F.C. and Nijman, T.E. (1993) Temporal Aggregation of GARCH Processes, *Econometrica*, 61, 909–927.

Duan, J. (1997) Augmented GARCH(p,q) Process and its Diffusion Limit, *Journal of Econometrics*, 79, 97–127.

Durbin, J. and Watson, G.S. (1950) Testing for Serial Correlation in Least Squares Regression I, *Biometrika*, 37, 409–428.

Durbin, J. and Watson, G.S. (1951) Testing for Serial Correlation in Least Squares Regression II, *Biometrika*, 38, 159–178.

Echenique, F. and Komunjer, I. (2009) Testing Models With Multiple Equilibria by Quantile Methods, *Econometrica*, 77, 1281–1297.

Efron, B. (1979) Bootstrap Methods: Another Look at the Jackknife, *Annals of Statistics*, 7, 1–26.

Ehrbar, H.G. (2000) Irrealist Lines of Defense in Econometrics, Working Paper, Economics Department, University of Utah.

Ehrlich, I. (1975a) The Deterrent Effect of Capital Punishment: A Question of Life and Death, *American Economic Review*, 65, 397–417.

Ehrlich, I. (1975b) Deterrence: Evidence and Inference, *Yale Law Journal*, 85, 209–227.

Ehrlich, I. (1977a) The Deterrent Effect of Capital Punishment: Reply, *American Economic Review*, 67, 452–458.

Ehrlich, I. (1977b) Capital Punishment and Deterrence: Some Further Thoughts and Additional Evidence, *Journal of Political Economy*, 85, 741–788.

Ehrlich, I. and Liu, Z. (1999) Sensitivity Analyses of the Deterrence Hypothesis: Let's Keep the Econ in Econometrics, *Journal of Law and Economics*, 42, 455–487.

Eisner, R. and Strotz, R.H. (1963) *Determinants of Business Investment*, Commission on Money and Credit, Impacts of Monetary Policy, Englewood Cliffs (NJ): Prentice Hall, 59–337.

Elliott, G., Gargano, A. and Timmerman, A. (2013) Complete Subset Regressions, *Journal of Econometrics*, 177, 357–373.

Elliott, R.J., van der Hoek, J. and Malcolm, W.P. (2005) Pairs Trading, *Quantitative Finance*, 5, 271–276.

Elsby, M.W., Hobin, B. and Sahin, A. (2013) The Decline of the US Labor Share, *Brookings Papers on Economic Activity*, Fall, 1–63.

Enders, W. (1988) ARIMA and Cointegration Tests of PPP under Fixed and Flexible Exchange Rate Regimes, *Review of Economics and Statistics*, 70, 504–508.

Engel, C., Mark, N. and West, K. (2007) Exchange Rate Models are Not as Bad as You Think, *NBER Macroeconomics Annual*, 22, 381–441.

Engle, R.F. (1982) Autoregressive Conditional Heteroscedasticity, with Estimates of the Variance of United Kingdom Inflation, *Econometrica*, 50, 987–1007.

Engle, R.F. (1990), Discussion: Stock Market Volatility and the Crash of '87, *Review of Financial Studies*, 3, 103–106.

Engle, R.F. (2002a), Dynamic Conditional Correlation: A Simple Class of Multivariate GARCH Models, *Journal of Business and Economic Statistics*, 20, 339–350.

Engle, R.F. (2002b), New Frontiers for ARCH Models, *Journal of Applied Econometrics*, 17, 425–446.

Engle, R.F. and Bollerslev, T. (1986) Modeling the Persistence of Conditional Variances, *Econometric Reviews*, 5, 1–50.

Engle, R.F. and Gonzalez-Rivera, G. (1991) Semiparametric ARCH Models, *Journal of Business and Economic Statistics*, 9, 345–359.

Engle, R.F. and Granger, C.W.J. (1987) Cointegration and Error-Correction: Representation, Estimation and Testing, *Econometrica*, 55, 251–276.

Engle, R.F. and Lee, G.G.J. (1999) A Permanent and Transitory Component Model of Stock Return Volatility, in R.F. Engle and H. White (eds) *Cointegration, Causality, and Forecasting: A Festschrift in Honor of Clive W.J. Granger*, Oxford: Oxford University Press, 475–497.

Engle, R.F. and Manganelli, S. (2004) CAViaR: Conditional Autoregressive Value-at-Risk by Regression Quantiles, *Journal of Business and Economic Statistics*, 22, 367–381.

Engle, R.F. and Ng, V.K. (1993) Measuring and Testing the Impact of News on Volatility, *Journal of Finance*, 48, 1749–1778.

Engle, R.F. and Rangel, J.G. (2008) The Spline-GARCH Model for Low Frequency Volatility and its Global Macroeconomic Causes, *Review of Financial Studies*, 21, 1187–1221.

Engle, R.F. and Rosenberg, J. (1995) GARCH Gamma, *Journal of Derivatives*, 17, 229–247.

Engle, R.F. and Russell, J.R. (1998) Autoregressive Conditional Duration: A New Model for Irregularly Spaced Transaction Data, *Econometrica*, 66, 1127–1162.

Engle, R.F., Hendry D.F. and Richard, J.F. (1983) Exogeneity, *Econometrica*, 51, 277–304.

Engle, R.F., Lilien, D.M. and Robbins, R.P. (1987) Estimating Time

Varying Risk Premia in the Term Structure: The ARCH-M Model, *Econometrica*, 55, 391–407.

Engle, R.F., Lilien, D.M. and Watson, M. (1985) A Dymimic Model of Housing Price Determination, *Journal of Econometrics*, 28, 307–326.

Engle, R.F., Ng, V.K. and Rothschild, M. (1990) Asset Pricing with a Factor-ARCH Covariance Structure: Empirical Estimates for Treasury Bills, *Journal of Econometrics*, 45, 213–238.

Escanciano, J.C. and Velasco, C. (2010) Specification Tests of Parametric Dynamic Conditional Quantiles, *Journal of Econometrics*, 159, 209–221.

Eun, C.S. and Shin, S. (1989) International Transmission of Stock Market Movements, *Journal of Financial and Quantitative Analysis*, 24, 41–56.

Evans, G.W. (1989) Output and Unemployment Dynamics in the United States: 1950–1985, *Journal of Applied Econometrics*, 4, 213–238.

Evans, M. and Lyons, R. (2005) Meese–Rogoff Redux: Micro-Based Exchange Rate Forecasting, *American Economic Review*, 965, 405–414.

Fair, R. (1970) The Estimation of Simultaneous Equation Models with Lagged Endogenous Variables and First Order Serially Correlated Errors, *Econometrica*, 3, 507–516.

Fair, R. (2008) Estimating Exchange Rate Equations Using Estimated Expectations, Yale University ICF Working Paper No. 07–18.

Falk, G. (1995) How Does Econometrics Contribute, if at all, to the Scientific Status of Economics? https://www.tcd.ie/Economics/assets/pdf/SER/1995/Gavin_Falk.html (accessed 5 March 2016).

Farmer, J.D. and Foley, D. (2009) The Economy Needs Agent-Based Modelling, *Nature*, 460, 685–686.

Fatás, A. and Summers, L.H. (2015) Macroeconomics and Growth and Monetary Economics and Fluctuations, CEPR Discussion Papers, No. 10902.

Fauver, L. and McDonald, M.B. (2015) Culture, Agency Costs, and Governance: International Evidence on Capital Structure, *Pacific Basin Finance Journal*, 34, 1–23.

Fergusson, A. (2010) *When Money Dies* (revised edition), New York: Public Affairs.

Fisher, F.M. (1966) *The Identification Problem in Econometrics*, New York: McGraw-Hill.

Fisher, I. (1892) *Mathematical Investigations in the Theory of Value and Prices*, New York: Augustus M. Kelley (Reprinted in 2016 by Cosimo, New York).

Fisher, I. (1930) *The Theory of Interest*, New York: Macmillan.

Fisher I. (1933) Statistics in the Service of Economics, *Journal of the American Statistical Association*, 28, 1–13.

Fisher, I. (1937) Note on a Short-Cut Method for Calculating Distributed Lags, *Bulletin de l'Institut International de Statistique*, 29, 323–327.

Flaherty. J.C., Gourgey, G. and Natarajan, S. (2013) Five Lessons Learned: Risk Management After the Crisis, *European Financial Review*, 30 April.

Flood, R. and Rose, A. (2008) Why so Glum? The Meese–Rogoff Methodology Meets the Stock Market, CEPR Discussion Papers, No. 6714.

Florens, J.P. and van Bellegem, S. (2015) Instrumental Variable Estimation in Functional Linear Models, *Journal of Econometrics*, 186, 465–476.

Focardi, S. and Fabozzi, F. (2010) The Reasonable Effectiveness of Mathematics in Economics, *American Economist*, 49, 3–15.

Folger, J. (2014) Guide to Pairs Trading, Investopedia. http://www.investopedia.com/university/guide-pairs-trading/ (accessed 1 September 2016).

Fornari, F. and Mele, A. (1996) Modeling the Changing Asymmetry of Conditional Variances, *Economics Letters*, 50, 197–203.

Fox, J. (2009) *The Myth of the Rational Market*, New York: Harper Collins.

Francq, C., Wintenberger, O. and Zakoian, J.M. (2013) GARCH Models without Positivity Constraints: Exponential or Log GARCH? *Journal of Econometrics*, 177, 34–46.

Frankel, J. and Rose, A. (1995) Empirical Research on Nominal Exchange Rates, *Handbook of International Economics*, Vol. 3, Amsterdam: Elsevier.

Friedman, B.M., Laibson, D.I. and Minsky, H.P. (1989) Economic Implications of Extraordinary Movements in Stock Prices, *Brookings Papers on Economic Activity*, 137–189.

Friedman, M. (1957) *A Theory of the Consumption Function*, Princeton: Princeton University Press.

Frisch, R. (1933a) Editorial, *Econometrica*, 1, 1–4.

Frisch, R. (1933b) *Pitfalls in the Statistical Construction of Demand and Supply Curves*, Leipzig: Hans Buske Verlag.

Frydenberg, S. (2008) Theory of Capital Structure: A Review. http://papers.ssrn.com/sol3/papers.cfm?abstract_id=556631 (accessed 5 March 2016).

Gallant, A.R. and Tauchen G. (1998) SNP: A Program for Nonparametric Time Series Analysis. www.econ.duke.edu/~get/wpapers/index.html (accessed 10 June 2016).

Galvao, A.F. (2009) Unit Root Quantile Autoregression Testing Using Covariates, *Journal of Econometrics*, 152, 165–178.

Galvao, A.F. (2011) Quantile Regression for Dynamic Panel Data with Fixed Effects, *Journal of Econometrics*, 164, 142–157.

Galvao, A.F. and Kato, K. (2016) Smoothed Quantile Regression for Panel Data, *Journal of Econometrics*, 193, 92–112.

Garratt, A., Lee, K., Pesaran, M.H. and Shin, Y. (2003) Forecast Uncertainty in Macroeconometric Modelling: An Application to the

UK Economy, *Journal of the American Statistical Association*, 98, 829–838.

Garratt, A., Lee, K. Pesaran, M.H. and Shin, Y. (2006) *Global and National Macroeconometric Modelling: A Long-Run Structural Approach*, Oxford: Oxford University Press.

Garrone, G. and Marchionatti, R. (2004) Keynes on Econometric Method: A Reassessment of his Debate with Tinbergen and other Econometricians (1938–1943), Universita di Torino, Working Paper No. 01/2004.

Gatev, E., Goetzmann, W.N. and Rouwenhorst, K.G. (2006) Pairs Trading: Performance of a Relative-Value Arbitrage Rule, *Review of Financial Studies*, 19, 797–827.

Gautier, E. and Kitamura, Y. (2013) Nonparametric Estimation in Random Coefficients Binary Choice Models, *Econometrica*, 81, 581–607.

Geary, R.C. (1949) Studies in Relations between Economic Time Series, *Journal of the Royal Statistical Society*, Series B, 10, 140–158.

Gelman, A. and Stern, H. (2006) The Difference Between "Significant" and "Not Significant" is Not Itself Statistically Significant, *American Statistician*, 60, 328–331.

Georgopoulos, G. (2008) The J-Curve Revisited: An Empirical Analysis for Canada, *Atlantic Economic Journal*, 36, 315–332.

Geweke, J.F. (1986) Modeling the Persistence of Conditional Variances: A Comment, *Econometric Reviews*, 5, 57–61.

Geweke, J.F., Horowitz, J.L. and Pesaran, M.H. (2006) Econometrics: A Bird's Eye View, IZA Discussion Papers, No. 2458.

Ghali, K.L. (1999) Government Size and Economic Growth: Evidence from a Multivariate Cointegration Analysis, *Applied Economics*, 31, 975–987.

Ghosh, A. (1993) Hedging with Stock Index Futures: Estimation and Forecasting with Error Correction Model, *Journal of Futures Markets*, 13, 743–752.

Gilbert, C.L. (1986) Professor Hendry's Econometric Methodology, *Oxford Bulletin of Economics and Statistics*, 48, 283–307.

Glosten, L.R., Jagannathan, R. and Runkle, D. (1993) On the Relation Between the Expected Value and the Volatility of the Nominal Excess Return on Stocks, *Journal of Finance*, 48, 1779–1801.

Godfrey, L.G. and Wickens, M.R. (1982) Tests of Mis-Specification Using Locally Equivalent Alternative Models, in G.C. Chow and P. Corsi (eds) *Evaluation and Reliability of Macro-economic Models*, New York: Wiley, 71–99.

Goertzel, T. (2002) Econometric Modeling as Junk Science, *The Skeptical Inquirer*, 26, 19–23.

Gonzalez-Rivera, G. (1998) Smooth Transition GARCH Models, *Studies in Nonlinear Dynamics and Econometrics*, 3, 61–78.

Gonzalo, J. (1994) Comparison of Five Alternative Methods of Estimating Long-Run Equilibrium Relationships, *Journal of Econometrics*, 60, 203–233.

Gordon, R.J. (1984) Unemployment and Potential Output in the 1980s, *Brooking Papers on Economic Activity*, 15, 537–564.

Gordon, R.J. (2010) The Demise of Okun's Law and of Procyclical Fluctuations in Conventional and Unconventional Measures of Productivity, Presentation at the CREI/CEPR Macro-Labor Conference, Barcelona, 5 November.

Gospodinov, N. and Otsu, T. (2012) Local GMM Estimation of Time Series Models with Conditional Moment Restrictions, *Journal of Econometrics*, 170, 476–490.

Gourieroux, C. and Jasiak, J. (2008) Dynamic Quantile Models, *Journal of Econometrics*, 147, 198–205.

Gourieroux, C. and Monfort, A. (1992) Qualitative Threshold ARCH Models, *Journal of Econometrics*, 52, 159–199.

Granger, C.W.J. (1969) Investigating Causal Relations by Econometric Models and Cross-Spectral Methods, *Econometrica*, 37, 424–438.

Granger, C.W.J. (1986) Developments in the Study of Co-Integrated Economic Variables, *Oxford Bulletin of Economics and Statistics*, 48, 213–228.

Granger, C.W.J. and Newbold, P. (1974) Spurious Regression in Econometrics, *Journal of Econometrics*, 2, 111–120.

Gray, S.F. (1996) Modeling the Conditional Distribution of Interest Rates as a Regime-Switching Process, *Journal of Financial Economics*, 42, 27–62.

Griliches, Z. (1986) Economic Data Issues, in Z. Griliches and M.D. Intriligator (eds) *Handbook of Econometrics*, Vol. III, Amsterdam: North Holland, 1465–1514.

Guégan, D. and Diebolt, J. (1994) Probabilistic Properties of the ARCH Model, *Statistica Sinica*, 4, 71–87.

Guidotti, P.E. and Rodriguez, C.A. (1992) Dollarization in Latin America – Gresham Law in Reverse, *International Monetary Fund Staff Papers*, 39, 518–544.

Guisan, M.C. (2001) Causality and Cointegration between Consumption and GDP in 25 OECD Countries: Limitations of the Cointegration Approach, *Applied Econometrics and International Development*, 1, 39–61.

Gulen, S.G. (1998) Efficiency in the Crude Oil Futures Market, *Journal of Energy Finance and Development*, 3, 13–21.

Guscina, A. (2006) Effects of Globalization on Labor's Share in National Income, *IMF Working Papers*, WP/06/294.

Haavelmo, T. (1943) Statistical Testing of Business Cycle Theories, *Review of Economics and Statistics*, 25, 13–18.

Haavelmo, T. (1944) The Probability Approach in Econometrics, *Econometrica*, Supplement to Volume 12: 1–118.

Hall, R.L. and Hitch, C.J. (1939) Price Theory and Business Behaviour, *Oxford Economic Papers*, 2, 12–45.

Hamilton, J. and Jordá, O. (2002) A Model of the Federal Funds Rate Target, *Journal of Political Economy*, 110,1135–1167.

Hansen, B.E. (1994) Autoregressive Conditional Density Estimation, *International Economic Review*, 35, 705–730.

Hansen, B.E. (2007) Least Squares Model Averaging, *Econometrica*, 75, 1175–1189.

Hansen, B.E. (2011) *Econometrics*, University of Wisconsin. http://www. ssc.wisc.edu/~bhansen/econometrics/Econometrics2011.pdf (accessed 7 April 2016).

Hansen, L.P. (1982) Large Sample Properties of Generalized Method of Moments, *Econometrica*, 50, 1029–1054.

Hansen, L.P. and Singleton, K.J. (1982) Generalized Instrumental Variables Estimation of Nonlinear Rational Expectations Models, *Econometrica*, 50, 1269–1286.

Hansen, L.P. and Singleton, K.J. (1983) Stochastic Consumption, Risk Aversion, and the Temporal Behavior of Asset Returns, *Journal of Political Economy*, 91, 249–265.

Harris, M. and Raviv, A. (1991) The Theory of Capital Structure, *Journal of Finance*, 46, 297–355.

Harris, R.D.F., Stoja, E. and Tucker, J. (2007) A Simplified Approach to Modeling the Comovement of Asset Returns, *Journal of Futures Markets*, 27, 575–598.

Harris, R.I.D. (1995) *Using Cointegration Analysis in Econometric Modelling*, London: Prentice Hall.

Harvey, A. (1989) *Forecasting, Structural Time Series Models and Kalman Filter*, Cambridge: Cambridge University Press.

Harvey, A., Ruiz, E. and Sentana, E. (1992) Unobserved Component Time Series Models with ARCH Disturbances, *Journal of Econometrics*, 52, 129–157.

Harvey, C.R., Liu, Y. and Zhu, H. (2015) . . . and the Cross-Section of Expected Returns, *Journal of Financial Studies* (published online, 9 October).

Haug, S. and Czado, C. (2007) An Exponential Continuous-Time GARCH Process, *Journal of Applied Probability*, 44, 960–976.

Hausman, J.A. (1978) Specification Tests in Econometrics, *Econometrica*, 46, 1251–1272.

Hausman, J.A., Hall, B.H. and Griliches, Z. (1984) Econometric Models for Count Data with Application to the Patents–R&D Relationship, *Econometrica*, 52, 909–1038.

Heckman, J.J. (2001) Econometrics and Empirical Economics, *Journal of Econometrics*, 100, 3–5.

Heckman, J.J. and Singer, B. (1984) Econometric Duration Analysis, *Journal of Econometrics*, 24, 63–132.

Hendricks, K. and Porter, R.H. (1988) An Empirical Study of an Auction with Asymmetric Information, *American Economic Review*, 78, 865–883.

Hendry, D.F. (1980) Econometrics – Alchemy or Science?, *Economica*, 47, 387–406.

Hendry, D.F. (2004) The ET Interview: Professor David F. Hendry: Interviewed by Neil R. Ericsson, *Econometric Theory*, 20, 743–804.

Hendry, D.F. and Clements, M.P. (2001) Economic Forecasting: Some Lessons from Recent Research, European Central Bank, Working Paper No. 82.

Hendry, D.F. and Ericsson, N. (1991) An Econometric Analysis of UK Money Demand in Monetary Trends in the United States and the United Kingdom by Milton Friedman and Anna J. Schwartz, *American Economic Review*, 81, 8–38.

Hendry, D.F. and Richard, J.F. (1982) On the Formulation of Empirical Models in Dynamic Econometrics, *Journal of Econometrics*, 20, 3–33.

Henrekson, M. (1992) *An Economic Analysis of Swedish Government Expenditure*, Aldershot: Avebury.

Hentschel, L. (1995) All in the Family: Nesting Symmetric and Asymmetric GARCH Models, *Journal of Financial Economics*, 39, 71–104.

Heston, S.L. and Nandi, S. (2000) A Closed-Form GARCH Option Valuation Model, *Review of Financial Studies*, 13, 585–625.

Higgins, M.L. and Bera, A.K. (1992) A Class of Nonlinear ARCH Models, *International Economic Review*, 33, 137–158.

Hilsenrath, J.E. (2004) Stock Characters: As Two Economists Debate Markets, the Tide Shifts, *Wall Street Journal*, 18 October.

Hjalmarsson, E. and Österholm, P. (2007) Testing for Cointegration Using the Johansen Methodology when Variables are Near-Integrated, IMF Working Papers, June.

Hoffman, D.L. and Rasche, R.H. (1996) Assessing Forecast Performance in a Cointegrated System, *Journal of Applied Econometrics*, 11, 495–517.

Hongyan, Y. (2008) The Determinants of Capital Structure of the SMEs: An Empirical Study of Chinese Listed Manufacturing Companies, School of Management, Beijing Union University, Working Paper.

Hood, W.C. and Koopmans, T.C. (eds) (1953) *Studies in Econometric Method*, Cowles Commission for Research in Economics, Monograph No. 14, New York: Wiley.

Hooker, R.H. (1901) Correlation of the Marriage Rate with Trade, *Journal of the Royal Statistical Society*, 44, 485–492.

Horn, K. (2009) The Serendipity of Genius, Standpoint, October. http://www.standpointmag.co.uk/node/2164/full (accessed 14 February 2016).

Horwitz, S. (2012) The Empirics of Austrian Economics, *Cato Unbound*, 5 September. http://www.cato-unbound.org/2012/09/05/steven-horwitz/empirics-austrian-economics (accessed 5 September 2016).

Hsiao, C., and Pesaran, M.H. (2006) Random Coefficient Panel Data Models, in L. Matyas and P. Sevestre (eds) *The Econometrics of Panel Data*, London: Kluwer Academic Publishers, 185–213.

Huang, R. and Ritter, J.R. (2005) Testing the Market Timing Theory of Capital Structure, Working Paper. http://bear.warrington.ufl.edu/ritter/TestingOct2805(1).pdf (accessed 3 January 2016).

Huang, S. and Song, F.M. (2002) The Determinants of Capital Structure: Evidence from China. http://papers.ssrn.com/sol3/papers.cfm?abstract_id=320088 (accessed 23 May 2017).

Hussain, M. and Brookins, O.S. (2001) On the Determinants of National Saving: An Extreme Bounds Analysis, *Weltwirtschaftliches Archiv*, 137, 151–174.

Hwang, S. and Satchell, S.E. (2005) GARCH Model with Cross-Sectional Volatility: GARCHX Models, *Applied Financial Economics*, 15, 203–216.

Im, K.S., Pesaran, M.H. and Shin, Y. (2003) Testing for Unit Roots in Heterogenous Panels, *Journal of Econometrics*, 115, 53–74.

Imai, S., Jain, N. and Ching, A. (2009) Bayesian Estimation of Dynamic Discrete Choice Models, *Econometrica*, 77, 1865–1899.

IMF (2010) Unemployment Dynamics During Recessions and Recoveries: Okun's Law and Beyond, *World Economic Outlook*, April.

Islam, A.M. (2001) Wagner's Law Revisited: Cointegration and Exogeneity Tests for USA, *Applied Economics*, 8, 509–515.

Jensen, M. (1978) Some Anomalous Evidence Regarding Market Efficiency, *Journal of Financial Economics*, 6, 95–101.

Jensen, M. and Maheu, J.M. (2013) Bayesian Semiparametric Multivariate GARCH Modeling, *Journal of Econometrics*, 176, 3–17.

Jevons, W.S. (1871) *The Theory of Political Economy*, London: Macmillan.

Jin, X. and Maheu, J.M. (2016) Modeling Covariance Breakdowns in Multivariate GARCH, *Journal of Econometrics*, 194, 1–23.

Johansen, S. (1988) Statistical Analysis of Cointegration Vectors, *Journal of Economic Dynamics and Control*, 12, 231–254.

Johansen, S. (1991) Estimation and Hypothesis Testing of Cointegrating

Vectors in Gaussian Vector Autoregressive Models, *Econometrica*, 59, 1551–1580.

Jorgenson, D.W. (1966) Rational Distributed Lag Functions, *Econometrica*, 34, 135–149.

Kalli, M. and Griffin, J.E. (2014) Time-Varying Sparsity in Dynamic Regression Models, *Journal of Econometrics*, 178, 779–793.

Karabell, Z. (2013) The "Laws of Economics" Don't Exist, *The Atlantic*, 11 April.

Karabournis, L. and Neiman, B. (2014) The Global Decline of the Labor Share, *Quarterly Journal of Economics*, 129, 61–103.

Kasahara, H. and Shimotsu, K. (2012) Sequential Estimation of Structural Models with a Fixed Point Constraint, *Econometrica*, 80, 2303–2319.

Kasparis, I. and Phillips, P.C.B. (2012) Dynamic Misspecification in Nonparametric Cointegrating Regression, *Journal of Econometrics*, 168, 270–284.

Kaufman, H. (2009) *The Road to Financial Reformation: Warnings, Consequences, Reforms*, New York: Wiley.

Kawakatsu, H. (2006) Matrix Exponential GARCH, *Journal of Econometrics*, 134, 95–128.

Kearns, A. (1995) Econometrics and the Scientific Status of Economics: A Reply. https://www.tcd.ie/Economics/assets/pdf/SER/1995/Allan_Kearns.html (accessed 6 May 2016).

Keuzenkamp, H.A. (1995) Keynes and the Logic of Econometric Method, Working Paper, Department of Economics, Tilburg University.

Keuzenkamp, H.A. (2000) *Probability, Econometrics and Truth: The Methodology of Econometrics*, Cambridge: Cambridge University Press.

Keuzenkamp, H.A. and Magnus, J.R. (1995) On Tests and Significance in Econometrics, *Journal of Econometrics*, 67, 5–24.

Keynes, J.M. (1936) *The General Theory of Employment, Interest, and Money*, London: Macmillan.

Keynes, J.M. (1939) Professor Tinbergen's Method, *Economic Journal*, 49, 558–568.

Keynes, J.M. (1940) Comment, *Economic Journal*, 154–156.

Kilian, L. and Taylor, M.P. (2003) Why is it so Difficult to Beat the Random Walk Forecast of Exchange Rates?, *Journal of International Economics*, 60, 85–107.

Kim, J.H. (2016) Stock Returns and Investors' Mood: Good Day Sunshine or Spurious Correlation, Working Paper, La Trobe University.

Kim, J.H. and Choi, I. (2016) Unit Roots in Economic and Financial Time Series: A Re-Evaluation at the Optimal Level of Significance, Working Paper, La Trobe University.

Kim, J.H. and Ji, P.I. (2015) Significance Testing in Empirical Finance: A Critical Review and Assessment, *Journal of Empirical Finance*, 34, 1–14.

Kim, K. and Pagan, A.R. (1995) The Econometric Analysis of Calibrated Macroeconomic Models, in M.H. Pesaran and M. Wickens (eds) *Handbook of Applied Econometrics: Macroeconomics*, Oxford: Basil Blackwell, 356–390.

Klein, D.B. and Romero, P.P. (2007) Model Building versus Theorizing: The Paucity of Theory in the Journal of Economic Theory, *Economics in Practice*, 4, 241–271.

Klein, L.R. (1947) The Use of Econometric Models as a Guide to Economic Policy, *Econometrica*, 15, 111–151.

Klein, L.R. (1950) *Economic Fluctuations in the United States 1921–1941*, Cowles Commission Monograph No. 11, New York: Wiley.

Klein, L.R. (1951) The Life of J.M. Keynes, *Journal of Political Economy*, 59, 443–451.

Klein, L.R. (1971) Whither Econometrics, *Journal of the American Statistical Association*, 66, 415–421.

Kling, A. (2010) Macroeconometrics: The Lost History, Unpublished Paper. http://arnoldkling.com/essays/macroeconometrics.doc (accessed 3 July 2016).

Kling, A. (2011) Macroeconometrics: The Science of Hubris, *Critical Review*, 23, 123–133.

Klüppelberg, C., Lindner, A. and Maller, R. (2004) A Continuous Time GARCH Process Driven by a Lévy Process: Stationarity and Second Order Behaviour, *Journal of Applied Probability*, 41, 601–622.

Knetsch, T.A. (2007) Forecasting the Price of Crude Oil via Convenience Yield Prediction, *Journal of Forecasting*, 26, 273–306.

Kodres, L.E. (1993) Test of Unbiasedness in Foreign Exchange Futures Markets: An Examination of Price Limits and Conditional Heteroskedasticity, *Journal of Business*, 66, 463–490.

Kolluri, B.R., Panik, M.J. and Wahab, M.S. (2000) Government Expenditure and Economic Growth: Evidence from G7 Countries, *Applied Economics*, 32, 1059–1068.

Koop, G., Leon-Gonzalez, R. and Strachan, R.W. (2011) Bayesian Inference in a Time Varying Cointegration Model, *Journal of Econometrics*, 165, 210–220.

Koopmans, T.C. (1937) *Linear Regression Analysis of Economic Time Series*, Haarlem: De Erven F. Bohn for the Netherlands Economic Institute.

Koopmans, T.C. (1949) Identification Problems in Economic Model Construction, *Econometrica*, 17, 125–144.

Koopmans, T.C. (ed.) (1950) *Statistical Inference in Dynamic Economic Models*, Cowles Commission Monograph No. 10, New York: Wiley.

Koopmans, T.C., Rubin, H. and Leipnik, R.B. (1950) Measuring the Equation Systems of Dynamic Economics, in T.C. Koopmans (ed.) *Statistical Inference in Dynamic Economic Models*, Cowles Commission Monograph No. 10, New York: Wiley, 54–237.

Kourlas, J. (2012) Lessons Not Learned From the Housing Crisis, *The Atlas Society*, 12 April.

Koutsoyiannis, A. (1977) *Theory of Econometrics: An Introductory Exposition of Econometric Methods*, London: Macmillan.

Koyck, L.M. (1954) *Distributed Lags and Investment Analysis*, Amsterdam: North-Holland.

Krämer, H.M. (2011) Bowley's Law: The Diffusion of an Empirical Supposition into Economic Theory, *Papers in Political Economy*, 61, 19–49.

Kremers, J.J.M., Ericsson, N.R. and Dolado, J.J. (1992) The Power of Cointegration Tests, *Oxford Bulletin of Economics and Statistics*, 54, 325–348.

Kroner, K.F. and Sultan, J. (1993) Time-Varying Distributions and Dynamic Hedging with Foreign Currency Futures, *Journal of Financial and Quantitative Analysis*, 28, 535–551.

Krugman, P. (2009) How Did Economists Get it So Wrong, *New York Times Magazine*, September 6. http://www.nytimes.com/2009/09/06/magazine/06Economic-t.html (accessed April 9, 2016).

Krugman, P. (2015) Demand Creates its Own Supply, *New York Times*, 3 November.

Kuersteiner, G.M. (2012) Kernel-Weighted GMM Estimators for Linear Time Series Models, *Journal of Econometrics*, 170, 399–421.

Kumar, M. (1992) The Forecasting Accuracy of Crude Oil Futures Prices, *IMF Staff Papers*, 39, 432–461.

Kumar, S., Webber, D. and Fargher, S. (2010) Wagner's Law Revisited: Cointegration and Causality Tests for New Zealand, Department of Business Economics, Auckland University of Technology.

Kydland, F.E. and Prescott, E.C. (1996) The Computational Experiment: An Econometric Tool, *Journal of Economic Perspectives*, 10, 69–85.

Laffont, J.J., Ossard, H. and Vuong, Q. (1995) Econometrics of First-Price Auctions, *Econometrica*, 63, 953–980.

Lasak, K. (2010) Likelihood Based Testing for no Fractional Cointegration, *Journal of Econometrics*, 158, 67–77.

Lavoie, M. (2000) A Post Keynesian View of Interest Parity Theorems, *Journal of Post Keynesian Economics*, 23, 163–179.

Lawson, T. (2015) *Essays on the Nature and State of Modern Economics,* London: Routledge.

Leamer, E. (1978) *Specification Searches: Ad Hoc Inference with Non-experimental Data,* New York: John Wiley.

Leamer, E. (1983) Let's Take the Con out of Econometrics, *American Economic Review,* 73, 31–43.

Leamer, E. and Leonard, H. (1983) Reporting the Fragility of Regression Estimates, *Review of Economics and Statistics,* 65, 307–317.

LeBaron, B. (1992) Some Relations between Volatility and Serial Correlation in Stock Market Returns, *Journal of Business,* 65, 199–219.

Ledoit, O., Santa-Clara, P. and Wolf, M. (2003) Flexible Multivariate GARCH Modeling with an Application to International Stock Markets, *Review of Economics and Statistics,* 85, 735–747.

Lee, J. and Robinson, P.M. (2015) Panel Nonparametric Regression with Fixed Effects, *Journal of Econometrics,* 188, 346–362.

Lee, S. and Taniguchi, M. (2005) Asymptotic Theory for ARCH-SM Models: LAN and Residual Empirical Processes, *Statistica Sinica,* 15, 215–234.

Lee, T.H. (1994) Spread and Volatility in Spot and Forward Exchange Rates, *Journal of International Money and Finance,* 13, 375–382.

Lenoir, M. (1913) *Etudes sur la formation et le mouvement des prix,* Paris: Giard et Brière.

Leonard, J. (2014) Torture the Data, and it will Confess to Anything. https://www.linkedin.com/pulse/20140908144907-4149707--torture-the-data-and-it-will-confess-to-anything-ronald-coase (accessed 26 April 2016).

Leontief, W. (1971) Theoretical Assumptions and Nonobserved Facts, *American Economic Review,* 61, 1–7.

Levin, A., Lin, C. and Chu, C.J. (2002) Unit Root Tests in Panel Data: Asymptotic and Finite Sample Properties, *Journal of Econometrics,* 108, 1–24.

Levine, D.K. (2012) Why Economists are Right: Rational Expectations and the Uncertainty Principle in Economics, *Huffington Post,* 26 January.

Levinovitz, A.J. (2016) The New Astrology. https://aeon.co/essays/how-economists-rode-maths-to-become-our-era-s-astrologers (accessed 11 September 2018).

Li, C.W. and Li, W.K. (1996) On a Double Threshold Autoregressive Heteroskedastic Time Series Model, *Journal of Applied Econometrics,* 11, 253–274.

Li, M., Li, W.K. and Li, G. (2015) A New Hyperbolic GARCH Model, *Journal of Econometrics,* 189, 428–436.

Li, K., Yue, H. and Zhao, L. (2009) Ownership, Institutions, and Capital

Structure: Evidence from China, *Journal of Comparative Economics*, 37, 471–490.

Lien, D.D. (1996) The Effect of the Cointegration Relationship on Futures Hedging: A Note, *Journal of Futures Markets*, 16, 773–780.

Lin, J.L. and Tsay, R.S. (1996) Cointegration Constraint and Forecasting: An Empirical Examination, *Journal of Applied Econometrics*, 11, 519–538.

Lin, Z. and Brannigan, A. (2003) Advances in the Analysis of Non-Stationary Time Series: An Illustration of Cointegration and Error Correction Methods in Research on Crime and Immigration, *Quality and Quantity*, 37, 151–168.

Litterman, R.B. (1985) Forecasting with Bayesian Vector Autoregressions: Five Years of Experience, *Journal of Business and Economic Statistics*, 4, 25–38.

Liu, S.M. and Brorsen, B.W. (1995) Maximum Likelihood Estimation of a GARCH Stable Model, *Journal of Applied Econometrics*, 10, 272–285.

Liu, Y., Ren, J. and Zhuang, Y. (2009) An Empirical Analysis on the Capital Structure of Chinese Listed IT Companies, *International Journal of Business and Management*, 4, 46–51.

Lopez-Iturriaga, F.J. and Rodriguez-Sanz, J.A. (2008) Capital Structure and Institutional Setting: A Decompositional and International Analysis, *Applied Economics*, 40, 1851–1864.

Lott, J. (2000) *More Guns, Less Crime: Understanding Crime and Gun Control Laws*, Chicago: University of Chicago Press.

Lott, J. and Mustard, D. (1997) Crime, Deterrence and the Right to Carry Concealed Handguns, *Journal of Legal Studies*, 26, 1–68.

Lubik, T.A. and Surico, P. (2006) The Lucas Critique and the Stability of Empirical Models, Federal Reserve Bank of Richmond, Working Papers, No. 06-05.

Lucas, R.E. (1976) Econometric Policy Evaluation: A Critique, *Carnegie Rochester Conference Series on Public Policy*, 1, 19–46.

Lucas, R.E. and Sargent, T.J. (eds) (1981) *Rational Expectations and Econometric Practice*, London: Allen and Unwin.

Lyttkens, E. (1970) Symmetric and Asymmetric Estimation Methods, in E. Mosback and H. Wold (eds) *Interdependent Systems*, Amsterdam: North-Holland, 434–459.

Ma, C. (1989) Forecasting Efficiency of Energy Futures Prices, *Journal of Futures Markets*, 9, 393–419.

Maddala, G.S. (1983) Limited Dependent and Qualitative Variables in Econometrics, Cambridge: Cambridge University Press.

Maddala, G.S. (1986) Disequilibrium, Self-Selection, and Switching

Models, in Z. Griliches and M.D. Intriligator (eds) *Handbook of Econometrics*, Vol. 3, Amsterdam: North-Holland, 1633–1688.

Maddala, G.S. (1999) Econometrics in the 21st Century, in C.R. Rao and R. Szekeley (eds) *Statistics for the 21st Century*, New York: Marcel Dekker, 265–284.

Magableh, M.A. (2006) A Theoretical and Empirical Analysis of the Wagner Hypothesis of Public Expenditure Growth, PhD Thesis, School of Economics and Finance, University of Western Sydney.

Magnus, J.R. (1999) The Success Of Econometrics, *De Economist*, 147, 55–71.

Maharaj, E.A, Moosa, I.A., Dark, J. and Silvapulle, P. (2008) Wavelet Estimation of Asymmetric Hedge Ratios: Does Econometric Sophistication Boost Hedging Effectiveness? *International Journal of Business and Economics*, 7, 213–230.

Maheu, J.M. and McCurdy, T.H. (2004) News Arrival, Jump Dynamics, and Volatility Components for Individual Stock Returns, *Journal of Finance*, 59, 755–793.

Malinvaud, E. (1966) *Statistical Methods of Econometrics*, Amsterdam: North-Holland.

Malliaris, A.G. and Urrutia, J.L. (1992) The International Crash of October 1987: Causality Tests, *Journal of Financial and Quantitative Analysis*, 27, 353–364.

Manski, C.F. (1975) Maximum Score Estimation of the Stochastic Utility Model of Choice, *Journal of Econometrics*, 3, 205–228.

Manski, C.F. (1985) Semiparametric Analysis of Discrete Response: Asymptotic Properties of the Maximum Score Estimator, *Journal of Econometrics*, 27, 313–334.

Manski, C.F. (1995) *Identification Problems in the Social Sciences*, Cambridge (MA): Harvard University Press.

Manski, C.F. (2003) *Partial Identification of Probability Distributions*, New York: Springer.

Manski, C.F. and McFadden, D. (1981) *Structural Analysis of Discrete Data with Econometric Applications*, Cambridge (MA): MIT Press.

Mason, P.M., Steagall, J.W. and Fabritiust, M.M. (1992) Publication Delays in Articles in Economics: What to Do about Them?, *Applied Economics*, 24, 859–874.

Mathur, T. and Subrahmanyam, V. (1990) Interdependencies among the Nordic and US Stock Markets, *Scandinavian Journal of Economics*, 92, 587–597.

Matzkin, R.L. (2015) Estimation of Nonparametric Models with Simultaneity, *Econometrica*, 83, 1–66.

McAleer, M. (1994) Sherlock Holmes and the Search for Truth: A Diagnostic Tale, *Journal of Economic Surveys*, 8, 317–370.

McAleer, M., Pagan, A.R. and Volker, P.A. (1985) What will Take the Con out of Econometrics? *American Economic Review*, 75, 293–307.

McCloskey, D.N. (1985) The Loss Function has been Mislaid: the Rhetoric of Significance Tests, *American Economic Review*, 75, 201–205.

McCloskey, D.N. (1998) *The Rhetoric of Economics*, Madison (WI): University of Wisconsin Press.

McCulloch, J.H. (1985) Interest-Risk Sensitive Deposit Insurance Premia: Stable ARCH Estimates, *Journal of Banking and Finance*, 9, 137–156.

McFadden, D. (1989) A Method of Simulated Moments for Estimation of Multinomial Probits without Numerical Integration, *Econometrica*, 57, 995–1026.

McNeil, A.J. and Frey, R. (2000) Estimation of Tail-Related Risk Measures for Heteroskedastic Financial Time Series: An Extreme Value Approach, *Journal of Empirical Finance*, 7, 271–300.

McWilliams, A. and Siegel, D. (2001) Corporate Social Responsibility: A Theory of the Firm Perspective, *Academy of Management Review*, 26, 117–127.

Medeiros, M.C. and Veiga, A. (2009) Modeling Multiple Regimes in Financial Volatility with a Flexible Coefficient GARCH(1,1) Model, *Econometric Theory*, 25, 117–161.

Meese, R. and Rogoff, K. (1983a) Empirical Exchange Rate Models of the Seventies: Do They Fit Out-of-Sample? *Journal of International Economics*, 14, 3–24.

Meese, R. and Rogoff, K. (1983b) The Out-of-Sample Failure of Empirical Exchange Rate Models: Sampling Error or Misspecification?, in J. Frenkel (ed.) *Exchange Rates and International Macroeconomics*, Chicago (IL): University of Chicago Press, 67–112.

Meyer, B. and Tasci, M. (2012) An Unstable Okun's Law, Not the Best Rule of Thumb, Federal Reserve Bank of Cleveland, *Economic Commentary*, 7 June.

Mihm, S. (2008) Dr Doom, *New York Times Magazine*, 15 August.

Mills, F.C. (1940) Quantification: The Quest for Precision, in L. Wirth (ed.) *Eleven Twenty-Six: A Decade of Social Science Research*, Chicago (IL): University of Chicago Press, 153–193.

Mitchell, W.C. (1928) *Business Cycles: The Problem in its Setting*, New York: National Bureau of Economic Research.

Mitchell, W.C. (1937) *Quantitative Analysis in Economic Theory*, New York: McGraw-Hill.

Mizon, G. (1995) A Simple Message for Autocorrelation Correctors: Don't, *Journal of Econometrics*, 69, 267–288.

Moon, H.R. and Schorfheide, F. (2009) Estimation with Overidentifying Inequality Moment Conditions, *Journal of Econometrics*, 153, 136–1 54.

Moore, H.L. (1914) *Economic Cycles: Their Law and Cause*, New York: Macmillan.

Moore, H.L. (1917) *Forecasting the Yield and the Price of Cotton*, New York: Macmillan.

Moosa, I.A. (1994) The Monetary Model of Exchange Rates Revisited, *Applied Financial Economics*, 4, 279–287.

Moosa, I.A. (1997) A Cross-Country Comparison of Okun's Coefficient, *Journal of Comparative Economics*, 24, 335–356.

Moosa, I.A. (2000) *Exchange Rate Forecasting: Techniques and Applications*, London: Macmillan.

Moosa, I.A. (2002) *Foreign Direct Investment: Theory, Evidence and Practice*, London: Palgrave.

Moosa, I.A. (2003) The Sensitivity of the Optimal Hedge Ratio to Model Specification, *Finance Letters*, 1, 15–20.

Moosa, I.A. (2004) Is Covered Interest Parity an Arbitrage or a Hedging Condition? *Economia Internazionale*, 57, 189–194.

Moosa, I.A. (2011a) The Failure of Financial Econometrics: Estimation of the Hedge Ratio as an Illustration, *Journal of Financial Transformation*, 31, 67–72.

Moosa, I.A. (2011b) The Failure of Financial Econometrics: Assessing the Cointegration "Revolution", *Journal of Financial Transformation*, 32, 113–122.

Moosa, I.A. (2011c) Undermining the Case for a Trade War between the US and China, *Economia Internazionale*, 64, 365–388.

Moosa, I.A. (2011d) On the US–Chinese Trade Dispute, *Journal of Post Keynesian Economics*, 34, 85–111.

Moosa, I.A. (2012) The Failure of Financial Econometrics: "Stir-Fry" Regressions as an Illustration, *Journal of Financial Transformation*, 34, 43–50.

Moosa, I.A. (2013) Why is it so Difficult to Outperform the Random Walk in Exchange Rate Forecasting?, *Applied Economics*, 45, 3340–3346.

Moosa, I.A. (2014) Direction Accuracy, Forecasting Error and the Profitability of Currency Trading: Simulation-Based Evidence, *Economia Internazionale*, 68, 413–423.

Moosa, I.A. (2016a) Blaming Suicide on NASA and Divorce on Margarine: the Hazard of Using Cointegration to Derive Inference on Spurious Correlation, *Applied Economics* (Published online, 16 August).

Moosa, I.A. (2016b) Covered Interest Parity: The Untestable Hypothesis, School of Economics, Finance and Marketing, RMIT, Working Paper.

Moosa, I.A. (2016c) Futures Crude Oil Prices as Predictors of Spot Prices: Lessons from the Foreign Exchange Market, School of Economics, Finance and Marketing, RMIT, Working Paper.

Moosa, I.A. and Al-Loughani, N.E (1994) Unbiasedness and Time-Varying Risk Premia in the Crude Oil Futures Market, *Energy Economics*, 16, 99–105.

Moosa, I.A. and Burns, K. (2012) Can Exchange Rate Models Outperform the Random Walk? Magnitude, Direction and Profitability as Criteria, *Economia Internazionale*, 65, 473–490.

Moosa, I.A. and Burns, K. (2014a) Error Correction Modelling and Dynamic Specifications as a Conduit to Outperforming the Random Walk in Exchange Rate Forecasting, *Applied Economics*, 46, 3107–3118.

Moosa, I.A. and Burns, K. (2014b) A Reappraisal of the Meese–Rogoff Puzzle, *Applied Economics*, 46, 30–40.

Moosa, I.A. and Burns, K. (2014c) The Unbeatable Random Walk in Exchange Rate Forecasting: Reality or Myth? *Journal of Macroeconomics*, 40, 69–81.

Moosa, I.A. and Burns, K. (2015) *Demystifying the Meese–Rogoff Puzzle*, London: Palgrave.

Moosa, I.A. and Cardak, B.A. (2006) The Determinants of Foreign Direct Investment: An Extreme Bounds Analysis, *Journal of Multinational Financial Management*, 16, 199–211.

Moosa, I.A. and Ma, M. (2015) Is the Chinese Currency Undervalued?, *International Journal of Economics*, 9, 81–99.

Moosa, I.A. and Ma, M. (2017) Linear and Nonlinear Attractors in Purchasing Power Parity, School of Economics, Finance and Marketing, *Economia Internazionale* (forthcoming).

Moosa, I.A. and Vaz, J.J. (2015) Why is it so Difficult to Outperform the Random Walk? An Application of the Meese–Rogoff Puzzle to Stock Prices, *Applied Economics*, 47, 398–407.

Moosa, I.A. and Vaz, J.J. (2016a) Cointegration as an Explanation for the Meese–Rogoff Puzzle, *Applied Economics*, 48, 4201–4209.

Moosa, I.A. and Vaz, J.J. (2016b) Cointegration, Error Correction and Exchange Rate Forecasting, *Journal of International Financial Markets, Institutions and Money*, 44, 21–34.

Moosa, I.A., Li, L. and Naughton, T. (2011) Robust and Fragile Determinants of the Capital Structure of Chinese Firms, *Applied Financial Economics*, 21, 1331–1343.

Müller, U.A. and Watson, M.W. (2008) Testing Models of Low-Frequency Variability, *Econometrica*, 76, 979–1016.

Müller, U.A., Dacorogna, M.M., Davé, R.D. Olsen, R.B., Puctet, O.V. and von Weizsäcker, J. (1997) Volatilities of Different Time Resolutions – Analyzing the Dynamics of Market Components, *Journal of Empirical Finance*, 4, 213–239.

Mundlak, Y. (1961) Empirical Production Function Free of Management Bias, *Journal of Farm Economics*, 43, 44–56.

Mundlak, Y. (1978) On the Pooling of Time Series and Cross Section Data, *Econometrica*, 46, 69–85.

Murphy, R.P. (2002) Econometrics: A Strange Process, *Mises Daily Articles*, 15 July. https://mises.org/library/econometrics-strange-process (accessed 26 April 2016).

Musgrave, R.A. and Peacock, A.T. (1958) *Classics in the Theory of Public Finance*, London: Macmillan.

Myers, S. and Majluf, N.S. (1984) Corporate Financing and Investment Decisions when Firms have Information that Investors Do not Have, *Journal of Financial Economics*, 13, 187–221.

Nam, K., Pyun, C.S. and Arize, A.C. (2002) Asymmetric Mean-Reversion and Contrarian Profits: ANST-GARCH Approach, *Journal of Empirical Finance*, 9, 563–588.

Nassar, I.A., Almsafir, M.K. and Al-Mahrouq, M.H. (2014) The Validity of Gibrat's Law in Developed and Developing Countries (2008–2013): Comparison Based Assessment, *Social and Behavioral Sciences*, 129, 266–273.

Neely, C. and Sarno, L. (2002) How Well Do Monetary Fundamentals Forecast Exchange Rates, *Economic Review of the Federal Reserve Bank of St. Louis*, September, 51–74.

Neftci, S.N. (1984) Are Economic Time Series Asymmetric over the Business Cycle? *Journal of Political Economy*, 92, 307–318.

Nelson, D.B. (1991) Conditional Heteroskedasticity in Asset Returns: A New Approach, *Econometrica*, 59, 347–370.

Nelson, D.B. (1996) Asymptotically Optimal Smoothing with ARCH Models, *Econometrica*, 64, 561–573.

Nelson, R.H. (2001) *Economics as Religion: From Samuelson to Chicago and Beyond*, State College (PA): Penn State University Press.

Nerlove, M. (1958a) Adaptive Expectations and the Cobweb Phenomena, *Quarterly Journal of Economics*, 72, 227–240.

Nerlove, M. (1958b) *Distributed Lags and Demand Analysis*, USDA, Agriculture Handbook No. 141, Washington, DC.

Nevo, A. and Whinston, M.D. (2010) Taking the Dogma out of Econometrics: Structural Modeling and Credible Inference, *Journal of Economic Perspectives*, 24, 69–82.

Nocera, J. (2009) Poking Holes in a Theory on Markets, *New York Times*, 5 June.

Noureldin, D., Shephard, N. and Sheppard, K. (2014) Multivariate Rotated ARCH Models, *Journal of Econometrics*, 179, 16–30.

Nowicka-Zagrajek J. and Weron, A. (2001) Dependence Structure of Stable R-GARCH Processes, *Probability and Mathematical Statistics*, 21, 371–380.

Nyblom, J. (1989) Testing for the Constancy of Parameters over Time, *Journal of the American Statistical Association*, 84, 223–230.

Okui, R. (2011) Instrumental Variable Estimation in the Presence of Many Moment Conditions, *Journal of Econometrics*, 165, 70–86.

Okun, A. (1962) Potential GNP: Its Measurement and Significance, *Proceedings of the Business and Economic Statistics Section of the American Statistical Association*, 89–104.

Orcutt, G.H. (1948) A Study of the Autoregressive Nature of the Time Series Used for Tinbergen's Model of the Economic System of the United States, 1919–1932, *Journal of the Royal Statistical Society*, Series B, 10, 1–45.

Pagan, A.R. (1984) Econometric Issues in the Analysis of Regressions with Generated Regressors, *International Economic Review*, 25, 221–247.

Pagan, A.R. (1987) Twenty Years After: Econometrics, 1966–1986, Paper presented at CORE's 20th Anniversary Conference, Louvain-la-Neuve.

Pakes, A. and Pollard, D. (1989) Simulation and the Asymptotics of Optimization Estimators, *Econometrica*, 57, 5 1027–1058.

Palley, T.I. (1993) Okun's Law and the Asymmetric and Changing Cyclical Behaviour of the USA Economy, *International Review of Applied Economics*, 7, 144–162.

Park, B.J. (2002) An Outlier Robust GARCH Model and Forecasting Volatility of Exchange Rate Returns, *Journal of Forecasting*, 21, 381–393.

Passell, P. and Taylor, J.B. (1977) The Deterrent Effect of Capital Punishment: Another View, *American Economic Review*, 67, 445–451.

Patinkin, D. (1976) Keynes and Econometrics: On the Interaction between the Macroeconomics Revolutions in the Interwar Period, *Econometrica*, 44, 1091–1123.

Pesaran, B. and Pesaran, M.H. (2009) *Time Series Econometrics: Using Microfit 5.0*, Oxford: Oxford University Press.

Pesaran, M.H. (1990) Econometrics, in J. Eatwell, M. Milgate and P. Newman (eds) *The New Palgrave: Econometrics*, New York: Norton, 25–26.

Pesaran, M.H. and Shin, Y. (1995) Long Run Structural Modelling, Working Paper, University of Cambridge.

Pesaran, M.H. and Shin, Y. (1996) Cointegration and the Speed of Convergence to Equilibrium, *Journal of Econometrics*, 71, 117–143.

Pesaran, M.H. and Smith, R. (1985) Keynes on Econometrics, in T. Lawson and M.H. Pesaran (eds) *Keynes' Economics: Methodological Issues*, London: Croom Helm, 134–150.

Pesaran, M.H. and Smith, L.V. (2013) Panel Unit Root Tests in the Presence of a Multifactor Error Structure, *Journal of Econometrics*, 175, 94–115.

Pesaran, M.H. and Timmermann, A. (2005) Small Sample Properties of Forecasts from Autoregressive Models under Structural Breaks, *Journal of Econometrics*, 129, 183–217.

Pesaran, M.H. and Timmermann, A. (2007) Model Instability and Choice of Observation Window, *Journal of Econometrics*, 137, 134–161.

Pesaran, M.H. and Weeks, M. (2001) Non-Nested Hypothesis Testing: An Overview, in B.H. Baltagi (ed.) *Companion to Theoretical Econometrics*, Oxford: Basil Blackwell, 279–309.

Pesaran, M.H., Schuermann, T. and Smith, V. (2009) Forecasting Economic and Financial Variables with Global VARs, *International Journal of Forecasting*, 25, 642–675.

Pesaran, M.H., Shin, Y. and Smith, R.J. (2001) Bounds Testing Approaches to the Analysis of Level Relationships, *Journal of Applied Econometrics*, 16, 289–326.

Phillips, P.C.B. (1983) Exact Small Sample Theory in the Simultaneous Equations Model, in Z. Griliches and M.D. Intrilgator (eds) *Handbook of Econometrics*, Vol. 1, Amsterdam: North-Holland, 449–516.

Phillips, P.C.B. (1986) Understanding Spurious Regression in Econometrics, *Journal of Econometrics*, 33, 311–340.

Phillips, P.C.B. (1991) Optimal Inference in Cointegrated Systems, *Econometrica*, 59, 283–306.

Phillips, P.C.B. and Hansen, B.E. (1990) Statistical Inference in Instrumental Variables Regression with I(1) Processes, *Review of Economic Studies*, 57, 99–125.

Pollock, S. (2014) Econometrics: An Historical Guide for the Uninitiated, University of Leicester, Department of Economics, Working Paper No. 14/05.

Powell, J.L. (1984) Least Absolute Deviations Estimation for the Censored Regression Model, *Journal of Econometrics*, 25, 303–325.

Powell, J.L. (1986) Censored Regression Quantiles, *Journal of Econometrics*, 32, 143–155.

Powell, J.L. (1994) Estimation of Semiparametric Models, in R.F. Engle and D. McFadden (eds) *Handbook of Econometrics*, Vol. 4, Amsterdam: North Holland, 2443–2521.

Prachowny, M.F.J. (1993) Okun's Law: Theoretical Foundations and Revised Estimates, *Review of Economics and Statistics*, 75, 331–336.

Prasad, S.J., Green, C.J., and Murinde, V. (2001) Company Financing,

Capital Structure, and Ownership: A Survey and Implications for Developing Economies, *SUERF Studies,* No. 12, February.

Qian, Y., Tian, Y. and Wirjanto, T.S. (2009) Do Chinese Publicly Listed Companies Adjust their Capital Structure Toward a Target Level? *China Economic Review*, 20, 662–676.

Quan, J. (1992) Two-Step Testing Procedure for Price Discovery Role of Futures Prices, *Journal of Futures Markets*, 12, 139–149.

Quandt, R.E. (1982) Econometric Disequilibrium Models, *Econometric Reviews*, 1, 1–63.

Ram, R. (1987) Wagner's Hypothesis in Time-Series and Cross-Section Perspectives: Evidence from "Real" Data for 115 Countries, *Review of Economics and Statistics*, 69, 194–204.

Ramsey, J.B. (1969) Tests for Specification Errors in Classical Linear Least Squares Regression Analysis, *Journal of the Royal Statistical Society*, Series B, 31, 350–371.

Rashid, S. (2007) The "Law" of One Price: Implausible, yet Consequential, *Quarterly Journal of Austrian Economics*, 10, 79–90.

Reiersol, O. (1941) Confluence Analysis by Means of Lag Moments and other Methods of Confluence Analysis, *Econometrica*, 9, 1–24.

Reiersol, O. (1945) *Confluence Analysis by Means of Instrumental Sets of Variables*, Stockholm: Almqvist and Wiksells Boktryckeri.

Reimers, H.E. (1991) Comparison of Tests for Multivariate Cointegration, Christian-Alberchts University, Discussion Paper No. 58.

Relander, P. (2011) Gibrat's Law Revisited – A Study on Gibrat's Law with Models of Industry Dynamics, Department of Economics, Aalto University. http://epub.lib.aalto.fi/en/ethesis/pdf/12487/hse_ethesis_12487.pdf (accessed 15 May 2016).

Rigobon, R. (2002) The Curse of Non-Investment Grade Countries, *Journal of Development Economics*, 69, 423–449.

Ritholtz, B. (2009) The Hubris of Economics, *EconoMonitor*, 4 November. http://www.economonitor.com/blog/2009/11/the-hubris-of-economics/ (accessed 4 June 2016).

Robinson, P.M. (1991) Testing for Strong Serial Correlation and Dynamic Conditional Heteroskedasticity in Multiple Regression, *Journal of Econometrics*, 47, 67–84.

Rogoff, K., Froot, K.A. and Kim, M. (2001) The Law of One Price over 700 Years, IMF Working Papers, No. WP/01/174.

Rolnick, A.J. and Weber, W.E. (1986) Gresham's Law or Gresham's Fallacy, *Journal of Political Economy*, 94, 185–199.

Romer, C. and Bernstein, J. (2009) The Job Impact of the American Recovery and Reinvestment Plan, 9 January. http://otrans.3cdn.net/45593e8ecbd339d074_l3m6bt1te.pdf (accessed 17 August 2016).

Romer, P.M. (2015) Mathiness in the Theory of Economic Growth, *American Economic Review*, 105, 89–93.

Rothenberg, T.J. (1984) Approximating the Distributions of Econometric Estimators and Test Statistics, in Z. Griliches and M.D. Intriligator (eds) *Handbook of Econometrics*, Vol. 2, Amsterdam: North-Holland, 881–935.

Rothman, P. (1991) Further Evidence on the Asymmetric Behaviour of Unemployment Rates over the Business Cycle, *Journal of Macroeconomics*, 13, 291–298.

Rowley, R. (1988) The Keynes–Tinbergen Exchange in Retrospect, in O.F. Hamouda and J.N. Smithin (eds) *Keynes and Public Policy after Fifty Years*, Vol. 2, Aldershot, UK and Brookfield (VT): Edward Elgar Publishing, 23–31.

Samii, M.V. (1992) Oil Futures and Spot Markets, *OPEC Review*, 4, 409–417.

Samuels, J.M. (1965) Size and the Growth of Firms, *Review of Economic Studies*, 32, 105–112.

Samuelson, P.A. (1946) Lord Keynes and the General Theory, *Econometrica*, 14, 187–200.

Samuelson, P.A. (1947) *Foundations of Economic Analysis*, Cambridge (MA): Harvard University Press.

Samuelson, P.A. (1952) Economic Theory and Mathematics: An Appraisal, *American Economic Review*, 42 (Papers and Proceedings), 56–66.

Samuelson, P.A. (1965) Proof that Properly Anticipated Prices Fluctuate Randomly, *Industrial Management Review*, 6, 41–49.

Samuelson, P.A., Koopmans T.C. and Stone, R. (1954) Report of the Evaluative Committee for Econometrica, *Econometrica*, 22, 141–146.

Samuelson, R.J. (2011) Reckless Optimism, *Claremont Review of Books*. http://www.claremont.org/crb/article/reckless-optimism/ (accessed 27 May 2017).

Sargan, J.D. (1958) The Estimation of Economic Relationships Using Instrumental Variables, *Econometrica*, 26, 393–415.

Sargan, J.D. (1964) Wages and Prices in the United Kingdom: A Study in Econometric Methodology, in P.E. Hart, G. Mills and J.K. Whitaker (eds) *Econometric Analysis for National Economic Planning*, London: Butterworths, 25–63.

Sargent, T.J. and Wallace, N. (1976) Rational Expectations and the Theory of Economic Policy, *Journal of Monetary Economics*, 2, 169–183.

Savin, N.E. (1973) Systems k-Class Estimators, *Econometrica*, 41, 1125–1136.

Say, J.B. (1834) *A Treatise on Political Economy*, Philadelphia (PA): Grigg and Elliot.

Scarpa, E. and Manera, M. (2006) Pricing and Hedging: An Application to the JCC Index, Working Paper 130.2006, Nota Dilavoro.

Schinasi, G.J. and Swamy, P.A. (1989) The Out-of-Sample Forecasting Performance of Exchange Rate Models when Coefficients are Allowed to Change, *Journal of International Money and Finance*, 8, 375–390.

Schmidt, A.D. (2008) Pairs Trading: A Cointegration Approach, Honours Thesis, University of Sydney. http://ses.library.usyd.edu.au/bitstream/2123/4072/1/Thesis_Schmidt.pdf (accessed 7 September 2016).

Schneider, E. (1952) Okonometrie, *Weltwirtschaftliches Archiv*, 68, 59–70.

Scholes, M. and Williams, J. (1977) Estimating Betas for Nonsynchronous Data, *Journal of Financial Economics*, 5, 309–327.

Schultz, H. (1938) *The Theory and Measurement of Demand*, Chicago (IL): University of Chicago Press.

Schumpeter, J.A. (1954) *History of Economic Analysis*, London: Allen and Unwin.

Schumpeter, J.A. (1978) Economic Methodology, in F. Machlup (ed.) *Methodology of Economics and Other Social Sciences*, New York: Academic Press, 461–474.

Schwert, G.W. (1989) Why Does Stock Market Volatility Change Over Time?, *Journal of Finance*, 44, 1115–1153.

Schwert, G.W. (1990) Stock Volatility and the Crash of '87, *Review of Financial Studies*, 3, 77–102.

Sellin, T. (1959) *The Death Penalty*, Philadelphia (PA): American Law Institute.

Sentana, E. (1995) Quadratic ARCH Models, *Review of Economic Studies*, 62, 639–661.

Serletis, A. (1991) Rational Expectations, Risk and Efficiency in Energy Futures Markets, *Energy Economics*, 13, 11–115.

Serletis, A. and Banack, D. (1990) Market Efficiency and Cointegration: An Application to Petroleum Markets, *Review of Futures Markets*, 9, 373–385.

Shen, G. (2008) The Determinants of Capital Structure in Chinese Listed Companies, PhD Thesis, University of Ballarat.

Shiller, R.J. (2007) Bubble Trouble, *Project Syndicate*, 7 July.

Shojai, S. (2009) Economists' Hubris: The Case of Mergers and Acquisitions, *Journal of Financial Transformation*, 26, 4–12.

Shojai, S. and Feiger, G. (2009) Economists' Hubris: The Case of Asset Pricing, *Journal of Financial Transformation*, 27, 9–13.

Shojai, S. and Feiger, G. (2010) Economists' Hubris: The Case of Risk Management, *Journal of Financial Transformation*, 28, 25–35.

Shojai, S., Feiger, G. and Kumar, R. (2010) Economists' Hubris: The Case of Equity Asset Management, *Journal of Financial Transformation*, 29, 9–16.

Sideris, D. (2007) Wagner's Law in 19th Century Greece: A Cointegration and Causality Analysis, Bank of Greece Working Papers, No. 64.

Sills, D.L. and Merton, R.K. (2000) *Social Science Quotations: Who Said What, When and Where*, New Brunswick (NJ): Transaction Publishers.

Sims, C.A. (1972) Money, Income and Causality, *American Economic Review*, 62, 540–552.

Sims, C.A. (1980) Macroeconomics and Reality, *Econometrica*, 48, 1–48.

Sims, C.A. (1982) Policy Analysis with Econometric Models, *Brookings Papers on Economic Activity*, 1, 107–164.

Sinha, D. (2007) Does Wagner's Law hold for Thailand? A Time Series Study. http://econpapers.repec.org/paper/pramprapa/2560.htm (accessed 12 February 2016).

Smets, F. and Wouters, R. (2003) An Estimated Stochastic Dynamic General Equilibrium Model of the Euro Area, *Journal of the European Economic Association*, 1, 1123–1175.

Smith, Y. (2010) *Econned: How Unenlightened Self Interest Undermined Democracy and Corrupted Capitalism*, New York: Palgrave Macmillan.

Solow, R.M. (1960) On a Family of Lag Distributions, *Econometrica*, 28, 393–406.

Solow, R.M. (1988) The Wide, Wide World Of Wealth, in J. Eatwell and M. Milgate (eds) *The New Palgrave: A Dictionary of Economics*, New York: Stockton Press, 3251–3252.

Soros, G. (2008) The Worst Market Crisis in 60 Years, *Financial Times*, 22 January.

Spanos, A. (1986) *Statistical Foundations of Econometric Modelling*, Cambridge (MA): MIT University Press.

Srivastava, V.K. (1971) Three-Stage Least-Squares and Generalized Double k-Class Estimators: A Mathematical Relationship, *International Economic Review*, 12, 312–316.

Stigler, G.J. (1939) The Limitations of Statistical Demand Curves, *Journal of the American Statistical Association*, 34, 469–481.

Stigler, G.J. (1962) Henry L. Moore and Statistical Economics, *Econometrica*, 30,1–21.

Stigler, G.J., Stephen, J., Stigler, M. and Friedland, C. (1995) The Journals of Economics, *Journal of Political Economy*, 103, 331–359.

Stock, J.H. and Watson, M.W. (1996) Evidence on Structural Instability in Macroeconomic Time Series Relations, *Journal of Business and Economic Statistics*, 14, 11–30.

Stock, J.H., Wright, J.H. and Yogo, M. (2002) A Survey of Weak

Instruments and Weak Identification in Generalized Method of Moments, *Journal of Business and Economic Statistics*, 20, 518–529.

Stone, R. (1945) The Analysis of Market Demand, *Journal of the Royal Statistical Society*, Series A, 108, 286–382.

Stone, R. (1978) Keynes, Political Arithmetic and Econometrics, *Proceedings of the British Academy*, Vol. 64, Oxford: Oxford University Press.

Strachan R.W. and van Dijk, H.K. (2006) Model Uncertainty and Bayesian Model Averaging in Vector Autoregressive Processes, Discussion Papers in Economics, No. 06/5, Department of Economics, University of Leicester.

Stroe-Kunold, E. and Werner, J. (2009) A Drunk and her Dog: A Spurious Relation? Cointegration Tests as Instruments to Detect Spurious Correlations between Integrated Time Series, *Quality and Quantity*, 43, 913–940.

Summers, L. (1991) The Scientific Illusion in Empirical Macroeconomics, *Scandinavian Journal of Economics*, 93, 129–148.

Sutter, D and Pjesky, R. (2007) Where Would Adam Smith Publish Today? The Near Absence of Math-Free Research in Top Journals, *Economics in Practice*, 4, 230–240.

Swamy, P.A. (1970) Efficient Inference in a Random Coefficient Regression Model, *Econometrica*, 38, 311–323.

Swanson, N.R. (2002) Comments on "A Vector Error-Correction Forecasting Model of the US Economy", *Journal of Macroeconomics*, 24, 599–606.

Syll, L.P. (2012a) David K Levine is Totally Wrong on the Rational Expectations Hypothesis, 14 February. https://rwer.wordpress.com/2012/02/16/david-k-levine-is-totally-wrong-on-the-rational-expectations-hypothesis/ (accessed 14 May 2016).

Syll, L.P. (2012b) Keynes's Critique of Econometrics, 4 July. https://larspsyll.wordpress.com/2012/07/04/keyness-critique-of-econometrics/ (accessed 14 May 2016).

Syll, L.P. (2012c) Randomization is a Poor Substitute for Real Science, 3 July. https://larspsyll.wordpress.com/2012/07/03/randomization-is-a-poor-substitute-for-real-science/ (accessed 14 May 2016).

Syll, L.P. (2012d) Probabilistic Econometrics – Science without Foundations (part I), 21 February. https://larspsyll.wordpress.com/2012/02/21/probabilistic-econometrics-science-without-foundations-part-i/ (accessed 14 May 2016).

Taleb, N.N. (2009) Ten Principles for a Black Swan Proof World, *Financial Times*, 7 April. http://www.ft.com/cms/s/0/5d5aa24e-23a4-11de-996a-00144feabdc0.html#axzz360kcijDN (accessed 8 February 2016).

Tawadros, G. (2001) The Predictive Power of the Monetary Model of Exchange Rate Determination, *Applied Financial Economics*, 11, 279–286.

Taylor, M.P. (1988) An Empirical Examination of Long-Run Purchasing Power Parity Using Cointegration Techniques, *Applied Economics*, 20, 1369–1381.

Taylor, M.P. (1995) The Economics of Exchange Rates, *Journal of Economic Literature*, 33, 13–47.

Taylor, M.P. and Tonks, I. (1989) The Internationalisation of Stock Markets and the Abolition of UK Exchange Control, *Review of Economics and Statistics*, 71, 332–336.

Taylor, S.J. (1986) *Modeling Financial Time Series*, Chichester: Wiley.

The Economist (2008) Joseph and the Amazing Technicalities, 26 April, 16–18.

The Economist (2012) The Mathematics of Markets, 14 January.

The Economist (2013) Labour Pains, 2 November.

The Economist (2015) What's Wrong with Finance, 1 May.

Theil, H. (1954) Estimation of Parameters of Econometric Models, *Bulletin of International Statistics Institute*, 34, 122–128.

Theil, H. (1958) *Economic Forecasts and Policy*, Amsterdam: North-Holland.

Thompson, J.R., Baggetts, L.S., Wojciechowski, W.C. and Williams, E.E. (2006) Nobels for Nonsense, *Journal of Post Keynesian Economics*, 29, 3–18.

Tinbergen, J. (1930) Bestimmung und Deutung von Angebotskurven: ein Beispiel, *Zeitschrift für Nationalökonomie*, 1, 669–679.

Tinbergen, J. (1937) *An Econometric Approach to Business Cycle Problems*, Paris: Herman and Cie Editeurs.

Tinbergen, J. (1939a) *Statistical Testing of Business-Cycle Theories*, Vol. I: *A Method and Its Application in Investment Activity*, Geneva: League of Nations.

Tinbergen, J. (1939b) *Statistical Testing of Business-Cycle Theories*, Vol. II: *Business Cycles in the USA, 1919–1932*, Geneva: League of Nations.

Tinbergen, J. (1951) *Econometrics*, London: Allen and Unwin.

Tintner, G. (1953) The Definition of Econometrics, *Econometrica*, 21, 31–40.

Titman, S, and Wessels, R. (1988) The Determinants of Capital Structure Choice, *Journal of Finance,* 43, 1–19.

Tobin, J. (1958) Estimation of Relationships for Limited Dependent Variables, *Econometrica*, 26, 24–36.

Treadway, A.B. (1971) On the Multivariate Flexible Accelerator, *Econometrica*, 39, 845–855.

Tse, Y.K. (1998) The Conditional Heteroskedasticity of the Yen–Dollar Exchange Rate, *Journal of Applied Econometrics*, 13, 49–55.

Tse, Y.K. and Tsui A.K.C. (2002) A Multivariate GARCH Model with Time-Varying Correlations, *Journal of Business and Economic Statistics*, 20, 351–362.

Turner, D.S. (1990) The Role of Judgement in Macroeconomic Forecasting, *Journal of Forecasting*, 9, 315–345.

van Dam, L. (2012) Why I Won't Teach Pair Trading to my Students, *Market Watch*, 1 October. http://www.marketwatch.com/story/why-i-wont-teach-pair-trading-to-my-students-2012-10-01 (accessed 22 April 2016).

van der Weide, R. (2002) GO-GARCH: A Multivariate Generalized Orthogonal GARCH Model, *Journal of Applied Econometrics*, 17, 549–564.

Varian, H.R. (2014) Big Data: New Tricks for Econometrics. http://people.ischool.berkeley.edu/~hal/Papers/2013/ml.pdf (accessed 28 July 2016).

Velupillai, K.V. (2005) The Unreasonable Ineffectiveness of Mathematics in Economics, *Cambridge Journal of Economics*, 29, 849–872.

Verdoorn, P.J. (1980) Verdoorn's Law in Retrospect: A Comment, *Economic Journal*, 90, 382–385.

Vogelsang, T.J. and Wagner, M. (2014) Integrated Modified OLS Estimation and Fixed-Inference for Cointegrating Regressions, *Journal of Econometrics*, 178, 741–760.

von Mises, L. (1978) The Inferiority Complex of the Social Sciences, in F. Machlup (ed.) *Methodology of Economics and Other Social Sciences*, New York: Academic Press, 333–344.

von Mises, L. (1998) *Human Actions: A Treatise on Economics*, Auburn (AL): Ludwig von Mises Institute.

Wallis, K.F., and Whitley, J.D. (1991) Sources of Error in Forecasts and Expectations: UK Economic Models, 1984–1988, *Journal of Forecasting*, 10, 231–253.

Wang, Q. and Phillips, P.C.B. (2009) Structural Nonparametric Cointegrating Regression, *Econometrica*, 77, 1901–1948.

Weber, C.E. (1995) Cyclical Output, Cyclical Unemployment and Okun's Coefficient: A New Approach, *Journal of Applied Econometrics*, 10, 433–445.

Wegge, L.L. (1965) Identifiability Criteria for a System of Equations as a Whole, *Australian Journal of Statistics*, 7, 67–77.

White, H.L. (1980) A Heteroskedasticity-Consistent Covariance Matrix Estimator and a Direct Test for Heteroskedasticity, *Econometrica*, 48, 817–838.

Wickens, M.R. (1996) Interpreting Cointegrating Vectors and Common Stochastic Trends, *Journal of Econometrics*, 74, 255–271.

Wold, H.O.A. (1949) Causality and Econometrics, *Econometrica*, 22, 162–177.

Wong, C.S. and Li, W.K. (2001) On a Mixture Autoregressive Conditional Heteroskedastic Model, *Journal of the American Statistical Association*, 96, 982–995.

Wood, D. (1991) Corporate Social Performance Revisited, *Academy of Management Review*, 16, 691–718.

Wood, D. (2008) A Model Model?, *OpRisk & Compliance*, March, 35–37.

Working, E.J. (1927) What Do Statistical 'Demand Curves' Show?, *Quarterly Journal of Economics*, 41, 212–235.

Wright, P.G. (1915) Review of Economic Cycles by Henry Moore, *Quarterly Journal of Economics*, 29, 631–641.

Wright, P.G. (1928) *The Tariff on Animal and Vegetable Oils*, London: Macmillan.

Wu, D. (1973) Alternatives Tests of Independence between Stochastic Regressor and Disturbances, *Econometrica*, 41, 733–750.

Wu, T. and McCallum, A. (2005) Do Oil-Futures Prices Help Predict Future Oil Prices?, *Federal Reserve Bank of San Francisco Economic Letter*, No. 2005-38.

Xiao, Z. (2009a) Functional-Coefficient Cointegration Models, *Journal of Econometrics*, 152, 81–92.

Xiao, Z. (2009b) Quantile Cointegrating Regression, *Journal of Econometrics*, 150, 248–260.

Yang, M. and Bewley, R. (1995) Moving Average Conditional Heteroskedastic Processes, *Economics Letters*, 49, 367–372.

Young, C. and Kroeger, K. (2015) Model Uncertainty and Robustness: A Computational Framework for Multi-Model Analysis, Working Paper, Stanford University. http://web.stanford.edu/~cy10/public/mrobust/Model_Robustness.pdf (accessed 30 June 2016).

Yule, G.U. (1895) On the Correlation of Total Pauperism with Proportion of Out-Relief, *Economic Journal*, 5, 603–611.

Zakoïan, J.M. (1994) Threshold Heteroskedastic Models, *Journal of Economic Dynamics and Control*, 18, 931–955.

Zellner, A. (1962) An Efficient Method of Estimating Seemingly Unrelated Regressions and Tests for Aggregation Bias, *Journal of the American Statistical Association*, 57, 348–368.

Zellner, A. and Theil, H. (1962) Three-Stage Least Squares: Simultaneous Estimation of Simultaneous Equations, *Econometrica*, 30, 54–78.

Zimring, F. and Hawkins, G. (1997) Concealed Handguns: The Counterfeit Deterrent, *The Responsive Community*, 7, 46–60.

Index

Printed and bound by CPI Group (UK) Ltd, Croydon, CR0 4YY

23/04/2025

14660984-0005